June 2014

Fr Teri Cissé
with affection from

Emily

THE LEGACY OF SIMONE DE BEAUVOIR

The Legacy of Simone de Beauvoir

Edited by

Emily R. Grosholz

CLARENDON PRESS · OXFORD

OXFORD

UNIVERSITY PRESS

Great Clarendon Street, Oxford OX2 6DP

Oxford University Press is a department of the University of Oxford.
It furthers the University's objective of excellence in research, scholarship,
and education by publishing worldwide in

Oxford New York

Auckland Bangkok Buenos Aires Cape Town Chennai
Dar es Salaam Delhi Hong Kong Istanbul Karachi Kolkata
Kuala Lumpur Madrid Melbourne Mexico City Mumbai Nairobi
São Paulo Shanghai Taipei Tokyo Toronto

Oxford is a registered trade mark of Oxford University Press
in the UK and in certain other countries

Published in the United States
by Oxford University Press Inc., New York

British Library Cataloguing in Publication Data

Data available

Library of Congress Cataloging in Publication Data

Data available

ISBN 0–19–926535–6

1 3 5 7 9 10 8 6 4 2

Typeset by Kolam Information Services Pvt. Ltd., Pondicherry, India
Printed in Great Britain
on acid-free paper by
Biddles Ltd.,
King's Lynn, Norfolk

This volume is dedicated to Paula Deitz, with thanks for her example as a writer, her collegiality and encouragement as editor of *The Hudson Review,* and her friendship. Her devotion to the education of women, shared by Simone de Beauvoir and all the contributors to this volume, was honored by the John M. Greene Award bestowed by Smith College in 1995, and her efforts on behalf of that institution have only intensified since then. She, and *The Hudson Review,* also support The Young Women's Leadership School in New York City.

Editor's Preface

The year 1999 marked the fiftieth anniversary of the publication of Simone de Beauvoir's *The Second Sex*. When I was reminded of that half-centenary, I started planning a conference as a homage that would achieve two related ends. First, Beauvoir's book should receive greater recognition as a work of philosophy, to encourage more systematic reflection on her methods and aims, on the place of her book in the canon, and on its role in generating social change. Theoretically, *The Second Sex* offers new problems for reflection and novel means for appropriating older texts, and thus plays a central role in the profound shift in philosophy's self-understanding that took place in the latter half of the twentieth century. Its reflective iconoclasm can be compared to that of Descartes's *Meditations*. At the same time it has had an enormous, directly discernible, impact on our social world, and so can also be compared to Locke's *Two Treatises of Government*. Thus I wanted to invite scholars to the conference who could illuminate Beauvoir's place in the canon: Susan James, Catherine Wilson, and Michèle Le Doeuff (known for their work on the seventeenth and eighteenth centuries), and Claude Imbert and Seyla Benhabib (known for their work on the nineteenth and twentieth centuries). I also wanted to invite scholars concerned with the intersection of theory and practice, and this made Toril Moi, Michèle Le Doeuff, and Seyla Benhabib obvious choices. Many of these scholars were concerned with feminist issues, but some had never before published on the work of Simone de Beauvoir, so I hoped to find new commentators on her.

The second of my intentions is related to the search for new commentary. Simone de Beauvoir has always inspired me, not just because she was an important philosopher, deeply concerned with the critical and creative powers of reason as well as with the betterment of our suffering world, but also because she worked in a variety of genres, including the novel, political journalism, and the memoir. In this respect, she strikingly resembles W. E. B. Du Bois, who has also commanded my attention and the homage of an edited volume. I understand the multiplicity of her voices to be closely related to her philosophical project, which is (to use Nancy Bauer's formulation) 'to see whether we can come up with a new way of doing philosophy, one that is rigorous and generalized enough really to count as philosophy but at the same time is tethered in the right way to the sorts of everyday, real-life problems of sexism that are the raison d'être of feminism' (Bauer 2001: 25). Moreover, Beauvoir's method proceeds from her own experience: 'I am a woman.' Her reflections thus had to find expression sometimes as narrative, sometimes as autobiography, sometimes as argument, if the philosophical issues themselves were to be addressed adequately; and this was also true for Du Bois. So I wanted to invite scholars for whom philosophical reflection sometimes took the form of historiography, literary criticism, and even fiction or poetry. This was another reason why I invited Toril Moi, Catherine Wilson, and Michèle Le Doeuff, and later added an essay by Anne Stevenson, and wrote my own essay in a literary vein. Broadly stated, I wanted the conference and the present volume to demonstrate the many ways in which Beauvoir's writings, in particular *The Second Sex*, can serve as resources for thought, for the life of the mind which is as concerned with the past and future as it is with the present.

Four of the essays in this volume were written for and delivered at the conference held at the Pennsylvania State University on 19–21 November 1999 entitled 'The Legacies of Simone de Beauvoir'. The idea was first suggested to me by Susan Reighard, Senior Staff Assistant at the Institute for the Arts and Humanistic Studies at Penn State; she is (and was then) pursuing a BA in Women's Studies and is also an active member of the Commission for Women, as I am. I invited two colleagues in the philosophy department, Shannon Sullivan and Susan Schoenbohm, to organize the conference with me; as a result of their efforts, other papers from the conference were collected in *The Journal of Speculative Philosophy* 13/1 (1999), guest-edited by Shannon Sullivan. It includes excellent papers by Margaret Simons (whose scholarly dedication to Beauvoir's work is unmatched), Emily Zakin, Elaine Miller, and Tina Chanter. The conference took place in large part because of the support of two people, my husband Robert R. Edwards, then Director of the Institute, and the Associate Vice-President for Outreach and Executive Director of Continuing Education Patricia Book, whose encouragement and enthusiasm I once again acknowledge with gratitude.

One of the readers of the manuscript of this volume for Oxford University Press characterized the conference as 'the most important commemoration in the English-speaking world of the fiftieth anniversary of *The Second Sex*', and I am happy to think that it was. Toril Moi delivered a version of her trenchant essay on the Parshley translation that, building on Margaret Simons's earlier essay, made everyone sit up and take note. Catherine Wilson, Claude Imbert, and Susan James gave versions of the essays that appear in this volume, which they have since recast and rethought with characteristic intellectual energy. Michèle Le Doeuff and Seyla Benhabib were unfortunately unable to attend; I was present as an organizer. Nancy Bauer attended the conference as well; although at that time I was unfamiliar with her work, I have since come to esteem it highly and am grateful for the chance to include it here. Toril Moi generously wrote a second, more theoretical, essay for the volume, and I invited Anne Stevenson to reply to it. Michèle Le Doeuff kindly and retrospectively offered an essay for the volume; the task of translating it, as well as the essay by Claude Imbert, I found pleasant and thought-provoking. Seyla Benhabib is represented in the dedication of my essay.

I have divided the essays into three sections, which consider Simone de Beauvoir's legacy from three perspectives: historical, philosophical, and literary. The first section begins with Claude Imbert's 'Simone de Beauvoir: A Woman Philosopher in her Generation'. Claude Imbert has devoted much of her career to the philosophical study of logic. Her recent book *Pour une histoire de la logique* makes use of texts by Plato and Aristotle, as well as the Stoic logicians, and from the modern era texts by Descartes, Kant, and Gauss. She has written extensively on Frege, and his devotion to and rupture with Kant's conception of logic. In the past decade, perhaps as a consequence of trying to think through the insights of Frege and Wittgenstein, she has turned to the period in France that originally sparked her own fascination with philosophy. Her partly historical, partly theoretical book (to be entitled *Années 30: le point de non retour*) examines the radical rethinking of philosophy exemplified in the writings of Sartre, Merleau-Ponty, and Lévi-Strauss. The very first issues of *Les Temps Modernes*, which anyone interested in Simone de Beauvoir should spend time perusing, give a good indication of the stir produced by these philosophers: they left Imbert's sense of her profession permanently altered and unsettled by a profound discontent with 'l'incapacité de la philosophie classique à traiter de l'actuel'. It was thus a short step from her work on this book to her essay on Beauvoir, which illuminates the novelty of both *The*

Ethics of Ambiguity and *The Second Sex* by setting them in historical context.

Imbert begins by making a fascinating comparison between Simone de Beauvoir and Simone Weil. Both of them belonged to the first generation of professionally trained women philosophers, which followed hard on the heels of universally established education for young girls in post-Napoleonic nineteenth-century France. The group included the brilliant but more conventional scholars Jacqueline de Romilly, Simone Pétremont, Florence Ramnoux, and Geneviève Rodis-Lewis, and was also linked to a group of philosophers who published a series of highly original books during the latter half of the 1940s: Sartre, Merleau-Ponty, Lévi-Strauss. Beauvoir felt very competitive with Weil, but at the same time enjoyed their common ability to beat the men at their own game. While Beauvoir scorned Weil's lack of aesthetic sense and was wary of her radical politics, she shared with her the conviction that philosophy must be *engagée*. And although they both began their careers as teachers, both Weil and Beauvoir were driven by the inability of genius to stay within established bounds, putting their talents in the service of a cause invisible to the university establishment. They shared with Sartre and Merleau-Ponty a desire to bring philosophy into novel relation with the reality of history, with concrete situations, partly as a reaction to the just-ended world war, above whose horrors philosophy seemed to drift like a helpless cloud.

Yet, Imbert argues, Beauvoir's attempt to forge this novel relation was even more radical than Sartre's, so radical in fact that it called the very program of existentialism into question. All of them were trying to distentangle themselves from the philosophical projects of Kant and Hegel; but even Sartre still fell under the influence of his nineteenth-century models (including Flaubert as well as Hegel and Marx) and failed to understand the extent to which his existentialist hero, bravely taking up a radical freedom, was in fact male and not universally human. As Beauvoir carried out the writing and research that ended up as *The Second Sex*, she came more and more to see that a woman in the real world is almost never radically free, but confronts her life as an imposed destiny. In a sense, the only behavior appropriate to her situation is bad faith, yet precisely that internalized combination of hysteria, narcissism, and emotional abandonment in conjunction with externally imposed barriers prolongs her imprisonment. The destiny of women is, after all, a social construction, but one whose reality women have learned to manage, as they manage their husbands. Beauvoir writes: 'One is not born a woman, but becomes one.' Yet the project of becoming a woman, or for that matter the project of trying to invent a different spectrum of lives for women, escapes the analytic nets of existentialism.

Thus, Imbert writes of *The Second Sex*, the enterprise could not be carried out without a radical revision of existentialist concepts and methods. Beauvoir's stubborn, scholarly examination of the facts of the historical life of women put in question the very philosophical procedures she was using. One collateral consequence of this, Imbert notes, was the disappearance of existentialism during the 1960s. Another was a tension in Beauvoir's book: it treats a consciousness that must struggle for its very recognition as a consciousness—the choices are pretending to be an object, pretending to enjoy domination, or nothingness. This turns *Being and Nothingness*, like Kant's *Critique of Practical Reason* and indeed Locke's *Two Treatises of Government*, into rather shabby pretence, if it cannot be applied to half of humanity. But then, how to proceed? Imbert ends her essay by looking again at the perspectives on the situation of women that have been uncovered by biology on the one hand and anthropology on the other. She argues that just as Beauvoir brings philosophy into novel relation with history, so too does she establish a new tangency with the sciences that treat human beings; and that indeed Beauvoir's task would have been easier if she knew then what we know now. To imagine the liberation of women, it is useful to think of a woman as organism and member of society as well as an isolated mind. To adjoin these other disciplines to academic philosophy is to oppose its small-mindedness. Beauvoir, by her writing and her example, helps us to do both.

Michèle Le Doeuff, like Claude Imbert, decided early on to become a philosopher. For Le Doeuff, however, reflection on the status of women and her own place as a woman in philosophy were central to her writings, along with a commitment to philosophical reason. How, she often asks, can one celebrate reason's ability to criticize and revise, and its ability to think impartially and universally, and at the same time resist the temptation to totalize and dominate? Her search for an acceptable rationalism has developed in tandem with a search for a philosophical feminism: Mary Wollstonecraft and Simone de Beauvoir are her two mainstays in both searches, and so are Bacon (many of whose works she has translated into French) and Descartes. One reason why she found *The Second Sex* so helpful as a young woman and philosopher starting out to fashion an unconventional life was Beauvoir's universalism.

Beauvoir, analyzing the situation of women—as subjects whose subjectivity is systematically constrained, unrecognized, or denied—with particular clarity, revealed to a whole generation of women that their difficulties were not the result of some idiosyncratic, personal failing but were rather reflections of a generalizable social problem. As a writer, Beauvoir also refused the authoritarian, judgmental stance Sartre assumes in *Being and Nothingness*. Her aim, as she says at the beginning of *The Second Sex*, is to understand, in the hope that understanding will speed the end of oppression. And what she wants to examine is the widespread bad faith of women, not condemned as a failing but understood as the normal and almost inescapable response to a social environment that punishes women for the exercise of their autonomy, along with the (normal and almost inescapable) fear and arrogance of men that leads them to punish autonomous women. Indeed, Le Doeuff's argument is the converse of Imbert's. Whereas Imbert criticizes Sartre for having failed to disentangle himself from a Hegelian universalism from which Beauvoir's concern for the concrete social problems of women freed her, Le Doeuff criticizes him for his parochial 'masculinism' and lack of theoretical empathy—the ability to entertain the perspective of the other as well as to admit its opacity. For Le Doeuff, Beauvoir achieves a greater universality—and rationality—than Sartre because of the way she transforms existentialism by making it ethical and then rewriting her existentialist ethics to include the lives of women.

In her essay 'Towards a Friendly, Transatlantic Critique of *The Second Sex*' Michèle Le Doeuff recounts her experience teaching that book in 1976 to her students at Fontenay, when the Ecoles Normales Supérieures were still divided. She and her students were looking for a philosophical discourse that would illuminate questions about the status of women, and examining existentialism (so unfriendly to women in the thought of Sartre) to see what it might offer, as reworked by Beauvoir. Le Doeuff began to lecture on *The Second Sex*, often explicating its philosophical strengths at the expense of Sartre, as she does in the central section of *Hipparchia's Choice*. On Beauvoir's initiative, she and Le Doeuff engaged directly in conversation that was, however, oddly inconsequential for the development of Le Doeuff's reflections, since at that point the older philosopher had left her own book behind and seemed unwilling to countenance criticism of Sartre. Beauvoir did nonetheless lend her voice and prestige to French feminism throughout the last years of her life, and Le Doeuff came to feel close to her in the context of the political struggle for reproductive rights—the freedom of women to make choices about their own fertility.

Le Doeuff's essay in this volume explains two often overlooked aspects of the political context in which Simone de Beauvoir wrote *The Second Sex* in the late 1940s. The first is that French women before World War II did not have the vote and were also not politically organized; French women were given the vote after the war almost as a gift or accident, because De Gaulle's new government did not want their enfranchisement to be imposed by the Allies. Thus French women, including Beauvoir, felt ambivalent about the new political role that was thrust upon them, as well as about the Anglo-American culture that had proposed it. So too Beauvoir seems to have had mixed feelings about feminism in England and America, and was reluctant to admit her debt to that tradition. Le Doeuff, by contrast, whose cosmopolitan professional life has often involved her in Anglo-American feminism and philosophical culture, suggests that the mutual acknowledgment of indebtedness would be an important contribution. As Michèle Le Doeuff observes in *Hipparchia's Choice*, nowhere in *The Second Sex* does Beauvoir seem to think of feminism as a social movement; rather, it is a struggle that each woman, understanding the universality of her dilemma as a subject whose subjectivity is in question or under attack, must work out for herself. By contrast, Anglo-American feminism has always had a political dimension, going back to the thought of Mary Wollstonecraft, Harriet Taylor, and John Stuart Mill. During the 1970s Le Doeuff and her compatriots also found an effective political organization for feminism in France, an organization which Le Doeuff (as her essay in the Fall 2000 issue of *Hypatia* makes clear) is keenly interested in keeping alive. Thus one task for feminism which remains, and which Beauvoir herself did not attempt, is the synthesis of the insights of *The Second Sex* with the political vigor of Anglo-American feminism; indeed, given the current political landscape, we might suppose that the latter itself needs reinvigorating, and that the dispassionate passion of Beauvoir may be especially rewarding just now.

The first generation of professionally trained women philosophers in Europe produced the monumental figures Simone de Beauvoir,

Simone Weil, and Hannah Arendt. (No one up till now has done a good job of analyzing their commonalities and differences as philosophers, nor their failures to collaborate and admire each other, which are just as hard to come to terms with as their complex relations to Sartre, God, and Heidegger.) The latter two have been well edited and translated (when necessary) into English, but the work of Simone de Beauvoir has suffered for various reasons. One is the multiplicity of genres in which she wrote, and her own tendency to represent herself as a writer rather than a philosopher. Three years ago, when I was preparing some of the material for this volume, I went into the famous philosophy bookstore maintained by the publishing house VRIN next to the Sorbonne and asked for a copy of *Le Deuxième Sexe*. 'Ah, Beauvoir,' said the young female salesclerk scornfully, 'you won't find her here, this is a philosophy bookstore. Go next door to FNAC and look in the literature section.' I responded somewhat heatedly that Beauvoir certainly was a philosopher and that it was a scandal they didn't carry her books—Toril Moi recalled her own experiences when I told her this story—and then went next door only to discover that FNAC was out of *Le Deuxième Sexe* and would be for many months. Somehow no one at Gallimard had realized that the fiftieth anniversary of the publication of that book might inspire an increased demand for it. Another reason is that the sole English version of *The Second Sex* is severely flawed both as an edition and as a translation, in ways that profoundly obscure its philosophical import. It has long disappointed and misled philosophers who try to make use of it in English translation.

Toril Moi, in her essay 'While We Wait: Notes on the English Translation of *The Second Sex*', describes a long process of scholarly protest against H. M. Parshley's translation of *The Second Sex*. It begins with Margaret Simons's essay 'The Silencing of Simone de Beauvoir: Guess What's Missing from *The Second Sex*', published in 1983, which first raised the issue by pointing out that more than 10 per cent (actually closer to 15 per cent) of the original two-volume book was omitted in Parshley's translation; cuts that are nowhere signalled in the text. Combining her own research with recent work by Elizabeth Fallaize, Moi describes in even greater detail what can be called without hyperbole a hatchet job. In fairness, Parshley deserves to be acknowledged as a supporter of feminism at a time when it was distinctly unfashionable for a man of science to be interested in the status of women. Moreover, Parshley was required to make substantial cuts in the text by Alfred Knopf in order to produce a book of more manage-able (marketable) size, and perhaps he was in no position to contest this decision. But it is also true that his limitations as a thinker deter-mine the shape of the result. Avuncular and patronizing even while supportive of feminism, he cuts out descriptions of women's anger, conflict, and oppression. Hostile to socialism, he eliminates almost every reference to socialist feminism in the history section, along with seventy-eight women's names. Trained not as a historian, philosopher, or man of letters but as a scientist, he routinely eliminates copious literary references, which support many of Beauvoir's arguments as important sources of evidence. Moi observes, such cuts are not ideo-logically innocent, for they impoverish Beauvoir's book by depriving us of the rich variety of women's voices that make up the French text. They also rob us of the insights produced by Beauvoir's brilliant way of juxtaposing philosophical and literary texts, a gift she enjoyed because she was both a writer and a philosopher.

Indeed, Moi's most serious criticism of Parshley as a translator is that he had little philosophical background, and thus the philosophical vocabulary and concepts essential to Beauvoir's arguments are lost on him. He simply does not recognize them for what they are: traces of Beauvoir's long interrogation of the philosophical tradition. Beauvoir uses words that are standard French translations of German terms from the technical vocabularies of Kant, Hegel, Marx, Husserl, and Heidegger, terms that are taken up in turn by her French contempor-aries for use in developing existententialism and phenomenology. (I would add, in light of Susan James's essay and my own training, that I believe this exercise could also be carried out with respect to the philosophical vocabulary of Descartes and Malebranche, and perhaps also Pascal, Arnauld, Leibniz, Montesquieu, and Rousseau. Why has no one attempted it?) As Moi is at pains to show, Beauvoir's use of these terms is always exact and thoughtful, and often—most import-antly—subversive in that it both ties her to the tradition and her contemporaries and reveals her distance from them. Parshley cannot even recognize the technical existentialist use of the terms *sujet, pour-soi* and *en-soi*, or *réalité humaine*, the special sense of the Hegelian term *poser*, or the Marxist and Lacanian notion of *aliénation*, much less Beauvoir's subversion of this usage, and so it is all lost for us in English translation. Moreover, Parshley's lack of comprehension is often taken by readers to be Beauvoir's own; this is ironic because, as Imbert points out, Simone de Beauvoir was one of the earliest and most accurate interpreters of Lévi-Strauss and Merleau-Ponty, and as a star student at the Sorbonne she always got the doctrines of her philosophical forebears straight as a precondition for departing from them.

Finally, Toril Moi makes the case that Parshley's translation also substantively distorts Beauvoir's positions on many important issues. It makes Beauvoir appear, for example, to be masculinist and anti-motherhood, when in fact what she champions is a woman's right to *choose* her own path rather than have a ready-made destiny thrust upon her. And it makes her appear to hold essentialist doctrines when in fact, as an existentialist and a maverick existentialist at that, she opposes essentialism on every front. More generally, it collapses the richness and irony, the multivocality and subtlety, of *The Second Sex*, qualities valuable in the work of any writer and thinker but indispensable to Beauvoir's project of making the condition of women visible. The essay ends with an implied plea to Knopf/Vintage to reconsider their position. Many feminist scholars, in many countries, stand ready to seek funding for and to carry out a new edition and English translation of *The Second Sex*; they have only to get the green light to begin.

The second section of this collection of essays examines *The Second Sex* and Beauvoir's related writings in philosophical context, as a great book that has assumed its place in the canon and whose position there provokes reflection. Despite the obstacles just discussed, the 1990s saw a resurgence of interest in Simone de Beauvoir as a philosopher, which in the past few years has resulted in important books by Margaret Simons, Eva Gothlin, Toril Moi, Michèle Le Doeuff, Debra Bergoffen, and Nancy Bauer *inter alia*. The Select Bibliography in this volume records much of the growing body of literature, but this is just a beginning. Simone de Beauvoir's philosophical legacy must still be recovered: the transmission of texts must be corrected, and Beauvoir's legitimacy as a philosopher must be re-established. And it must be revived: philosophers female and male should simply make much more use of the resources for thought she provides. Why should it be that *The Second Sex*, a book whose political and philosophical consequences have been so overwhelming, particularly in the anglophone world, has been allowed to languish for decades in a shoddy edition and translation, relatively neglected by the philosophical community for whom it was written? The question itself is food for thought.

Susan James scrutinizes the history of philosophy through the prism
of a neglected topic, that of passion, a term which in the theoretical
proportions of the seventeenth century is opposed to action and juxta-
posed with the body, matter, error, and women. (I see her choice here
as parallel to that of the philosopher Jorge Gracia, who examines the
neglected term 'the individual' in his historical writings, and then
makes use of those insights when he writes about race.) Her book
Passion and Action is a subtly feminist analysis of the inconsistencies
and untapped resources of seventeenth-century philosophy, particularly
the work of Descartes and Malebranche, Hobbes and Spinoza. She is
also a general editor of the Oxford Readings in Feminism series. When
she was invited to the conference at Penn State, however, she had
never before written on Beauvoir; she accepted with the hope of inte-
grating the study of Beauvoir and her feminist themes into the history
of philosophy, without creating a counter-canon or denigrating the
achievement of male philosophers. Already interested in the way in
which conceptions of the self are gendered, she had become increasingly interested in how our passions are shaped by relationships of
scale (size, distance, power), and was then surprised to find this theme
salient in *The Second Sex*. In her essay 'Complicity and Slavery in *The
Second Sex*', she examines how Beauvoir takes up the theme for her
own purposes and transforms it, deploying traditional resources for
feminist ends, and at the same time developing a series of what have
become quite familiar insights about the gendering of the self, how a
woman is socially constructed. 'One is not born a woman, but becomes one.'

Social hierarchies are built on the unequal distribution of power
and, as Aristotle observed, every constitution (and political power generally) is situated between the demand for equality and the inevitability
of hierarchy. Susan James's essay has two cognate aims. The first is to
locate Beauvoir's arguments vis-à-vis the social reality of hierarchy—in
this case the domination of men over women—and political theories
that take hierarchy as a given to be dealt with rather than an accident
of history to be abolished. The second is to locate such arguments not
in the context of Hegel's master–slave dialectic (and Sartre's appropriation of it)—as Eva Lundgren-Gothlin and Nancy Bauer have so admir-
ably done—but rather in the French tradition where Antoine Arnauld,
Pierre Nicole, Jean de La Bruyère, and especially Nicolas Malebranche
analyze the relations between passion and action in a social code that

is embodied as well as conceptualized. This is a significant move, I think, because current accounts of mid-twentieth-century European philosophy tend to overemphasize the influence of German thinkers in France, and to forget the ongoing engagement of French philosophers with Descartes and Cartesianism, and with the socio-political doctrines of the French Enlightenment, Voltaire, Montesquieu, and Rousseau. Perhaps because of the robust French tradition of materialism, this tradition also tends to honor better the claims of the body in its philosophical discourse.

James's approach also underlines Simone de Beauvoir's own reservations and conflicts about the existentialist program, with its relentless emphasis on agency, authenticity, and freedom. To answer the question why we find ourselves in a social world populated by transcendent men and immanent women—when existentialism exhorts all of us regardless of gender to strive for transcendence—Beauvoir instructs us to apply Hegel's master–slave dialectic. However, as James observes, Beauvoir's construal of the analogy between master and slave and man and woman is not straightforward. The complicity of women in their own domination cannot be understood in Hegelian terms as defeat or in Sartrean terms as bad faith; rather, for Beauvoir, complicity is conceived as a condition of an embodied self whose abilities, and therefore options, have been formed by its social circumstances. Thus there is a tension in *The Second Sex* between Beauvoir's understanding of embodiment and her Sartrean conception of humans as split between transcendence and immanence. Beauvoir makes it clear that in the everyday gendered experience of women constraints so severe they appear to be destiny, passions, and the negotiation of dominance by a more powerful group are facts that must be acknowledged, both in theory and in practice. The task of philosophy is not only the optimistic analysis of progressive freedom, but also the more sober analysis of power, especially power opposed to or indifferent to one's own interests.

James makes a compelling case that it would be just as illuminating to set Simone de Beauvoir back into the older, French tradition of philosophical inquiry concerning the character of social hierarchy— and the passions of embodied as well as thoughtful beings that create and sustain it. This is not just a claim about the influences that shaped Beauvoir's project, but an outgrowth of James's own project for reviving the philosophical investigation of the passions, for which she now enlists Beauvoir as a collaborative partner. As James observes, in

French philosophy of the late seventeenth century hierarchical social relations are widely held to depend on affects of admiration and contempt that operate on and through the body. In the resulting economy of the passions people are construed as complicit in their domination in a sense very like the one articulated by Beauvoir.

Malebranche, like Beauvoir, explains the acceptance of social subordination by pointing to relatively unyielding and thoroughly embodied differences of power that shape the exchange of esteem and admiration: the role of subordinates is not to exact esteem but to furnish it. At the same time, those who rule require and reward the admiration of their subordinates: the grandeur of the prince or husband rubs off on the indispensable courtier or wife. Indeed, the intimacy of life at court or within marriage gives the subordinate special, critical insight into the private failings of the *grand homme* who must always be honored publicly, as La Bruyère observed. The pleasant mutual illusions of hierarchy thus always risk degenerating into slavishness and hypocrisy: as Aristotle and Machiavelli warned, every constitution requires vigilant maintenance. One advantage of placing Beauvoir's arguments into this context is to be reminded that men can also be enslaved and trapped within socially imposed structures of complicity, in ways that are physical as well as psychical; and that history teaches that such subordination based on unalterable biological conditions (in this case, blood lines) can be revised. Thus, James concludes, just because woman's subordination is written on her body does not make it ineluctable, or intractable to philosophical reflection or political remedy. Part of the remedy is the tough-minded acknowledgment of forms of social hierarchy that must be assessed and negotiated, and that can be transformed but never abolished. The genocidal political experiments of the twentieth century that tried to impose pure egalitarianism and eliminate the messy maintenance of always imperfect constitutions are the tragic proof of Aristotle's wisdom.

Catherine Wilson was working on Leibniz and the relations between seventeenth-century philosophy and the emerging sciences of physics and biology in the late 1980s when she was asked to teach a course on feminism. Out of a sense of duty she agreed, and soon became fascinated by *The Second Sex*, at first as a work of literature and then as a philosophical text when she began systematically to reflect on the causes of female subordination and its remedies. In recent years she has turned her attention both to such questions in the context of moral theory and to Kant. Many critics of Kant, she observes, complain that his moral philosophy is too abstract and fails to take situation and interpersonal dependency into account, and thus to pertain to the lives of most women. One response to this criticism has been the development of an ethics of care, but Wilson discerned in Beauvoir's writings an alternative response. In *The Second Sex* Beauvoir argues that people are often unfree because of what others are doing to or thinking about them: it is often not merely up to the subject himself whether or not he can achieve free self-determination, or fall prey to bad faith. In this light, Sartre exhibits psychological and historical naivety about the possibility of human freedom. Wilson realized that a parallel objection could be made against Kant, for Kantian autonomy both idealizes and substitutes for the real autonomy that women (and peasants) lack. To improve the status of women in the public realm this distinction must be clearly drawn, and consequences drawn on the basis of it.

Catherine Wilson's essay 'Simone de Beauvoir and Human Dignity' thus locates Beauvoir's work in a neo-Kantian tradition already beset by an internal tension that *The Second Sex* stretches to breaking point. Kant's moral philosophy insists that those lacking in social prestige nonetheless enjoy intrinsic worth as human beings. Kant, Wilson points out, was offended by the classical Greek (and particularly Aristotelian) habit of associating virtue with high social standing; but his injunction to treat every human being as worthy of respect (as autonomous, rational, an end rather than a means) leaves the relation between the metaphysical and the social unclear, and fails to answer certain important questions. Why are women—almost invariably and ubiquitously—treated as less worthy of respect than men? Is it because members of society constantly and inexplicably fail to detect that feature (respect-worthiness) in a woman which she really possesses, or because they neglect to postulate it in her? But then what is the epistemological difference? Kant's egalitarian approach actually makes it more difficult to discern and diagnose the social ills that stem from belonging to a demeaned group. The boundary between symptoms of low socio-economic status and lesser dignity is an instance of the boundary between feature-detection and postulation, so the one is just as ill-defined as the other.

Usually we think of dignity as something that must be earned, accompanying maturity and achievement, and that may by the same token be lost; and yet we also think that any human being has an 'inner' dignity that should not be violated. The problem is, as Wilson argues, that although the law punishes certain violations of respect for the latter kind of dignity, it does nothing about the harm that befalls women because they are widely and unconsciously seen as devoid of the former kind of dignity; and Kant's ethical theory makes it appear that the possession of moral dignity ought to reconcile or comfort or inspire those who lack social dignity. Thus Beauvoir's approach, Wilson concludes, is superior to Kant's, for in showing how moral dignity might grow out of the same attitudes and activities that produce social dignity she blocks the ideological move of treating moral dignity as an adequate substitute for social dignity. Beauvoir makes it clear that the condition of women will improve only if the social perception of women, which includes the perception of themselves they have internalized, improves. And what is Beauvoir's prescription for improvement? Beauvoir, inspired by Marx on the one hand and by Sartre's existentialism on the other, urges women to a 'world-making' in which the value-adding power of human labor and the value-adding power of human consciousness combine to transcend, oppose, and alter nature. Wilson criticizes the stress on tools and labor in Beauvoir's analysis, but in the end finds her appeal to specialization suggestive. The explanation of social dignity in terms of specialization (and women's exclusion from both) is characteristic of Beauvoir, because it involves both a historical hypothesis and a theory of value: Beauvoir allows history to impinge upon philosophy and requires philosophy to answer to history.

Women tend to be generalists and amateurs, and this works against social honor. By contrast, Wilson observes, specialization involves the conspicuous display of extra resources: extra time, extra assistance, extra access. The specialist, in practising his craft, announces to the world his possession of a surplus, his status as a creator. Where investment and study are required as well as devotion and talent, and where access is controlled, work is specialized and confers status. This is the same insight that drives W. E. B. Du Bois's brief for the cultivation of the 'Talented Tenth' as essential to the general welfare and advancement of blacks, and Bernard Boxill's best arguments in support of the United States policy of affirmative action because it improves access to elite institutions and specialized training. As deep and important as this insight is, Wilson argues that maternity introduces complications that

Beauvoir does not fully address: women are the generalists of the world because they are mothers.

Beauvoir opposes the sentimentalization of motherhood for its deep hypocrisy, since it often masks social policies that damage children as well as women. All the same, Beauvoir's prescriptions are often vague or impractical, for she regularly underestimates the impact of children on the shape of a woman's life. Once this impact is factored in, it becomes clear that the workplace where specializing women learn to become consumers and producers of cultural resources must be re-structured to accommodate women and the children they can't set aside. It also suggests that men must be persuaded to moderate their demands for specialization and transcendence, and that philosophy (and the social world that slowly absorbs and then manifests philosoph-ical notions decades later) should revise its notion of dignity. For Kant, Wilson reminds us, dignity is a matter of purity, cleanliness, and un-touchability—to affront it a kind of *lèse-majesté*; perhaps there is an-other notion of dignity that would cover a philosophy or physics professor thoughtfully nursing her baby at her desk, changing its diaper and then settling it to sleep as she goes on thinking. What Kant does not admit, though it remains true, is that dignity is also a matter of power.

By examining Beauvoir's work in relation to Descartes and Male-branche on the one hand and Kant on the other, Susan James and Catherine Wilson make the case for Beauvoir's place in the philosoph-ical canon by showing how she recognizes, revises, and solves prob-lems that have persisted over centuries, and offers as well novel approaches to problems (both theoretical and practical) that concerned her peers fifty years ago, and now concern us. In her recent book *Simone de Beauvoir, Philosophy and Feminism* (2001) Nancy Bauer makes a similar case for Beauvoir's appropriation of Hegel. Working out the details of how Beauvoir brought philosophy to bear on the question of women's status in the world and in particular her own position, and thereby was forced to rethink both Hegel's master–slave dialectic and Sartre's treatment of it in *Being and Nothingness*, Bauer comes to radical conclusions. She argues that the use of philosophy to analyze the situation of women transforms the philosophical enterprise: it requires new methods and new problems, and generally 'a serious rethinking of what philosophy is', linked to a profound reappraisal of what it is to be human. In Beauvoir's *The Second Sex* Bauer finds a new model for doing philosophical work. In another recent article, 'Beauvoir's Heideggerian Ontology', she carries out a similarly instructive exercise with concepts central to Heidegger's *Being and Time*.

In the present essay, 'Must We Read Simone de Beauvoir?', Bauer reviews the ambivalent reception, often amounting to respectful neglect, that Beauvoir's masterwork has found among anglophone feminists. Like Toril Moi, she acknowledges that it is the result in part of the inadequacy of the only English translation. But, she points out, it is also the result of the demand for 'theory', and the tendency that theory has to unmoor itself from the earthly conditions of women's (and men's) lives. Whether such theorizing arises from the logical abstraction of analytic philosophy or the phenomenological abstraction of Continental philosophy, theories often give no indication of what we should do with them. And they often leave us unmoved and indifferent. Thus feminist theorists have a hard time focusing on the great virtue of *The Second Sex*, the way in which it goes far beyond theory construction without abandoning the premises of philosophical reflection. Feminist scholars also miss the point when they complain that Beauvoir really only applied Sartre's existentialism to a problem that Sartre happened to overlook, *and* when they assert that all Sartre's ideas were really stolen from Beauvoir, that it was Beauvoir who invented existentialism. Sartre's allegiance to the project of theory construction, Bauer argues, is precisely what Beauvoir learned to leave behind as she wrote *The Second Sex*. For example, when Beauvoir departs from Sartre's account of the self and other, his view of subject–object relations in which true reciprocity is impossible, she makes genuine mutual respect a central conceptual focus of both *The Ethics of Ambiguity* and *The Second Sex*. However, her arguments appeal not so much to metaphysics as to psychology, social reality, and anthropology. Beauvoir also locates a wealth of possibilities for bad faith in gender difference, a difference that cannot be explained without reference to our embodiment and social institutions, and indeed to our natural history; but then bad faith as well as the freedom it strives to escape no longer seem to exist simply at the level of metaphysics.

Bauer concludes that philosophical feminism, for its own sake, and indeed contemporary philosophy must turn again to Simone de Beauvoir not only for the problems she articulates but also for the methods she employs. The existence of this collection of essays as well as the scholarship on which these essays depend testify that many of

Beauvoir's ungrateful daughters (and sons) are coming around to this conclusion. To acknowledge the debt is to make use of her work, and to rethink her place in the canon: these essays show how closely connected the two forms of homage may be. At the end of her essay Bauer briefly reviews her own account of how usefully Beauvoir re-fashions Heidegger's notion of *Mitsein* for us, suggesting new strategies for avoiding philosophical and political inauthenticity, the way in which we internalize domination. Imbert sets Beauvoir in the context of Merleau-Ponty and Lévi-Strauss, suggesting that we return to many of those Parisian mid-century figures in search of a new conception of philosophical method. Moi reminds us to look again at Wittgenstein, Austin, and Cavell; James and Wilson send us back to neglected aspects of rationalism. I find in Beauvoir the impetus to revisit the philosoph-ical tradition of practical deliberation, which begins with Aristotle's combination of ethics, politics, and rhetoric and continues through Cicero, Machiavelli, Taylor and Mill, Ida B. Wells and W. E. B. Du Bois, Arendt, Habermas, and Luhmann. Beauvoir not only makes the world look different—that path along which we thread our way through the labyrinth of everyday life—but she also makes the philo-sophical canon look different, and more compelling.

The essays in the third and last part of this book put Beauvoir's thought into literary context. In the philosophical debates recorded above, where Beauvoir is shown to engage Descartes, Malebranche, Kant, and Hegel, as well as Sartre and Heidegger, the central term is not, as one might expect, 'justice' but rather 'respect'. The social conditions that hurt and disable women typically lie very close to home, which distinguishes them strongly from the conditions that oppress Marx's worker or Fanon's colonized person of color. This means, I think, that issues of respect are more central to feminism, and must be addressed prior to, or at least at the same time as, issues of justice. It also means that fictional and poetic accounts of the 'pri-vate' lives of women can play an especially important role in the quest for respect and justice. But the other side of the coin of respect is responsibility: those who have more social prestige are also generally speaking expected to put more on the line and do more for those around them. Beauvoir takes herself, and other professional women like her, to play a special role in the destiny of women. They are the hinge on which that destiny may swing around, for they belong to an unprecedented generation of women who earn their own living and acquire professional status; that is, some measure of public respect. They have become politically and socially active: one might call them catalysts, something added to a chemical reaction in small amounts that makes the reaction go faster, usually much faster. And with that visibility and efficacy comes responsibility, the topic of the interchange between Toril Moi and Anne Stevenson.

Toril Moi discovered *The Second Sex* (in a poor Norwegian translation) when she was in high school, and one of her first projects upon starting university at Bergen was to learn French and read Beauvoir properly: her old two-volume Blanche edition is underlined and annotated from start to finish. Beauvoir served as a model in two important ways: first as an independent and autonomous woman, and second as an intellectual who never allowed herself to become isolated in the ivory tower. Because she saw no divide between philosophy and life, Beauvoir showed Toril Moi how to think through the mundane and ordinary, how to produce theory from concrete experience, how to affirm a life and world that lends itself to reflective thought; the debt is amply repaid both in her 1994 biography of Beauvoir and in the already influential *What is a Woman?* (1999). A politically engaged writer, Toril Moi is impressed and comforted by the 'tremendous impact' of *The Second Sex*, and discusses Simone de Beauvoir as a writer who has clarified our understanding of the relationship between politics and intellectual work.

In her essay 'Meaning What We Say: The "Politics of Theory" and the Responsibility of Intellectuals' Moi tries initially to dispel certain myths about political efficacy and responsibility. Political correctness (in the words of Jonathan Culler) is the pursuit of theory that guarantees political radicalism, and often when reality fails to whip itself into shape in the light of their theories writers wonder if they shouldn't lay down their pencils and do something else more useful. Women writers may especially feel this way, surrounded as they are by a world of brutalized, threatened, coerced, suffering, illiterate, powerless, propertyless and voiceless women. As Sartre wrote, faced with a dying child, *Nausea* does not tip the scales.

Does this mean intellectual work has no political and ethical value? Moi dismisses Sartre's *cri de coeur* as the result of excessive and so inevitably disappointed optimism about the power and correctness of writing, and finds in a dictum of Beauvoir's a better guide, inviting us to consider the relation between theory and politics in more modest terms: 'I take words and the truth to be of value.' Beauvoir also says that to write is to appeal to the freedom of another person, the reader, whose reaction we can't control or foresee. Thus, Moi concludes, a politically committed writer must simply say what she has to say, and then and afterwards take responsibility for her words: she must own her words. This means that we must reject the fashionable dismissal of authorial authority and of intention. Moi argues that the writer must acknowledge her intentions, understood as the source of her responsibility for the work. The law takes intentions into account as it reckons responsibility for a crime; psychology takes intentions into account even as it registers the unconscious meaning of misspeaking or rash interpolations. We must take responsibility for what we say even when the effects are not those we foresaw or intended.

Indeed, we must be willing to engage in a process of rewriting and augmentation in which we explain and clarify what we meant; answer to rebuff and criticism; revise our positions without sacrificing our principles or integrity. To take responsibility for writing, especially when our intentions are political, is to enter into a process of practical deliberation, and that means to be willing to go on talking, even when or especially when one's interlocutors are opposed or uncomprehending or simply preoccupied with other (perhaps cognate) matters. It also entails, as Moi points out, that responsibility is tied to situation: we are not responsible to God, eternity, or some other abstract entity when we act, but rather to those human beings with whom we share a world. We write for readers who share a particular world with us, people who know enough about the concrete details to deliberate about how principles should be brought to bear on the messy circumstances of life, and for that matter which principles are pertinent. Improving the world is a common enterprise, and therein lies the risk of writing.

The interchange between Toril Moi and Anne Stevenson, both of them responding to Simone de Beauvoir, is a nice example of Moi's argument about responsibility, for each heeds and responds to the other as a writer who respects her own words, her interlocutor, the truth, and her wider audience. Like Catherine Wilson, Anne Stevenson came to Beauvoir's *The Second Sex* rather late and in response to a request: when Stevenson was a fellow of Lady Margaret Hall, Oxford, in 1975–6, Mary Jacobus asked her to deliver a lecture, which later became an essay in the collection *Women Writing and Writing about*

Women (1979). Like Beauvoir and her own mentor Elizabeth Bishop, Stevenson hadn't initially thought of herself as a woman writer, but once launched on this project found she had plenty to say. Rereading *The Second Sex* in 1998 she responded even more strongly to it, but as a work of literature. It seemed to her a book written under the pressure of experience, like *Middlemarch* or *To the Lighthouse*; a book moreover in which Beauvoir had discovered herself as she wrote, 'reading with her heart, and thinking her ideas out on her pulse'. Always wary of social theory and abstract philosophy, Stevenson found in *The Second Sex* a book that answered to her distrust of absolutes and liking for the particular, traits she shared with her mother Louise Destler and her father, the philosopher Charles Stevenson, who studied with Wittgenstein and G. E. Moore. He published his classic *Ethics and Language* in 1944, and was dismissed from Yale soon afterwards for his un-American rejection of absolute values.

In her responding essay, 'Saying What We Mean', Stevenson agrees that intellectual breast-beating is futile. She also observes that to say what we mean we have to know what we mean, and what we mean may be something that we work out as we go along. What we mean will be modified in the practical deliberation to which our sense of responsibility to a situation and interlocutors commits us, but it will also be modified and discovered in the internal dialogue a writer carries out with herself, where her language is itself a silent partner. Language makes possible a purchase on certain real things and aspects of reality, and even lends its metaphorical cast to express the indeterminacy that cannot, it seems, be chased from our relation to the world. And the intentions for which we take responsibility also include the conscientious search for words that will say what we mean. A writer may be able to answer Sartre's questions, 'What aspects of the world do you want to disclose?' and 'What change do you want to bring into the world by this disclosure?' before sitting down to her desk. On other occasions, however, the writer may be brought to her writing desk by an imperative but inchoate sense of what she wants to disclose and why.

Stevenson illustrates just such an occasion by one of her own poems, explained in terms of the process by which she came to it. The poem has in the meantime become the title poem of her most recent collection, *A Report from the Border* (2003). The poem, significantly, was triggered by precisely the kind of guilt that troubled Sartre when he weighed *Nausea* in the balance with a dying child, and that western intellectuals cannot after all escape: How can I enjoy my own life and works, how can they be meaningful, when I find myself in a sea of suffering? Stevenson recounts the way in which particular words, some borrowed from our common speech and some coined for the occasion, led her from thought to thought and finally to the last stanza, which expressed an insight essential to the poem and to her dilemma, and yet was somehow unexpected, as if the very process of expression had discovered it. The last stanza says, more or less, that the countries where injustice reigns and suffering is rampant often produce what is (to the poet) an essential good—literature. Literature is, of course, injustice and suffering fearlessly expressed—perhaps not directly but then in the beautiful veils of irony and metaphor and history. Stevenson chose a tight poetic form that put every single word under the truth-spotlight, and then had to be responsible for all of them. Some good can come from suffering; genius arises regularly among the poor and downtrodden; and this is no excuse for the rich and powerful who inflict suffering directly or by neglect, blight genius as it shows up here and there like wild flowers, and deserve the irony of the poet.

Anne Stevenson thus applauds the emphasis of both Beauvoir and Moi on situation, and their refusal to lay down theoretical requirements for what politically correct writing must look like. To suppose that we know what we mean before we try to say it, or argue for it with others, is to suppose that a correct theory can be devised beforehand and then imposed on the world to set us all straight; but this would be the death of art and, moreover, of the very politics that Locke and Mill, Beauvoir and Sartre, Moi and Stevenson, Boxill and Mandela, urge us to pursue. Whenever feminist philosophers denounce their predecessors as ideological and then claim to unmask all ideology by bringing forth 'facts' so as to furnish a correct account, borrowing the scientism of Marxism, they take as their model scientific theory rather than practical deliberation. But this is a big mistake, and both Moi and Stevenson recognize it as such, though the one has politics in mind and the other art. Social reality is not just given, to be studied by theory, but is also constructed in the processes of practical deliberation, which dialectically assess the moral significance of actions as we try to decide, in certain circumstances, what to do next. It refines our understanding of moral principles as they are brought to bear on particular situations, and it clarifies without disambiguating the 'essentially contested concepts' (to use W. B. Gallie's phrase) that define the meaning of actions in a process of attack and rebuttal. What a human action is—how it will bear on other events, what efficacy it has—is a function of what it means. If significance is worked out in practical deliberation, which is a social, conflictful, and cooperative assessment of action, then we determine the very being of social reality as we deliberate about it. Nor is this merely a matter of talk: if we want to get anything done, we must persuade other people to cooperate in the enterprise. Virtue must be effective, and to be effective it must be eloquent.

When I was in college at the University of Chicago I read the works of Simone de Beauvoir (and Germaine Greer, Betty Friedan, Susan Sontag, and others) as if my life depended on it. I was trying to invent a plan of life that did not resemble that of my mother (or father), and the example of Simone de Beauvoir as a successful, if maverick, philosopher, and as an independent intellectual who earned her own living was always before me. During my twenties, a rather unhappy period marked by my mother's death, I read through Beauvoir's memoirs, and at the same time most of the collected works of the novelist Colette, as well as a number of biographies of her long and complicated life. So I developed the habit of juxtaposing and weighing the lives of these two women, a habit I never outgrew. As the presence of children brought my own life closer than I ever expected to that of my mother, the ways in which Beauvoir and Colette came to terms with their mothers began to play a more central role in my reflections.

When I went back to *The Second Sex*, this time in search of traces of Colette, I was struck by the extremely literary surface of the first section of volume ii, that deals with the lifelines of women, its manifold references to fiction and its poetic diction. I was also struck by Beauvoir's nostalgia for early adolescence, and her negative assessment of her mother as a woman lacking in authority and autonomy, in contrast to Colette's description of her mother Sido. In *The Poetics of Space* Gaston Bachelard sketches a metaphysics that runs counter to Heidegger's 'ontology', for it emphasizes natality as well as mortality, and the way in which human life affords shelter as well as the way in which it casts us upon the waves. Colette seems to me in her writings to recognize and subvert the cold presuppositions of mid-twentieth-century existentialism (Heidegger's or Sartre's) perhaps even more accurately than Beauvoir, but then she was not a philosopher. I would like to see, or contribute to, a philosophizing that combines Beauvoir's novel appropriation of the philosophical tradition with the subversive insights of Colette and Sido; but that is a project for another day and year.

In writing *The Second Sex* Beauvoir had to avoid two snares, both pointed out by Claude Imbert: she had to avoid being caught in the scandalous embrace of female emotion and record dispassionately the everyday life of real women; and she had to prevent her treatise from turning into a literary 'author's book'. Yet the first section of volume ii of *The Second Sex*, entitled 'Formation', is strikingly literary, especially chapter II, 'The Young Girl', which runs parallel with much of the narrative in *Memoirs of a Dutiful Daughter.* In my essay 'The House We Never Leave: Childhood, Shelter, and Freedom in the Writings of Beauvoir and Colette' I argue that this chapter is deeply indebted to the writings of Colette, and is especially important to the book as a whole, because it is a clue about liberation. There Beauvoir treats the one period in a woman's life where she is not yet trapped by destiny, the brief transition between childhood and adulthood when even in traditional society she is allowed a limited autonomy. Thus every woman has in her memory the suggestion of what freedom and the creativity that comes with it taste like: it is delicious. Both Colette and Beauvoir wrote autobiographically about that period in their lives, as if seeking inspiration when they were just turning fifty, after a long period of great achievements and considerable losses. Beauvoir's characterization of the young girl should be studied carefully, because the philosopher recognizes in her the novel human type of modernity and sets her among Marlowe's Dr Faustus, Shakespeare's Hamlet, Rousseau's Emile, and Goethe's Werner. She is a poet, ironic and anxious, plunged in a self-conscious subjectivity that transforms itself into objectivity, and in a passive reflection that transforms itself into symbolic action; and so she stands in a special relation to nature.

As I argue, however, Beauvoir's construal of what this special relation to nature amounts to in *The Second Sex* is more biographical than she admits. On the one hand, her account registers her dissatisfaction with her mother: to escape into nature was to escape into a realm where she might be autonomous, a reader and writer, a lover discovering eros, but above all it was to elude her mother: 'In the paternal house, mother, laws, custom, routine, together rule: she [the young girl] wishes to tear herself away from this past, to become in turn a sovereign subject.' On the other hand, Beauvoir's account imagines a kind of shining mystical unity with an other whose dark side was abandonment, poetically recorded in one passage in terms of the moon. Beauvoir's early infatuations with the heroines of books and with her friend Zaza are conceptualized as mergings. In *Simone de Beauvoir: The Making of an Intellectual Woman* Toril Moi claims that this fantasy of merger accompanied by a violent fear of being left alone marked Beauvoir's erotic attachments through most of her adult life, and explains in part her ambivalent relationship with Sartre. The point here, however, is the way in which *The Second Sex* did sometimes become a literary 'author's book' in the embrace of female emotion, and this slippage both takes the edge off its objectivity and gives it added poignancy.

The limits of Beauvoir's perspective in this instance may best be seen not by somehow correcting her account to make it more 'objective', but by contrasting it with another parallel account, her own model in fact, written by a woman who was no philosopher but was a better writer and a deep thinker. In Colette's two memoirs about her mother, whom she loved and admired, we find another model of freedom for women struggling to make something of their odd position in the world. Sido, Colette's mother, is an adult woman severely constrained by poverty, the prejudices of her provincial neighbors, and the care of four children, a disabled husband, a house, a garden, and lots of animals. But Colette makes it clear that she is autonomous and creative, unencumbered by the usual feminine versions of bad faith except the faint residual traces of eros, like the vanity of perfume. The garden she cultivates is not a barrier but a way station, an antechamber between the house and the woods and fields that lie beyond it; she worries about her children, but she lets them roam wild all day long, and sometimes sends out the child Colette by herself at night as it ebbs into dawn. She doesn't bow to the local curé or the pretensions of rich neighbors, but willingly sacrifices her roses to a beautiful baby's haphazard appetite. So there is another way to represent the young girl as poet, and that is in relation to a mother who questions even if she cannot dominate, who judges but not according to custom, who reads even if she cannot publish, who gardens even if she cannot paint, who understands the patterns of seed and egg sac even if she has never set foot in a laboratory, and who does not resent but encourages the explorations of her children. Women, who have never had enough freedom, understand the advantages and opportunities provided by a house and garden, protected by walls and borders, and how the illusion of unhedged freedom may drive men to despair, or existentialism.

My hopes for this volume, and for the legacy of Simone de Beauvoir it celebrates, are many. I hope it will be a substantive addition to the Select Bibliography that provides the book with a coda and testifies to a resurgence of scholarly interest in Beauvoir's work during the past decade. I hope it will win renewed attention for her work among a younger generation of writers and scholars, and also among those of my generation who have put off a deeper acquaintance with her thought. I hope it will persuade scholars concerned with philosophical reflection on race to study her methods and formulations, as well as the way in which she urges the parallels between problems of race and gender. I hope it will contribute to the current widespread effort to provide the anglophone world with a scholarly edition and English translation of *The Second Sex*. And I hope it will count as interest on a debt I can never repay.

Bibliographical Note

All references to *Le Deuxième Sexe* will be given as *DS* 1949 or *DS* 1986 (followed by volume number and page number), depending on whether the author chooses to cite the original edition in two volumes (Paris: Gallimard, 1949) or the 1986 *Collection Folio* edition in two volumes (Paris: Gallimard). We have avoided the Gallimard *Collection Idées* edition and the 1979 *Collection Folio* edition, because they lack significant portions of the original. All references to the one-volume H. M. Parshley translation, *The Second Sex*, will be given as *SS* followed by the date of publication and then the page number, depending on which of the following the author chooses: New York: Alfred A. Knopf, 1953; Harmondsworth: Penguin, 1972/84; New York: Vintage Books, 1989; or London: Everyman's Library, 1993; the pagination differs somewhat from edition to edition.

Contents

Notes on Contributors

CLAUDE IMBERT is Professor of Philosophy at the Ecole Normale Supérieure, rue d'Ulm, Paris; she also teaches seminars at the Johns Hopkins University and the University of California at Davis on a regular basis. She has published *Phénoménologies et langues formulaires* (1992) and *Pour une histoire de la logique* (1999), and translations of two works of Gottlob Frege, *Fondements de l'arithmétique* and *Ecrits logico-philosophiques*. She is currently completing a book on philosophical developments in mid-twentieth-century Paris, *Années 30, le point de non retour*.

MICHÈLE LE DOEUFF is a director of research in philosophy at the Centre National de la Recherche Scientifique in Paris, and has taught at the University of Geneva. Her books include *Le Sexe du savoir* (1988), translated into English by Kathryn Hammer and Lorraine Code as *The Sex of Knowing* (2003); *L'Etude et le rouet* (1989), translated into English as *Hipparchia's Choice* (1991); and *L'Imaginaire philosophique* (1980), translated into English by Colin Gordon as *Philosophical Imaginary* (1989/2002). She has also translated into French two works of Francis Bacon, as well as Shakespeare's *Venus and Adonis*.

TORIL MOI is the James B. Duke Professor of Literature and Romance Studies at Duke University, and was a 2002–3 Radcliffe Institute Fellow. Her books include *What is a Woman? And Other Essays* (1999); *Simone de Beauvoir: The Making of an Intellectual Woman* (1994); *Feminist Theory and Simone de Beauvoir* (1990); and *Sexual/Textual Politics* (1985/2002). She is currently completing a book on Henrik Ibsen. She is also the editor of *The Kristeva Reader (1986)*, *French Feminist Thought* (1987), and co-editor of *Materialist Feminism* (1994).

SUSAN JAMES is Professor of Philosophy at Birkbeck College, University of London. She is the author of *Passion and Action: The Emotions in Seventeenth-Century Philosophy* (1997), and *The Content of Social Explanation* (1984), and co-editor of *Beyond Equality and Difference* (1992), *Visible Women* (2002), and *The Political Writings of Margaret Cavendish*

(2003). She is a general editor of the Oxford Readings in Feminism series.

CATHERINE WILSON is Professor of Philosophy and Distinguished University Scholar at the University of British Columbia. She is the author of *Moral Animals: Ideals and Constraints in Moral Theory* (2004); *Descartes' Meditations: A New Introduction* (2003); *The Invisible World: Early Modern Philosophy and the Invention of the Microscope 1620–1720* (1995/7); and *Leibniz's Metaphysics: A Historical and Comparative Study* (1989). She has also edited three collections: *Responsibility* (2003), *Leibniz: Critical Essays* (2000), and *Civilization and Oppression* (1999).

NANCY BAUER is Assistant Professor of Philosophy at Tufts University and was a 2002–3 Radcliffe Institute Fellow. She received her Ph.D. from Harvard University in 1997. She is the author of *Simone de Beauvoir, Philosophy and Feminism* (2001), and is currently writing a book on alternative ways of thinking philosophically about pornography.

ANNE STEVENSON is the author of fourteen books of poetry, most recently *Report from the Border* (2002), *Granny Scarecrow* (2000), and *Collected Poems 1955–1995* (1997). She is also the author of four books of biography and criticism, *Five Looks at Elizabeth Bishop; Between the Iceberg and the Ship: Selected Essays* (1998); *Bitter Fame, A Life of Sylvia Plath* (1989); and *Elizabeth Bishop* (1966). She won the Northern Rock Literary Award in 2002.

EMILY R. GROSHOLZ is the author of *Cartesian Method and the Problem of Reduction* (1991), co-author of *Leibniz's Science of the Rational* (1998), and co-editor of *The Growth of Mathematical Knowledge* (2000) and *W. E. B. Du Bois, On Race and Culture* (1996). She is the author of four books of poetry, most recently *The Abacus of Years* (2002) and *Eden* (1992), and editor of *Telling the Barnswallow: Poets on the Poetry of Maxine Kumin* (1997).

Ithaka

Penelope held off her ravenous suitors
by promising, tomorrow and tomorrow,
she'd finish lost Ulysses' winding sheet.
The Greek text says that she composed in light,

and analyzed in darkness. Woven figures
unravelled are not quite analysis,
rather a woman trying to understand
the altitude and basis of her island.

All day Penelope addressed the warp,
her shuttle a small craft with two directions.
All night her solitude relit the torch.
To analyze is to set life in question,

despite the crush of suitors at the door,
the cold synthetic wave raking the shore.

PART I

HISTORICAL CONTEXT

Simone de Beauvoir: A Woman Philosopher in the Context of her Generation

Claude Imbert

There are many ways of commemorating *The Second Sex*, fifty years after its publication. Since then, each generation has given it a new pertinence, increasing its long-range influence in the course of a debate which is nowhere near being over. I would like to contribute to that discussion by evoking the philosophical context in which the book first defined its intent. How was Simone de Beauvoir able to confront *philosophically* a question excluded by the very nature of the principles and positions in terms of which philosophy had traditionally justified itself? From this conflict stems a difficulty inherent in the project of *The Second Sex* which must not be forgotten if one is to do even minimal justice to the book. There is no doubt that Simone de Beauvoir was painfully aware of it, given that she found herself associated with those of her contemporaries who were most effective in redefining the methods and shape of philosophical activity.

In the first section I will reconstruct the context, both philosophical and academic, of Paris in the 1930s and 1940s, during which Simone de Beauvoir decided upon her commitments as a thinker and writer. A second section will set out to analyze the double bind which her project imposed upon her. In the final section I will investigate how and why arguments drawn from history, literature, and anthropology—far afield from philosophy—led Beauvoir to engage so early with questions which seem utterly contemporary; indeed, which seem to be our own.

PARIS IN THE 1930S AND 1940S

Simone de Beauvoir belonged to a generation of young women in France who for the first time could take up philosophy as a profession offering the privileged and secure status of a civil servant and an opportunity for financial and intellectual emancipation. During the period between the two world wars the philosophy *agrégation*, a competitive examination to recruit philosophical talent to teach at the high-school level, was opened for the first time to women. This outcome was the end of a long drama begun under Jules Ferry.[1] In the nineteenth century girls were given access first to high school and then to university-level education, mostly in order to obtain teaching diplomas: thus would France be endowed with schoolteachers of good quality. However, by the intelligent exploitation of legal possibilities and financial means that followed upon the decision to give women this access, it served their intellectual emancipation quite concretely, which was in fact the original intention of Jules Ferry. We should also recognize the role of certain prominent women, devout and active members of both the Protestant and the Catholic Churches, who helped initiate this legislation. Directors of public and private educational institutions, they prepared the way for what the Popular Front brought to completion. Madame Brunschvicg, a physicist married to one of the philosophers who left his mark on the decade of the 1930s, was Minister of Education and created the Centre National des Lettres. Thus the twentieth century revived and kept the promises of the Enlightenment, after the education of young women was suppressed and thwarted during the Restoration and the Second Empire of Napoleon III.

These facts belong to the prehistory of feminism. But the point where a vocation intersects historical circumstance is taken up quite insistently in various intellectual biographies of Simone de Beauvoir. She herself encouraged this survey provided by intellectual biography,

[1] Jules Ferry (1832–89) studied law. Journalist of the opposition, he was elected parliamentary deputy at the end of the First Empire. He was Mayor of Paris during the siege of 1870. Minister of Education from 1879 to 1889, he made elementary school mandatory for both girls and boys between the ages of 6 and 13. Concerned with the quality of schoolteachers, he created the Ecole Normale de Jeunes Filles at Sèvres, for secondary education. He also kept the promise he made at Paris in 1870: 'Among all the necessities imposed by the present time, amongst all the problems, I choose one to which I will dedicate myself with all my heart and soul, all my physical and moral being: that is the problem of the education of the people.' He ended his career as President of the Senate.

the narrative of a long life faithful to itself, which wished to remain without secrets. I don't deny the advantages. On the one hand, we may follow a well-documented trajectory, without lacunae, which Beauvoir herself related at every stage in minute detail. Her *Journal* is just as indispensable as it is extraordinary, for an understanding of herself, her contemporaries, and indeed the whole period. It is the testimony of a consciousness in its historical situation, as well as a defense and illustration of existentialism. On the other hand, to follow this trajectory of linked days as Beauvoir wished, that is as a correlate to the public figure of Sartre so that *The Second Sex* is kept within a strictly biographical perspective, is to assume that the philosophical location of the book is obvious. But is it?

On this assumption, the essential paradox of the book is obscured, a paradox which stems from the fact that the book must simultaneously affirm and deny that Simone de Beauvoir is a philosopher. No one ever accused her of any professional shortcoming, not even those who were scandalized by the book's purpose. Nor is the book in any way a manifesto that revolts against or belittles philosophy. There is much less irony than usually attributed to the title that Beauvoir chose for *Memoirs of a Dutiful Daughter* (*Mémoires d'une jeune fille rangée*). The paradox is rather inherent in the very structure of her philosophical position. That is, she raises a question both unnamed and unnameable in professional philosophy without offering a place or novel means for treating it. Because of this, the book took on a singularity, an isolation, which wasn't simply the result of its malicious rejection by academic philosophers, nor its rejection by a readership hostile on principle. *The Second Sex* enjoyed an unexpected success, both in French and in translation. Whatever the public response, it never lacked attention. But a book that ought to have taken its place beside the other philosophical essays of Beauvoir did not; it proved to be rather more atypical than provocative. An explanation must go more deeply into its lack of place, and its constitutive double bind.

We must keep in mind that the period between the two world wars in Europe was a moment of reflection and grief. Philosophers found themselves torn between the pursuit of the history of philosophy and a feeling of impotence: Simone de Beauvoir's generation was bitterly conscious of its inability to address the present. By contrast, the preceding generation had set out on the assumption that intellectual history is continuous, and that the development of the sciences is tied to the progress of the human spirit in bettering political and ethical thought. Her generation's disillusion was surely a response to the merciless violence, the barbarous acts, of the First World War. In the decades between the two wars the Academy never put in question the pursuit of a trajectory whose two bounds were Hellenism—with Athens as the rising sun of philosophy—and modern times, devoted to the perfection of a classicizing neo-Kantianism. This program also determined the stages of a philosophical education, which intersected in two different ways the study of Greek and Latin. First, as the site of philosophy's origin Greek conferred upon it a distinctive way of conceptualizing, which Latin then transmitted without interruption: recall that both the philosopher Henri Bergson and the socialist and writer Jean Léon Jaurés wrote dissertations in Latin. It seemed obvious that women, like the other students but with the special advantage of going through a ritual initiation long refused to them, would enter the newly opened discipline by that route. Second, the study of Greek offered the advantage of a discipline where philosophical studies and literary studies coincided. The study of Plato in particular was thus interdisciplinary, rather as his work is studied today in a classics department. It also happened that the *agrégation de lettres* open to women had recently added Greek as a subject in the competition.

The career of a Hellenist, philosophical or literary, thus appeared as a tempting and natural choice to this generation of women who wished to become intellectuals but weren't much interested in simply transmitting the patrimony of French letters. At the time it was still an audacity for a woman to aim at becoming a Hellenist, but one that might be tolerated and approved. Thus Jacqueline de Romilly, Simone Pétrement (the friend and biographer of Simone Weil), and Florence Ramnoux distinguished themselves in the study of Greek by their writings and their illustrious professional careers. The first was elected to the Collège de France for her translations and critical analysis of Thucydides. The second was Head Librarian at the Bibliothèque Nationale (as was Georges Bataille, who got his degree from the Ecole des Chartes, the School of Paleography and Archival Studies). Her work on gnosticism and Neoplatonism made its mark. The third achieved recognition through her research on the Presocratics. A bit later Geneviève Rodis-Lewis became a distinguished scholar of Descartes and Cartesianism; that is, in an area intensively studied by historians of philosophy. I'm not claiming that recognition came easily to them, but it came nevertheless, along with institutional honors to which these women could legitimately aspire. In this context, it was an act of independence, indeed of dissidence, to abandon the history of philosophy and its beginnings in Greek rationalism. This was precisely the audacity of Simone Weil and Simone de Beauvoir, to overtake their male counterparts and engage in contemporary philosophy when women had barely entered the discipline. But there was also a certain appearance of ingratitude, when such fine intellects made use of a university education at last bestowed upon them—and at which they so obviously excelled— outside the disciplines to which they were supposed to limit themselves.

In her *Memoirs of a Dutiful Daughter* Simone de Beauvoir talks about her failed encounter with Simone Weil. A rivalry for first place existed between them, though felt perhaps more strongly by Simone de Beauvoir, for whom it was also an emulation. Thus she prided herself on having obtained second place for the psychology certificate when Simone Weil obtained first place, not so much for the ranking, which wasn't important or consequential, but because together they had outshone the male candidates. Their intellectual rivalry in this instance was sensitive to the climate and context that I wish to describe: these two women wanted to make their male counterparts acknowledge that they were equal to or outstripped them, and this was in fact the case. They also imitated each other in the way they transgressed social boundaries. Both of them daughters of the bourgeoisie, they wanted a profession, a salary, and an intellectual independence that was without precedent, as were the means they employed to arrive at this aim. Simone de Beauvoir had really 'thrown her hat over the windmills'; that is, been especially shocking in her conduct and the company she kept during the years that preceded her decision to take the royal highway of a philosophical career. Simone Weil, all the while earnestly preparing for her university exams, including a competition for entering the Ecole Normale Supérieure (ENS), militated for working-class causes. This gave rise to a mutual distancing. Beauvoir, intent on fitting in with the small coterie of the best young philosophers of the time, was snubbed by Simone Weil, while she herself expressed surprise at Simone Weil's contempt for fashion, running about the corridors of the Sorbonne in a formless smock, her pockets full of tracts, as she recruited for working-class causes. Simone Weil's manner was more offhand and more provocative, an air allowed by her more prestigious position as a *normalienne*, a student at the ENS: witness this anecdote, reported by Simone

Pétrement. Simone Weil at one point insistently solicited the sociologist Bouglé, Director of the ENS, on behalf of a fund for some striking workers; he finally gave in, but he asked that his name not be mentioned. The next day Simone Weil hung up a poster in the entrance hall of the ENS ostentatiously exhorting her fellow students and the teachers to follow the example of the Director and contribute anonymously to the relief fund!

Having passed the *agrégation*, both asserted their independence by entering the teaching profession. According to many reports they were excellent teachers. And in both cases they showed a remarkable determination to push beyond the ordinary play of philosophy, to intervene in the current conventions without, however, ceasing to play the game very well. These two young women deliberately chose a philosophy *engagée*, though Simone de Beauvoir did so later than Simone Weil, who died at the age of 34 in 1943. Each put her talents in the service of a cause invisible to the university establishment, or at least not inscribed in the catalogue of concepts drawn from the history of philosophy, a history which Sartre and Merleau-Ponty also wished to modify from the inside. That these women had the means to carry out their engagement is beyond question. A complete edition of the works of Simone Weil is under way, and shows unequivocally her great philosophical ability, even though the editors initially solicited mystical texts and politically militant writings. Much has been made of Simone de Beauvoir's literary works and her allegiance to the philosophical project of Sartre; and she herself wanted it this way. But it is time to refine this view of her. Her *Ethics of Ambiguity* and the essay 'Must We Burn Sade?' eminently qualify her as a philosopher. In these works she articulates the existentialist ethics that Sartre promised at the end of *Being and Nothingness*, but never published, a lacuna that suggests he wasn't content with what he had written. When asked about it by her last biographer Deirdre Bair, Beauvoir gave her essays on ethics pride of place in her opus, followed by *The Second Sex*, her novels, and her journals. Let us also not forget that she wrote an important review of *The Phenomenology of Perception* at the very moment of its publication, in one of the first issues of *Les Temps modernes*: its competence and lucidity enjoin our admiration. Merleau-Ponty's book was novel in its conception, difficult, and received with great hostility by the academic establishment. Beauvoir read *Elementary Structures of Kinship* by Lévi-Strauss when it was still in proofs, and cited it a number of times in *The Second Sex*. This in itself shows the intellectual liveliness of a young woman whose education followed the usual rectilinear history of philosophy. Another mark of independence and philosophical maturity sets her in analogy with Simone Weil, who read Marx at a young age, and then Machiavelli and Clausewitz. Simone de Beauvoir read Hegel, Marx, Freud, and Lévinas. But both of them broke quite early with German philosophy.

And, to go one step further into a parallelism between the two women (set at odds by other choices), both perceived the impotence of any kind of dialectic to recapture not so much personal experience as the reality of historical situations. Simone de Beauvoir wrote: 'I remember feeling a great sense of peace while reading Hegel in the impersonal setting of the Bibliothèque Nationale during the period before 1940. But as soon as I took up my life again, outside the system, under the real sky, the system seemed completely useless: under the aspect of infinity, it offered only the consolations of death. And I was still hoping to live among living human beings.'[2] This *ambiguity*, which gave its name to her leading work, was also the novel concept which Merleau-Ponty used to undermine the canonicity of perception and its under-writing of clear and distinct ideas. Simone de Beauvoir was thus part of an enterprise which as it happened she went far beyond. She clearly held this attitude at a time when Sartre did not dare to publicly, and was still commited to the dialectic of bad faith. Moreover, in 1975, according to Sylvie le Bon, Beauvoir recalled that the fundamental concept of *The Second Sex* was not alterity or otherness (a Hegelian concept) but rather scarcity, a concept drawn from economics, and in so doing emphasized the blind spot of *Being and Nothingness* and the thesis towards which *The Critique of Dialectical Reason* later tended. Her anticipation of Sartre's rejection of Hegel thus came during the end of the 1940s while she was working on her own book.

Finally, another trait united these two women philosophers: their vivid resentment of all forms of oppression. During the 1930s Simone Weil wrote up and submitted to her former teacher, the philosopher Alain,[3] a text that was published only much later, *On the Principles of Oppression and Liberty*. This was the same theme taken up by Simone de Beauvoir in *The Second Sex*, though necessarily different in emphasis, focus, and mode of illustration. In sum, this philosophy invoked

[2] *Pour une morale de l'ambiguité, Collection Idées* (Paris: Gallimard, 1947), 221.
[3] Alain is a pseudonym for Emile Chartier. He was famous between the two wars for publishing erudite essays and notes in newspapers. He also taught Georges Canguilhem.

by present circumstance, before or after the war, was practiced by both of them in various genres—the newspaper article, the treatise, the academic essay, the political tract, as well as some book prefaces, later penned by Simone de Beauvoir perhaps a bit too generously. Both of them dared to become philosophers in a way that was not expected, not condoned. Neither would have been satisfied to insert herself into the network of academic philosophy, to occupy a place where she would be peripheral or merely tolerated. Rather, they undertook to treat the present, real world philosophically, and did so less prudently than their male contemporaries, and at the risk of colliding with the limits of their enterprise. Here I leave aside Simone Weil.

THE DOUBLE BIND

Begun in June 1946 and completed in 1949, *The Second Sex* took its place in a series of comprehensive works, veritable treatises, which marked the decade of the 1940s and the period immediately after the war: Sartre's *Being and Nothingness* (1944); Merleau-Ponty's *Phenomenology of Perception* (1945); Lévi-Strauss's *Elementary Structures of Kinship* (1947). All these works bore the stamp of a project to redesign experience—or rather to substitute for it something which could no longer be 'experience' but situation, existence, or structures of exchange—and in a manner that avoided the privileged position and a priori legislation of the transcendental subject. They were very different, and indeed their intensifying differences would occupy philosophical debate in France during the 1950s; but they all sought something like concreteness, a way of linking up with the real and ultimately of surmounting the European disaster, for which they held philosophy in part responsible because of its incompetence. They all endorsed an editorial published by Merleau-Ponty in the first issue of *Les Temps modernes* in November 1945 entitled 'La Guerre a eu lieu', on the shortcomings of pre-war academic philosophy: 'We were all pure consciousnesses'. They were announcing their rejection of philosophies of judgment, Cartesian or neo-Kantian. And yet it still seemed possible to make one last attempt, to take up the issue of civil society left open by Hegel at the end of *The Philosophy of Right*. They sought something like experience without Kantian organization; they wished to define a modernity like that glimpsed between the two wars, involving the mediation of the body (Merleau-Ponty), the concrete fabric of exchanges and social connection (Lévi-Strauss following Mauss), the inscription of freedom in existence (Sartre). Restored to the context of a quite telescoped history of philosophy, the question was how to leave Hegel behind without falling into the traps of Nietzsche, a question underscored by the inverse position of Georges Bataille, who claimed both as his mentors, and of Karl Löwith, more academic but no less enlightening, in his book *From Hegel to Nietzsche*.

So why might there not have been, in the midst of all this effort at concreteness and lucidity, a place for a consciousness made specific by its existence as a woman? Couldn't, indeed shouldn't, it have been added to that project whose method was supposed to be description and whose author a consciousness attentive to its own singularities? The intent of *The Second Sex* is clear. Beauvoir undertakes to exhibit how a consciousness which claims both its lucidity and its concreteness might enter into an existence where its life, work, and history are at stake. And yet, if one accords women the right of an engaged consciousness, it must somehow be granted without that moment ever occuring for them in which such a consciousness experiences, to use Sartre's terms, contingency and the radical freedom of its situation, or, to use Beauvoir's terms, the urgent opportunity to make use of its latent possibilities. For women in the real world are, for the most part, never radically free. There are thus two moments in the book's argument. The first conceptualizes the situation of women as existentialism requires, and in order to do so lifts the present condition of women up and out of history and myth. Here, Beauvoir must respond to a public opinion all too ready to suppose that the issue has already been decided: 'A great deal of ink has been spilled over the question of feminism, and now it is more or less closed, so let's not discuss it any more' (*DS* 1986: i. 11). The second moment, which concerns volume ii, discovers in the very writing of the book another and specific liberation: 'One is not born a woman, but becomes one' (*DS* 1986: ii. 13). Thus the education of young women must be reconsidered, so that it does not doom them to an essence or to the destiny of a 'true woman'. And here Simone de Beauvoir makes clear a specific condition of the life of women which reduces it to a caricature of the Sartrean situation, for it is closer to the closed quarters of a harem than to existentialist freedom. For many of them, *Les jeux sont faits*. To counter this, in the final pages of the book she gives a rough sketch of the path that led to freedom in her own life.

The coherence of this schema is faultless, but it is where the gravest difficulties originate. For my present purposes, and for those who have inherited something of Beauvoir's enterprise, it will be useful to set aside two kinds of objections to *The Second Sex*, in order to see more clearly the difficulties inherent in Simone de Beauvoir's project. We can easily ignore the crude objections, the vulgar and malicious jokes, hurtful intentions, and venomous insinuations, particularly those of François Mauriac, who took his revenge on her for articles in which Sartre had criticized his novels. We may ignore as well the political, thinly disguised resentment stemming from erstwhile partisans of the collaborationist government in Vichy. In retrospect these things are too obviously self-serving or simply funny to waste time over. It is less easy to dismiss other much more well-considered objections which have been raised to Simone de Beauvoir's use of historical, anthropological, and political documentation in *The Second Sex*. There is no doubt that the book is rather poorly documented and footnoted in all these areas, and especially with respect to feminist movements in Britain and the United States, about which she knew very little while she was writing the book and even afterwards. These criticisms are certainly legitimate, but they shouldn't prevent us from keeping in mind the circumstances under which the book was written, or its basic intentions. In fact, *The Second Sex* encompasses an impressive amount of documentation, which is, however, always woven into the warp threads of the argument and for that very reason rather less visible. Beauvoir certainly exhibits less concern for footnotes and bibliography than one might have been entitled to demand at an American university in the 1950s, where questions about feminism, industrial society, and anthropology were raised more openly. But we must keep in mind the conditions under which Simone de Beauvoir was working: imagine post-war Paris, where the only source of research material was the Bibliothèque Nationale, rich in nineteenth-century holdings but stripped of more recent books by two successive world wars. Moreover, during that period everyone struggled merely to find fuel and food. And although we might reproach her for publishing the book too soon, there were pressing circumstances that called for its publication: the French government had just given women the right to vote, but those same women who had kept the economy going quite well during the terrible war years were sent back home to the hearth-fires, and those who had been publicly recognized for their part in the fighting and the

Resistance were given a medal and told to leave the theater of history. At best, they were allowed to parade down the Champs-Elysées as the victorious Allied troops entered Paris, and then much later to see the names of their murdered friends inscribed on a marble plaque and bolted on a monument to the dead. At the moment Paris was liberated some people bought themselves a good conscience cheap on the open market, and were thus liberated from the memory of certain compromises with the occupying forces: they took revenge on the generally apolitical population of prostitutes who had plied their wares during economically difficult times with German soldiers. Sartre in *Les Temps modernes* wrote a fine article about the sadism of these pseudo-*Resistants* who emerged in the eleventh hour, rather nastily self-satisfied with pushing around and publicly humiliating such women; a powerful chapter of *The Second Sex* takes up this episode, whose historical import must not be ignored. So we can leave aside the tendentious debates among those who opposed the book on the grounds of their own self-righteousness, and the legitimate debates over the book's documentation. It is all too evident that the place of women in modern society, which concerns all of humanity, requires—now and in the future—more than a single book. *The Second Sex*, written in the middle of the twentieth century, was not meant to be just a manifesto: it must be read in the light of the precise philosophical project it represents. But this light reveals the internal obstacle to Simone de Beauvoir's enterprise, and can be formulated in two ways.

Briefly expressed, the enterprise could not be carried out in the philosophical terms which Simone de Beauvoir employs. To make the point a bit more clearly: her stubborn posing of the question of consciousness and existence in terms of the situation of women—a case extreme because singular—involving a difference never before taken into account, puts at issue the philosophical procedure that was essential to existentialism, a procedure which Simone de Beauvoir, however, never ceased to espouse and employ. To carry this exercise to its limit was to experience the malaise of a double bind. Beauvoir came up against the limit, the closed doors, of existentialism, and she made them apparent. She put the most recent philosophical 'revolution' to the test, and showed that it was unable to grasp the concrete reality of womanhood. On the one hand, this double bind helps us understand certain infelicities internal to Simone de Beauvoir's position, to which her principal line of argument inevitably led her. On the other hand, it also expresses how this book anticipated, or even perhaps directly brought about, the evaporation of the existentialist project during the 1960s.

Beauvoir was clearly committed to Sartrean existentialism, which put forward a convincing schematization of the relationship between consciousness and its situation. Caught up in intentionality and thrown into the world, consciousness was loosed from its essentialist mooring to a subject-substance. Simone de Beauvoir had Sylvie le Bon republish Sartre's first decisive text, *The Transcendence of the Ego* (1936), which argues that consciousness makes its intentionality dialectical in context, in the theater of situations. Sartre's opus sought to elaborate and revise this schema, throughout his books, his critical essays, and (with special mastery) his works of fiction: from *Emotions: Outline of a Theory* to *The Family Idiot*, from his novels to his plays, from *What is Literature?* to the last *Conversations* with Benny Levy.

Nevertheless a sole observation throws the whole existentialist philosophical stance into doubt. Simone de Beauvoir, in writing *The Second Sex*, denies that she herself and indeed all women have access to the instruments of Sartrean existentialism, a position that she continues to endorse. The central argument is blocked: instead of contingency and freedom of choice in the face of an open situation, a woman encounters a destiny, a necessity, a limited range of roles and figures in the closed chamber of history's conspiracy against her. Emotion, bad faith, narcissistic theatricality or hysteria, perhaps best displayed in *Les Sequestrés d'Altona*, are Sartre's way out, his 'exit', and no doubt sources of some of the strongest description in Sartre's writing. But for Simone de Beauvoir they are behaviors from which she wishes above all to liberate women. Those same terms—hysteria, emotional abandonment that leads to servitude, narcissism, and bad faith—become pejorative where women are concerned, not merely descriptive of the behavior or situation to which they are applied. To put it another way, Sartre exploits all the resources of nineteenth-century literature and philosophy, including its dialectical recurrences. Moreover, emotion—which posits a magical world in which it is both satisfied and abolished—is perhaps the truth of this kind of consciousness trapped in contingency. Sartre objectifies and vilifies a nineteenth century to which indeed he never ceased to belong. Baudelaire, Mallarmé, Flaubert, didn't measure up to the standards of 'engaged' literature, which Sartre himself happily did not write either. In Sartre's vast and incontestably inspired output there is nothing that might serve to constitute the philosophical consciousness, immediate and concrete, of a woman in her own situation, along the path of an existential freedom for which Beauvoir is nevertheless searching.

Beauvoir thus has to take up the challenge of philosophical existentialism literally, without allowing herself the range and dimensions of fiction available to Sartre. So, to avoid being caught in the scandalous embrace of feminine emotion, Beauvoir takes up quite adeptly the stance of the 'well-brought-up young lady' and cultivates the art of displaying the everyday in the present indicative. But Sartre's utopia stops here. The drama of bad faith cannot come to terms with a language set in the indicative mood of the everyday, or with the dispersed, interrupted domestic activity of real women which *The Second Sex* anticipates in its last chapters. The philosophical project as such exploded, Beauvoir could not avoid writing a montage of an accusatory report well-documented in history and a vivid description of what remained to be done in the subsequent post-war years. The book ends with the timid proposal of a new kind of fraternity between men and women, a far from realistic and perhaps not even very attractive program.

As a consequence of all that she denied herself while staying faithful to existentialism, Beauvoir wrote her novels in a style studded with dialogue, overloaded with candor and even flat-out indiscretion, far from her earlier philosophical achievement. There remained a certain grandeur in her comportment; for example, her courtroom testimony during a famous abortion trial, or her support of the feminist cause in defense of the most helpless and impoverished. But, for all that, it offered no means of circumventing the obstacle internal to the existentialist project.

Beauvoir couldn't ignore these problems completely. Evidence for this is what she says in a 1975 issue of *L'Arc* devoted to her work, where she takes up again the meaning of her book, with Sylvie le Bon as spokeswoman. She recalled quite emphatically that the book did not so much involve a narrow dialectic of alterity, the woman as 'other', as treat de facto that which constrains in advance the situation of women. This clarification, which sums up well and soberly her experience of the war years, underlines all the more clearly the philosophical difficulty inherent in the enterprise. While the situation of woman escapes the abstract dialectic of identity and otherness, it does have something to do with economics. But on this point Marx himself had little to say. Once again, Beauvoir doesn't take up any of Sartre's issues. It wasn't enough to give up positing the subject as a substance. The struggle of consciousnesses for recognition implied the subordination or rendering secondary of one of the two terms in conflict, and the term 'consciousness' itself became an uncertain or opaque philosophical topos. This is what Simone de Beauvoir painfully, persistently analyzes in her novels, where women are not consulted, are made peripheral, or are endlessly corralled into their non-place. *The Woman Destroyed* is the almost unreadable outcome of all this, a book which even Simone de Beauvoir criticized for its mediocrity. She would thus never forget her own fascination with *Madame Bovary* in which Baudelaire, with astonishing accuracy, identified Emma as the only masculine temperament in the novel; and yet, all the same, *poor Emma*. In *The Second Sex* what sustained Beauvoir's philosophical project also cornered it in the cul-de-sac of existentialism. Having lived out fiercely and passionately the philosophical position of existentialism, she felt betrayed by everything Sartre admitted to Benny Levy at the end of his life, for whatever good or bad reasons. While Beauvoir went on playing the game according to the rules most rigorously, Sartre overturned the chessboard.

The Second Sex, which was supposed to take up where *The Ethics of Ambiguity* left off, bears the burden of her decision. Of course, *ambiguity* sounds better than *bad faith*, but it was, however, no help in thinking about the singularity of a consciousness struggling for recognition of its singularity as effective. A female consciousness as such, taking into account her historical situation, succumbs to an oppressive relation that gives her second place, supposing it does not cast her down into nothingness or turn her into a thing. Beauvoir's choice of title for the book, which she happened upon in a conversation with Sartre and Bost after the latter had evoked the 'third sex' of transvestites, finds its meaning here. With respect to the situation that she describes at length in volume II of *The Second Sex*, the issues of existentialism offered only the worst kind of alibi. We know that the book was written during a period of doubt and must have allowed Beauvoir to understand herself better. In fact, it testifies to this moment, and indeed retains that feature of books she especially loved: 'each one of them carries on its lips the taste of its own life'.

THE BOUNDS OF PHILOSOPHY

The paradox of this atypical book sets it within that vexed emigration out of Hegelianism, where everything from phenomenology to (Marxist) dialectic was attempted. Beauvoir sought a philosophy of consciousness saturated with concreteness, and unencumbered by the trappings of that constitutive subjectivity that Merleau-Ponty (her old classmate) would later call 'the professional fraud of philosophy'. 'One day', Beauvoir writes in *The Force of Circumstance*, 'I had the impulse to explain, to analyze myself. I started to reflect and finally it occurred to me, with a kind of surprise, that the first thing I ought to say about myself was: I am a woman'.[4] But then, would she be able to prevent the treatise she wished to write from turning into a literary 'author's book'? This was also an issue for existentialism generally, as we see in the plays of Sartre or the novels of Queneau. In response to the publication of Heidegger's *What is Metaphysics?* in French translation, Queneau published *Couch Grass (Le Chiendent)* with a portmanteau title that ironically packs together bad fortune *(le mauvais sort)* and weeds *(la mauvaise herbe)*. That kind of literary comment was an ironic way out of the metaphysical existentialism of Heidegger and its tragic 'being towards death'.

But it would take a longer time to force the closed doors of the philosophical canon; that is, to make visible and consequential 'the outside of philosophy'—another phrase of Merleau-Ponty. Simone de Beauvoir's strategy, apparent just under the surface of her avowed existentialism, was to implicate history and to try to force the issue of history by means of history. If it is true that 'one is not born a woman, but becomes one' then what history has made—that history of humanity which covers over and sweeps away the life of individuals—history can unmake. Apropos of the woman 'who is not born a woman', of the issue is not so much biological as cultural. It entails that enough possibilities remain open so that one can 'become a woman' a thousand and one ways. Simone de Beauvoir's argument, which still lies at the heart of current debate, has suffered from being caught up in a mass of historical facts, testimony, chronicles, and citations, none of which is conclusive in itself. In order to do justice to her, let us take up the train of the argument once again.

Clearly, the new kind of education for young women which Beauvoir had just experienced ran counter to the destiny that Naziism and the collaborationist French government in Vichy envisaged for them. But this makes the point too narrowly; once it is granted, the project touches history at its two extremal bounds, biology and anthropology.

---

[4] *La Force des choses* (Paris : Gallimard (Coll. Folio), 1963), i. 259.

The *Phenomenology of Spirit* (and each individual *Bildungsroman*) emerges from the underbrush of nature as it once did for the Old Testament Adam. Hegelian history here loses the advantage of defining human history over against natural history because, quite simply, nature is no longer a metaphysical issue. The realm of biology is now a limit internal to our knowledge, since it is no longer something noumenal, a kind of sorceress casting lots, but only another science. And anthropology, opening up history to a field much vaster than the simple extent of Greece and Rome, robs Aristotelianism of its absolute power, along with the philosophical tropes it has bequeathed to us. So it is with respect to biology and anthropology *inter alia* that we may today reconsider the canvas painted by *The Second Sex*, even granted its loose brushwork.

By articulating the prejudice, ignorance, and terror that blocks all awareness of the sexual divide and sinks womankind in a vague, obtuse nature, and by contesting the classical naturalism that has mystified our origins, Simone de Beauvoir crossed a threshold from which there is no return. So it was good in a sense that there was such a rich catalogue of fantastic representations of the female sex available for satire. But in order to draw deeply on this one source, to denounce effectively certain tenacious prejudices, *The Second Sex* was restricted to a certain range of critical discourse. Greater biological knowledge was needed, more detailed attention to the processes of reproduction, to banish or at least turn back into street talk the vocabulary of abuse or of *action* and *passion* that underwrites the claims of the male sex. Of course, for a long time there was nothing better for conceptualizing the fact of two sexes than Aristotelian physiology, 'good for everything that ails you', and for conceptualizing femininity nothing much besides the Aristotelian notion of privation. Today, scientific investigation of the submicroscopic level of the cell and gene has improved to a degree the analysis of facts, replacing the terror of sex and generation with descriptions of specific sexual characteristics and incredibly diverse behaviors. It is all too clear that on this specific point not only the publication of *The Second Sex* was decisive but also what accompanied it: a half-century of basic genetics, pre- and post-natal medicine, sex education, and family planning have done more to counter prejudice and liberate women than two centuries of militant feminism. Simone de Beauvoir would have better counter-arguments today, since the argument from nature and the accusation of monstrosity for those who deny it have lost the authority of an a priori. Isn't it clear that, in the context of knowledge, the terms *nature* and *natural* risk the fate that historians of law save for the topos of *natural law*, which is, to carry the trace of a fossil concept? We have changed our frame of reference. The canvas of a philosophical depiction that was once learned or scientific and is today not even at the level of popular wisdom has been torn. Let's not forget that a comparable distress, following upon the loss of the physical basis governing our computation of time, and the shipwreck of Kantian experience, rattled Germany in the period between the two wars. It fed into Nazi ideology, which also wished to save 'German physics' from Einstein and Bohr; that is, to save some kind of fixed, unfathomable nature on which to build a novel and terrifying paganism. Indeed, we might surmise that the myth of feminity maintained by the Nazis was just its cynical and emotional double: that fear created a *Kitsch* womanhood, adding a fourth K to the three other emblems—*Kinder, Küche, Kirche*—of her fate according to Hitler's iconography. Of course, I'm not forgetting that anti-feminism has since moved on, to other economic motivations and other terrors.

The argument that Simone de Beauvoir drew from ethnography and anthropology is no less important and no less revisable. She treated it historically, on the evidence of an immemorial contempt for womanhood, but pointed also to the existence of matriarchal societies. However, this was only to step upon a rotten plank: matrilocality doesn't countermand the principle of the exchange of sisters for spouses. Leiris reported back to Simone de Beauvoir several objections made by Lévi-Strauss, who had himself played down the contestable claim of matriarchy. When Beauvoir's biographer Deirdre Bair wanted to interview him on this point Lévi-Strauss refused, saying that he had made his peace with *The Second Sex* a long time ago and moreover had never formulated the vigorous criticisms that were attributed to him by Leiris. He also said that he preferred not to go back to those problems which in any case were never very important to him.[5] And that's all there is to it? Maybe, but precisely because Lévi-Strauss himself profoundly transformed the question, by showing better than anyone else how in the process of exchange women are symbols and bearers of value, introducing culture into nature. In other words, such exchanges that disrupt the pure exercise of force might well have been a means

[5] Deirdre Bair, *Simone de Beauvoir: A Biography* (New York: Summit Books, 1990), 778.

(most likely universal) of bringing the master–slave dialectic to a close. The exchange of women is not just a detail of history, for it changes a great deal—almost everything—to have substituted for that crude ordinal hierarchy of first and second a relationship where there is preference and value. The very notion of value in a relation of exchange was already a great gain. Again and again, it sets in motion the ideas of nature and culture. In the conceptual schemes of the philosophers, exchange did in fact eliminate dialectic.[6] Social anthropology, which sets out a process where before a 'nature' was presupposed, would have served Beauvoir's argument better. Rather than go into it more deeply here, let us recall the penultimate conclusion of *Tristes Tropiques*. At the end of a long voyage through Islamic countries, the anthropologist evokes the harmful effects of the Crusades, which dragged the West through increasingly violent conflict into an imitation of Islam, and concludes enigmatically: 'And it was thus that the West lost its chance to remain female'.[7]

CONCLUSION

In order to memorialize Simone de Beauvoir I have chosen to evoke the first generation of professionally trained women philosophers in France, in which she and Simone Weil distinguished themselves. Indeed, she and Weil were the first women to assume the role of philosopher in the public eye, and that experience coincided with another, infinitely harder and more instructive, which the war imposed on them.[8] Both of them very quickly assessed the small-mindedness of the philosophy that was offered to them, not so much because they were women but because it made its own limits so obvious. Contemporary knowledge far surpassed the received forms of epistemology; criticism could not account for creativity; Hegel cast no light on politics; existentialism cross-examined psychoanalysis; the anxiety and injustice of the civil society they frequented was palpable. Clearly, it was necessary to bring down by several notches a philosophical pretension riveted to Kant's conditions of judgment, and, equally clearly, this work

[6] See Maurice Merleau-Ponty, *De Mauss á Levi-Strauss*, Signes (Paris: Gallimard, 1960).

[7] Claude Lévi-Strauss, *Tristes tropiques* (Paris: Plon, 1955), 473: 'C'est alors que l'Occident a perdu sa chance de rester femme.'

[8] See the article by Elizabeth A. Houlding, 'Simone de Beauvoir: From the Second World War to *The Second Sex*', in *L'Esprit créateur* 33/1 (1993), 39–57. See also Simone Weil's *L'Iliade, poème de la force* (Paris: Gallimard, 1941).

had just begun. I agree that the writings of those two women cannot be classified, but that is not the problem. For good or ill, they took part in the stylistic and philosophical inventiveness of their contemporaries. They also proposed a focusing, quite ethnographic, on some figures of contemporary society for which no points of reference or method were yet available.

After the war public opinion saw them as opposed. Camus published the last writings of Simone Weil, but was outraged by Beauvoir's book. The difference in their physical presentation and comportment is pertinent here too. Simone Weil exposed her body to long hours of work, danger, extreme fatigue, and hostile looks, all with the same passionate intensity. Militant and unabashed, she always stood out; she had nothing of the 'well-brought-up young woman' about her, not even in her appearance. The image of her striding about the Sorbonne which Simone de Beauvoir always recalled coincided with the judgment of the philosopher Jean Cavaillès, who refused to allow Weil to take part in Resistance activities despite her repeated pleas, on the grounds that she would be spotted immediately. Simone Weil had a kind of larger-than-life excessiveness, good for breaking through limits that she knew very well were there, and so making visible possibilities for action and thought never up till then attempted. Every aspect of the public presence of these two women, their writings and their comportment, revealed both an urgency and a kind of privation, and in the eyes of many did so quite outrageously. Their differences are undeniable, and yet mostly located not where gossip and received opinion set them. Despite the divergences of their bearing and engagement, despite the fact that one took the risk of life and the other the risk of death, what Simone de Beauvoir and Simone Weil had in common was political lucidity: neither one was mistaken in her choice to champion the education of women and to modify philosophical custom, even though the latter was pursued at a high cost. And both these projects are still eminently meaningful today.

2

Towards a Friendly, Transatlantic Critique of *The Second Sex*

Michèle Le Doeuff

I didn't participate much in celebrations of the fiftieth anniversary of *The Second Sex*. I felt I had done enough, since I began to address the work of Simone de Beauvoir in 1976, to defend her stature as a philosopher at a time when it wasn't at all fashionable to take her work seriously. Since this volume of essays seeks to put into perspective a life's work which merits the attention of both philosophers and historians of ideas, I would like to say a few words about the circumstances that led me to devote part of my seminar on women and philosophy at the Ecole Normale Supérieure at Fontenay to the study of Beauvoir. It was the couple Beauvoir and Sartre, allied in and by theory, who concerned my young women students, philosophers not much younger than myself. We were trying to explore a general question: Is there any one philosophical framework more appropriate than others for thinking about the liberation of women? This question was directly pertinent to the intellectual relations between Beauvoir and Sartre, since existentialism—at least in principle—produced *The Second Sex*.[1] And it hasn't ceased to preoccupy women philosophers today, even though one tends to find immediate responses to it rather than reflective work on the question itself. See, for example, Martha Nussbaum's *Sex and Social Justice*: with youthful enthusiasm, she assures us that the philosophical canon (Aristotle, Kant, Mill, Rawls) offers good perspectives for thinking about every kind of liberty, including that of women.[2] Other authors celebrate—without nuance—the thought of

[1] In *L'Etude et le rouet* (*Hipparchia's Choice*) (Paris: Seuil, 1989) I tried to show the complexity of the question itself.
[2] For a philosophical and feminist discussion of Martha Nussbaum's point of view see Nancy Bauer's *Simone de Beauvoir, Philosophy, and Feminism* (New York: Columbia, 2001), 30–4.

Lacan or postmodernism. For my own part, I believe the work potentially sparked by the question would really matter: as to the responses,
we must judge them case by case.

In this essay I approach *The Second Sex* differently, keeping in mind
today the students who might be daughters of my students at Fontenay in 1976. The interest of an ongoing interpretation of a text lies in
the fact that what must be *explained* in the text changes from generation to generation. Of course, this doesn't mean that the upcoming
generation poses radically new and different questions to feminism.
However, when a new generation takes up a book it may find certain
points and not others problematic, and expect certain kinds of clarification that the preceding generation didn't need. Let's proceed directly
to such a passage from *The Second Sex*, which seems more strange and
noteworthy now than it did twenty-five years ago, and whose explication will help to set the whole book in historical perspective: 'The
action of women has always been merely symbolic agitation; they won
only what men felt like conceding to them; they didn't take anything;
they received it' (*DS* 1986: i. 19).

My women students of 1976 didn't ask for any explication of this
passage. They and I passed over it with a melting smile, because in 1976
French women had every reason to think that she was just wrong, our
national treasure Simone, and it's human to err! We found it all rather
touching, that in this case she missed the point completely. *Voilà*: someone proposes a theoretical idea which then receives an emphatic refuta-
tion, since reality—historical or otherwise—is seldom what we say it is.
We had only a friendly smile for Simone and her possible flaws. From
1971 to 1975 there was an unprecedented mobilization in France, a
great women's movement for the right to abortion and to contraception, since access to contraception at that time was still very difficult.
Thus in 1976 any French woman knew that women could win what
most men did not in fact want to concede, and that we could claim
rights that no one yet recognized. For the women's movement in those
days didn't just consist in organized protest in order to get the fair
legislation that we wanted. We carried out abortions ourselves and
provided information about contraception, even though the law forbid-
ding this kind of promulgation was not overturned until 1991. It wasn't
symbolic agitation at all; courage was required to run the risk of twenty
years in prison, or more likely the censure of those close to us: courage
to seize collectively the right to manage our own fertility.

Our mobilization was a counter example to Beauvoir's idea that women don't take but only receive, and it bore no relation to the lines claiming that women 'do not have the concrete means to bring themselves together as a unity that would posit itself by its opposition [*se poserait en s'opposant*]', nor like the working class a solidarity based upon work and common interest. On the contrary, our whole experience at that point was of solidarity and the art of organizing ourselves as a unity, one which posits itself by its opposition. As a result, there was no need to explain to that generation of students that Beauvoir was wrong to describe the collective action of women as merely symbolic agitation. Simone herself, who from 1971 onwards joined us in the streets, didn't need to be told that. Surprised that I was writing about and teaching *The Second Sex*, she would say such things as: 'but others since then, especially the Americans, have gone much further'. The analyses of sexual oppression (oppressive relations that never cease to amaze us) carried out by Kate Millett and perhaps also Ti-Grace Atkinson, impressed her a great deal.

HISTORY'S UPHEAVAL

Today, by contrast, one must in fact explain why she wrote those lines at the end of the decade of the forties, and why at that time nobody contested her on that point, as if the idea were obvious, as if the book's first audience recognized itself there. Here is what can be said about the matter. Starting in 1944, by order of the provisional government which was still in Algiers, the right to vote and run for office was, as an especially urgent issue, conferred upon French women for the first time. According to an old Communist who was present at the meeting, even the night before they couldn't find the proper wording for this right and were splitting hairs: perhaps this should hold only for municipal, not national, government? Under the pressure of circumstance, they finally managed to write a version stating unequivocally that women should be given the right to vote and to stand for elections under exactly the same conditions as men; the wording recalls the language of certain groups in nineteenth-century Britain, when male suffrage itself was limited by certain conditions. Ultimately, the constitution of 1946 proclaimed the formal equality of the sexes: high time, you will say. Certainly, but it's not so simple. What kind of mobilization of French women for the right to vote existed between the two world wars? Let's compare comparable things: the French suffrage movement never had the popular support (among women of all classes), spirit, or determination of its Anglo-American counterpart. From the high point of its struggle for reproductive rights, my own generation might also have said that the pre-war movement for civic equality in France was comparatively anemic. Of course, some women—but not many—had demanded full citizenship; some men (a few) had even declared themselves ready to confer it one day. The majority of deputies supported it, without wanting to turn the issue into a *casus belli*; the senators opposed it, however, and the to and fro between the two chambers could have continued for a long time. Keep in mind also that in 1936 Louise Weiss was offered a place in the Popular Front government on condition that she give up her campaign for women's right to vote; she had the class to refuse the offer, saying that she wanted to be elected, not appointed. And she went on to write that feminism should be kicked out of the salons, where it merely strutted and preened: women must demonstrate for their rights in the streets. Her testimony, whether or not it was excessive, must at least be given a hearing.[3]

So, you will say, Beauvoir's dictum that 'the action of women has always been merely symbolic agitation, they only won what men felt like conceding to them' was a historically correct claim in France, at that time. The right to vote, eligibility for office, civil equality, fell upon French women like a gift on a parachute. Beauvoir therefore had local historical reasons to express such a view; her readership had the same reasons for not being surprised by it. And indeed, the admission of women to citizenship is a point that surfaces in the introduction to *The Second Sex*, between the ironic question 'Aren't harem girls happier than a woman voter?' (*DS* 1986: i. 31) and a tip of the hat to John Stuart Mill, whom she must have read superficially, like many another in France. Mill's title to fame was his stubborn defense of the right to vote. On other points he clearly lagged behind Harriet Taylor, Mary Wollstonecraft, and others. Later on in *The Second Sex* Beauvoir represents him as a founding father: 'Following his lead, English women began to organize politically under the leadership of Mrs. Fawcett' (*DS* 1986: i. 221). His lead? Not really. English women began to organize themselves in 1850,

---

[3] Cf. Louise Weiss, *Mémoires d'une Européenne* (Paris: Payot, 1968–76) iii. *Combats pour les femmes (1934–1939)*.

and in 1851 Harriet Taylor took up her pen in the service of the cause. The discourse written by Mill to which Beauvoir refers dates from 1867, and *The Subjection of Women* from 1869.[4]

EXILES

The Second Sex may thus seem, upon first analysis, like a local commentary on a ruling that was itself a local phenomenon. But the genesis of this ruling in Algiers was precisely not wholly local: therefore, if we relate the genesis of *The Second Sex* to the historical change introduced by it, we won't ascribe a purely French origin to that book at all. At the risk of annoying my compatriots, I want to maintain first that the right of women to vote was in France in effect a gift dropped from heaven, that it created an upheaval, and that we owe *The Second Sex* precisely to this divine surprise. And do not suppose for a moment that I give the credit for women's right to vote to De Gaulle personally, which would be futile; better to say that exile is formative. The French government in exile spent four years in London, in a country where women had had the vote for a generation; now, an idea that has been put into effect is always more credible than an unrealized project. Moreover, France was liberated by Americans, Canadians, and the British, all from countries that had conferred citizenship on women many years before, because the women themselves had been able to wrest it from them after a great struggle. In fact, French women in 1944 were the beneficiaries of their Anglo-American sisters, ironically through the intermediary of men, not to say men-at-arms. Beauvoir wasn't unaware of the long struggles of Anglo-American women; there are a few lines about Seneca Falls in the first volume of *The Second Sex*. Nonetheless, she minimizes them, reaffirming that 'the Anglo-Saxon suffragettes only succeeded in exerting pressure because the men were quite disposed to submit to it', and 'all of women's history is made by men' (*DS* 1986: i. 221). In the introduction, however, she is more ambiguous: 'We are no longer like our elder sisters, who put up a fight' (*DS* 1986: i. 29), which recognizes that the elder sisters were combatants, although Beauvoir erases the result of their action and the fact that it attained victory.

[4] Apropos of the intellectual relations between Harriet Taylor and J. S. Mill I might refer the reader to *Sexe du savoir*, p. III (Paris: Aubier, 1998, reissued by Flammarion in the *Champs* series, Paris, 2000).

So we must correct the statement? It wasn't 'the whole history of women that was made by men', but simply the history of French women after World War II that was made by men who had suffered exile and weren't even all French. In the United States as well during the course of the war many exiles reflected on what would be necessary to prevent future wars. The pan-European movement comes to mind, led by Coudenhove-Kalergi, living in the United States and a friend of Louise Weiss from the twenties on. In 1943 he published a work in New York entitled *Crusade for Pan-Europe: Autobiography of a Man and a Movement*. In the original edition we find these words: 'A world in which women would have a decisive influence on politics would certainly be more peaceful than a world directed by men. Therefore feminism is of vital importance for lasting peace. In the post-war world, women should be given not only theoretically but also practically political opportunities equal to men.'[5]

This passage articulates a principle that the Allies would impose after their victory. As for the aftermath, let's not go into raptures: the idea that a politics focused on peace should ally itself with feminism wasn't entirely original. Coudenhove-Kalergi saw feminism simply as a means; but all instrumentalism tends to produce doubtful or fragile effects. Still, it was a bold statement: after all, none of the pre-war pacifists in France would have endorsed feminism, even as a means to an end. In 1943 the idea was linked to the reality of the moment, so much so that it was suppressed when the book was reprinted, as if it were necessary to forget the reason why political status had been given or given back to European women, or to suppress intemperate praise for feminism, absent-mindedly reputed to be 'of vital importance for a durable peace'. Following Claude Barbey-Morand, let's note that this courageous statement only appeared in the original book; it wasn't reprinted in later editions or in any translations.[6] It was only valid in 1943, but afterwards became embarrassing, when the European countries resorted to war in order to try to hold on to their colonies, and when the cold war provided an opportunity to rearm. In any case, if we read it as a document testifying to what was being thought and discussed among the Allies during the war, we can understand why

[5] Richard de Coudenhove-Kalergi, *Crusade for Pan-Europe* (New York: Putnam & Sons, 1943), 301–2.

[6] Claude Barbey-Morand, *La Fiancée Orientale* (Geneva: Institut Européen de Genève, 1997), 79.

they and the provisional French government gave the right to vote as soon as possible to French women, and why it was given back to German women, whereas Switzerland remained the exception in Europe. If the rest of us had had to count only on our own forces, we might not have acquired political rights any faster than Swiss women did. Official history tells us that De Gaulle opposed the Allies meddling in the political reorganization of France. In this light, the haste with which the government settled the question of the vote for women can be explained: it was doubtless urgent to get rid of a potential element of discord between France and the Allies. Perhaps also the government wanted to overtake and pass the Allies, so that the latter wouldn't appear to be the 'authors' of the access of French women to the vote.

AFTERSHOCK

So it was in France after the war. Citizenship fell from heaven upon French women, even though during the years just before 1944 there hadn't been any public debate over that question or indeed any other, and the suffrage movement was so weak that it wasn't even recognized by the Popular Front. Moreover, after the Liberation everyday material problems took precedence over everything else. Citizenship wasn't an explicit or pressing expectation for most French women, even if a minority (who had been in the Resistance or were members of political parties) welcomed and claimed it as their due, and immediately made use of the right to run for office. Beauvoir didn't take any part in the suffrage movement before the war; indeed, it's not certain that after the war she often took advantage of her right to vote. Perhaps like many others she said to herself: 'Well, they gave me the vote, but to what end?' Maybe women were disconcerted to receive what they hadn't themselves demanded, something whose pertinence they didn't clearly see. On the other hand, even if the ruling of 1944 wasn't preceded by a public debate (for obvious reasons!), it certainly did engender debate after the fact. Indeed, what is striking about the introduction to *The Second Sex* is its tone of 'aftershock', not to say post-apocalypse. Adversaries of feminism complained: 'Woman is lost, woman is lost!' and 'Woman is in danger!' Beauvoir herself advised 'detachment'. Her book wasn't intended to begin a struggle, but to elucidate a situation. Her way of describing her project is quite clear: 'At the end of an era of chaotic polemic, this book is one attempt among others to take our bearings' (*DS* 1986: i. 30). Beauvoir basically saw herself as Hegel's owl, which flies in the twilight of an era.

Take our bearings, but with respect to what? About a personal concern, of course: Look! I've received what I didn't ask for. Who am I to receive this thing, I who never posited myself as the subject of the demand? Who am I, to have received something when the public discourse around me always tells me I'm not worthy of it? And also about a collective concern: many women must have asked themselves to what they owed the honor lately conferred upon them, while everywhere the misogynists flew into rages, as if at every advance in the rights of women—imposed by the State or wrested from it—something had been stolen from them. One of the enigmas which *The Second Sex* strives to elucidate is the latter, which remains enigmatic today, against which sooner or later every woman collides: But what is it exactly that men are deprived of when I have rights and become their equal? Or again: Since we have now achieved political representation and everything is settled, how does it happen that I have so much trouble inserting myself into, and participating in, the human *Mitsein*? The force of Beauvoir's book lies here, and its unchanging value. One could write the same thing now, at the beginning of a new century: Since everything is settled, how does it happen that everything still isn't settled? And with *The Second Sex* a new worry has appeared: 'What kind of life can our younger sisters expect?' To her own younger sisters (you and me) Beauvoir explains that if some things are unsettled, don't compound the problem by thinking the problem comes from us, from a feminine essence that dooms us to exclusion, but rather from . . . Well, read her book!

AT THE CROSSROADS

The paradox that allows *The Second Sex* to unfold (everything is settled and nothing is settled) may be viewed as precisely what determined the debates of the second half of the twentieth century. Indeed, starting off from this point two avenues are possible. The first, elaborated in the writings of Beauvoir's adversaries ('Woman is lost!'), embroiders the idea of a feminine nature that is allergic to civic rights and indifferent to freedom, a nature that turns away from equality because the latter would bestow rights on the same basis on which men enjoy them, so much so that equality would be equivalent to identity between men and women. Sexual difference would be lost, and women as such would disappear. This current of thought, which plays upon a crude conflation of equality and identity, wells up in the writings of Irigaray, Cixous, and Kristeva, with support at first from certain male French intellectuals, then from the 'new French feminism' on the other side of the Atlantic: as if in honor of the passage of time these new thinkers, being more recent than Beauvoir, must supplant her. In order to resist this current, it's not enough to criticize it as essentialist. One must also emphasize that the feminine essence it proposes is constituted to undermine community between men and women, and the equality of the sexes within that community. The most recent avatar of this tendency is thriving in anthropology, a field where some find it possible to claim that the fundamental cause of masculine domination is the consent of women to domination. We allegedly have a nature that wishes to be dominated![7] The second avenue is that of Beauvoir, who takes the paradox seriously, without looking for an immediate response to it, noting this enigma: men consider women as the other; women don't treat men in a similar fashion. She presents an inventory of the manifold difficulties that women must always face, and deciphers aspects of the enigma, not the totality. Making superb use of skepticism, she considers various explanations in order to reject them, one after another. Neither biology, nor the unconscious, nor economic circumstance is a foundation for the oppression of women, since the latter is not 'founded' but constructed in terms of the process by which 'one becomes a woman'.[8]

To do justice to Beauvoir's thought with full rigor we have to see that the issue is feminine identity (constructed, not given), and integrate her more materialist remarks with respect to it. Thus she writes; 'Men have always possessed all the concrete means and powers; since the first epoch of patriarchy, they have found it useful to keep women in a dependent state; their codes were set up against her', etc. (DS 1986: i. 237). Patriarchy exists; since it exists, the processes by which one becomes a woman require—of necessity and in a variety of manners—the internalization of modes and modalities of subordination. So we can admit that oppression finds one point of anchorage

[7] See Nicole-Claude Mathieu, 'Quand céder n'est pas consentir', in L'Arraisonnement des femmes (Paris: Editions de l'EHESS, 1985), reprinted in N-C. Mathieu, L'Anatomie politique (Paris: Editions Coté-Femmes), ch. V. See also my Le Sexe du savoir, 299 ff.

[8] I develop this point in Hipparchia's Choice.

(and only one among others, not its sole cause) in feminine identity thus constructed, but for Beauvoir no human being is, or should be, riveted to or frozen in a describable identity. The simple fact of inflicting any identity on women, whatever it is, must be contested.

ARISTOTLE AS HEARSAY

This explains, beyond her allusion to 'chaotic polemics', the abundance of citations, often without footnotes, at the beginning of *The Second Sex* which—on the authority of Pythagoras, Plato, Aristotle, Saint Thomas...up to Lévinas—pronounce upon a joyless identity for women. It's easy to reconstitute those polemics in imagination: they occurred not only in newspapers and literary journals. Beauvoir spent much of her life in bistros, with her friends and former fellow-students. Certain citations in the introduction can be understood as fragments of semi-learned conversations, where one throws in a reference to St Thomas or to Aristotle for effect, in order to comment on the present. 'You women may have citizenship, but, as Aristotle says, "woman is woman in virtue of a certain lack of qualities" '—things of that nature, which wound and are designed to humiliate. Might it not have been the Clairaut of Beauvoir's *Memoirs of a Dutiful Daughter* who offered, in a café near the Sorbonne, this medieval dictum: *tota mulier in utero?* The Simone of the late forties had doubtless not read medieval authors for a long time. She is citing not texts but cruel fragments of hearsay, living words of her time and place, and we may treat them as such. Indeed, during periods when by some accident of history the law arranges the feudalization of women less harshly, phallocrats can still draw upon culture, verbal violence and scholarly appeals to give women a negative idea of ourselves—to assign us a fossilized essence.

The reference to Plato deserves mention: 'Among the blessings for which Plato thanks the Gods, the first was that he was created a free citizen, and the second that he was created a man and not a woman.' The same opinion, likewise attributed to Plato, occurs in the writings of Gabrielle Suchon. But it isn't at all certain that Plato said exactly that, even though in the *Timaeus* a man who fails the tests of his life is destined to be reborn as a woman. Beauvoir doubtless came across this pseudo-Platonic thought in Poulain de la Barre, as did, by the way, Suchon. From this we may extract a methodological principle.

Although well trained in the history of philosophy, Beauvoir is not acting in that capacity here. Rather than verifying the citations in order to inscribe them in a history of philosophy, she offers them pell-mell, as fragments which were still thought meaningful in Paris at the time she was writing her book, and, as she forthrightly concluded: 'Legislators, priests, philosophers, writers, and scholars have tried desperately to demonstrate that the subordinate position of women is intended by heaven and profitable on earth. The religions invented by men reflect this will to domination... They put philosophy and theology in its service' (*DS* 1986: i. 23). I wish to acknowledge my own considerable debt to this thought. Yes, I read it when I was eighteen or twenty years old, and found there the energy I needed always to maintain a critical distance from philosophy, which is, however, very dear to me. I made the decision to write *L'Etude et le rouet* (translated into English as *Hipparchia's Choice*) on the day of Simone's funeral, in part because I wanted to give that debt expression, and keep Simone alive in memory. And, since I had inherited her concern for 'our younger sisters', I thought I had a legacy to keep alive too.

VIGNETTE

Two references in the introduction are contemporary with the drafting of *The Second Sex*: Lévinas's *Time and the Other*, and Lévi-Strauss's *Elementary Structures of Kinship*. Lévinas is cited in a footnote:

Couldn't there be a situation where otherness belonged to a being in a positive way, as an essence?... I think that the absolutely contrary, whose contrariety isn't affected at all by any relation that can be established between it and its correlative, the contrariety that allows a term to remain absolutely other, is the feminine... Otherness is fulfilled in the feminine. A term in the same rank, but with a sense opposed to consciousness.

Beauvoir comments: 'I suppose that Mr Lévinas hasn't forgotten that woman is also consciousness for herself [*pour soi*]' (*DS* 1986: i. 15–16). Doubtless she also read what follows this passage in *Time and the Other*, where Lévinas adds further on: 'I don't wish to ignore the legitimate claims of feminism.' But we have here in a nutshell the situation just after the war: a split between the juridico-political level, where things were getting better for women, and the metaphysical-imaginary level, where 'the feminine' is designated as the other and as an essence, a term opposed to consciousness.[9] When Lévinas 'writes that woman is mysterious, he tacitly assumes that she is mysterious for men', says Beauvoir. Just as she affirms later on that there isn't a problem about blacks—it is racist whites that are a problem—nor a Jewish question but rather a question of anti-Semitism (*DS* 1986: i. 221), so by analogy it could be said that 'feminine being' as other is a mere effect of what she calls patriarchy. The mystery for Beauvoir is the domination of one sex by another, and a 'key to the mystery' is offered in her book: superiority has been accorded not so much to men over women, but to the sex that kills over the sex that engenders. This has to do with function, not essence.

Beauvoir makes use of the assimilation of the feminine to the category of other in order better to unravel the alleged evidence for it. (1) The idea of a logic of the same and the other can be maintained without projecting a human subject on one of the terms. The duality day/night, for example, doesn't necessarily presuppose anthropomorphism. (2) The logic of the same and the other is used to describe the mutual relations among communities, not the relation between the sexes alone. It is, rather, a constitutive principle for any community, and Lévi-Strauss supports this claim by defining sociality in general—not bound to the duality of the sexes—in terms of this logic: 'duality, alternation, opposition, and symmetry' he describes as 'the fundamental, immediate data of social reality'. Beauvoir doesn't contest this, nor the inadequacy of this reduction to binary arithmetic: What about those social or symbolic systems structured by three terms, or n terms? She merely lets us feel a moral reticence: the antagonism between the same and the other wouldn't exist if human reality were the locus of friendship. Beauvoir lets Lévi-Strauss have his say, in order to approach Hegel and reciprocity within hostility. And there she finds her subject: In relations between the sexes, what is lacking is precisely reciprocity. Why?

The source of this moral reticence is most probably Bergson: the phrase 'immediate data of the social' in Lévi-Strauss seems also to be a

---

[9] At the time of writing this essay the Lévinas affair was pending in the courts. Shortly before his death, Lévinas signed a will leaving *le droit moral* (legal authority over his books and manuscripts) to his son, to the detriment of his daughter. The legal question is whether, at that moment, he was lucid enough to write a will. One day perhaps someone will write the history of this affair, emblematic of a question that concerns us: Is 'the feminine a metaphysical figure that doesn't lead to any consequences in the real world or is there a possible confusion of the two levels, and in this case what is the agency that organizes the confusion?

transposition of a title of Bergson's: *Time and Free Will: An Essay on the Immediate Data of Consciousness*. In fact, Bergson's philosophy could be deemed a major but veiled source of inspiration for the whole introduction to *The Second Sex*. Bergson's *The Two Sources of Morality and Religion* offers a distinction between a closed morality, attachment to the group to which one belongs and obligation to the members of the closed community to which one belongs, and open morality, a humane dynamic and love of humanity in general that goes beyond the interests of the closed group. This distinction could be applied to the view that Beauvoir has of men: most of them remain within sexism, which is closed. By contrast, she regards Poulain de la Barre and to a lesser degree Montaigne, Diderot, Condorcet, and Mill as men who transcended the corporate interests of their sex. She pays tribute to them with a greater warmth than she shows to any feminist women, as if the feminism of women represented a closed morality, in itself not worthy of praise because it is closed, and which moreover can't be genuine because women don't even constitute a group.

TRANSATLANTIC REFLECTIONS

At the beginning of 1947 Beauvoir was in the United States, where Lévi-Strauss was living; they met there, and would meet again. The many references to American life in the work even lead one to think that *The Second Sex*, begun the preceding year, took shape during that trip and Simone's sojourn at American universities. In a *New Yorker* interview from 22 February 1947 she announces that she is 'working on a very serious book about women', and adds: 'I talked to a great number of American women in order to understand their point of view. I find it very different from that of French women. But you will have to wait for my book. I can't explain it in three words.'[10] How exactly did the point of view of American women differ from that of French women in 1947? *The Second Sex* is hardly informative on this issue, as also Beauvoir's published correspondence. The introduction contains two rather nasty remarks about American women; according to Beauvoir, 'they willingly believe that woman as such no longer exists', and 'their hardened attitude of defiance proves they are haunted

---

[10] *Les Ecrits de Simone de Beauvoir*, ed. Claude Francis and Fernande Gontier (Paris: Gallimard, 1979), 144.

by the feeling of their femininity'. Her letters teem with anti-American sentiment; Americans irritated Simone by saying things like: 'It wasn't Stalin who gave you food to eat. Stalingrad? Meaningless. It was we who won the war for you.' Annoyed, she brands such people as 'pure American imperialists': she claims that the presence of dollars backing them up is palpable, and leaves her steak half eaten on her plate.[11]

This hostility seems to reflect the humiliation, muted but real, that France endured when it was liberated by a foreign army, indeed by a number of foreign armies. Was it this humiliation—redoubled in the case of the liberation of women—which echoed in the unkind remarks of Simone de Beauvoir, who among other things reproached Sartre for his indulgent approval of 'American women in general'? I would like to propose a conjecture: the academic women whom Simone encountered at Vassar and Wellesley, whom she described as 'old ladies', might precisely have tried to tell her that women occasionally make their own history, that their grandmothers had invented their own aims and attained their civil liberties themselves, something Beauvoir didn't want to hear. She had obviously read the beginning of A History of Woman's Suffrage.[12] It might even have happened that someone put this volume under her nose, a volume more easily found at Wellesley than in post-war France. In the New Yorker interview she alludes to 'the point of view of French women', which differs from that of American women. Was there indeed a point of view in France before the publication of The Second Sex? Apart from the Union des Femmes Françaises, created in November 1944 by women from the Resistance and soon to pass under the control of the Communist Party, there wasn't much. Indeed, it was because there wasn't really 'a point of view of French women' that The Second Sex filled a void, selling 20,000 copies in the first week.

A great book is not necessarily a book free from errors or ingenuousness. Any important philosophical work contains points whose fallibility gradually comes to light, and so it is with The Second Sex. Conversely, to reflect on what is not tenable in a book is not to dismiss the effort that went into it, nor its effects. As a student I read this book

---

[11] 7 February 1947, in Lettres à Sartre, ii (Paris: Gallimard, 1990), 29.

[12] A History of Woman's Suffrage, ed. Elizabeth Cady Stanton, Susan B. Anthony, and Matilda Joslyn Gage, i (New York, 1881). The Second Sex (DS 1986: i. 214) evokes the great inaugural event at Seneca Falls, though Beauvoir makes an error, for the Convention took place in 1848, not 1840.

as a direct address: 'Woman, know thyself'. Know the situation that made you what you are and constrains you, over against those discourses that imply there is nothing to know, or that others—certain others—know better than you what you must be. Having dramatized the question, Beauvoir makes it less dramatic, more practical. 'Watch out for that cliff-edge, just there', 'for that dead-end', 'for that nest of contradictions', the philosophical big sister advises, exhorting me to keep my eyes open. When we consider the extraordinary impact her book has had despite appalling, truncated translations and, even in France, mutilated editions, we have to suppose that a necessarily simple message is getting across, along with, far away at the horizon, hope for new relations between the sexes.

Since then I've read other books and had a variety of experiences, but I've never doubted that what feminism owes itself is to exist as an open politics, an open thought and practice, and to become so more and more. This is why we should leave behind once and for all appeals to nationalism and parochial labels. If *The Second Sex* threatens to become the emblem of a feminism completely 'made in France', forgetful of the encouragement that the American women's liberation movement gave Europe in 1970; if, as history is rewritten, the book were to obscure the spark received from the other side of the Atlantic Ocean; in that case, someone must write a more detailed history of the international exchanges within feminism.

ACKNOWLEDGEMENTS

This essay was first delivered as a paper at a conference organized by Ingrid Galster, 'Pour une édition critique du Deuxième Sexe', and held in Eichstätt, Germany, in November 1999.

3

While We Wait: Notes on the English Translation of *The Second Sex*

Toril Moi

That the English translation of Simone de Beauvoir's *The Second Sex* is bad has been well known ever since Margaret Simons published her ground-breaking essay 'The Silencing of Simone de Beauvoir: Guess What's Missing from *The Second Sex*' in 1983.[1] So why write another essay on the same topic twenty years later? The first and most obvious reason is that English-speaking readers still have to use the text so cogently criticized by Simons, namely H. M. Parshley's 'edition and translation'. Since Simons wrote her essay a new generation of readers have started reading Beauvoir. In 1983, 'French feminist theory' was usually taken to mean Irigaray, Kristeva, and Cixous. Today, it might just as well mean Beauvoir, for *The Second Sex* is again being widely read and discussed across the disciplines. A new wave of rigorous Beauvoir scholarship is in its first flourishing. This new wave has already produced increased recognition of Beauvoir's philosophical importance, but there is still a long way to go before her place in the history of philosophy is secure.[2]

---

[1] Margaret Simons, 'The Silencing of Simone de Beauvoir: Guess What's Missing from *The Second Sex*', *Women's Studies International Forum*, 6/5 (1983), 559–64.

[2] The philosophical revision of Beauvoir started in Europe with Michèle Le Doeuff, *Hipparchia's Choice: An Essay Concerning Women, Philosophy, etc.*, trans. Trista Selous (Oxford: Blackwell, 1991), first published in Paris in 1989, and continued with Sonia Kruks, *Situation and Human Existence: Freedom, Subjectivity and Society* (London: Unwin Hyman, 1990), Eva Lundgren-Gothlin, *Sex and Existence*, trans. Linda Schenck (Hanover, NH: Wesleyan, 1996), first published in Gothenburg in 1991, Karen Vintges, *Philosophy as Passion: The Thinking of Simone de Beauvoir*, trans. Anne Lavelle (Bloomington, Ind.: Indiana University Press, 1996), first published in Amsterdam in 1992, and Toril Moi, *Simone de Beauvoir: The Making of an Intellectual Woman* (Oxford: Blackwell, 1994). Recently so many books have been published

The renewed interest in Beauvoir means that more readers than ever are spending more time scrutinizing the fine details of Beauvoir's arguments. Inevitably, this has also increased the interest in the state of the translation. Over the years it has become clear to me that the translation is, if anything, even worse than Simons suspected. This is particularly true with respect to its philosophical shortcomings. Readers of Beauvoir in English need to know this. In French *The Second Sex* is almost a thousand pages long. In English there are mistakes and omissions on every page. Only a tome as long as the book itself could document all the flaws in this translation. Simons opened the way, but there is room for a lot more work on the subject. In Britain, for example, Elizabeth Fallaize has recently written an excellent paper on the cuts and omissions in the chapter on 'The Married Woman'.[3] More work will surely follow, until the day that there is a new, reliable English text of this feminist classic.[4]

---

on Beauvoir's philosophy that I can't mention more than a few: Debra B. Bergoffen, *The Philosophy of Simone de Beauvoir: Gendered Phenomenologies, Erotic Generosities* (Albany, NY: State University of New York Press, 1997), Margaret A. Simons, *Beauvoir and* The Second Sex*: Feminism, Race, and the Origins of Existentialism* (Lanham, Md.: Rowman & Littlefield, 1999), Toril Moi, *What Is a Woman? And Other Essays* (Oxford: Oxford University Press, 1999), and Nancy Bauer, *Simone de Beauvoir, Philosophy, and Feminism* (New York: Columbia, 2001) all focus on the philosophical strengths of *The Second Sex*. Finally, I should mention three recent anthologies of essays on Beauvoir, which taken together give a splendid overview of the energy and passion of contemporary Beauvoir studies: Margaret A. Simons (ed.), *Feminist Interpretations of Simone de Beauvoir* (University Park, Penn.: Pennsylvania State University Press, 1995); Ruth Evans (ed.), *Simone de Beauvoir's* The Second Sex*: New Interdisciplinary Essays* (Manchester: University of Manchester Press, 1998); Elizabeth Fallaize (ed.), *Simone de Beauvoir: A Critical Reader* (London: Routledge, 1998).

[3] In this essay I shall be quoting from Elizabeth Fallaize's unpublished English manuscript entitled 'The Housewife's Destiny: Translating Simone de Beauvoir's "The Married Woman"' (written in 1999). A French translation of this text was published in 2002 as Elizabeth Fallaize, 'Le Destin de la femme au foyer: traduire "la femme mariée" de Simone de Beauvoir', in *Cinquantenaire du Deuxième Sexe*, ed. Christine Delphy and Sylvie Chaperon, with assistance from Kate and Edward Fullbrook (Paris: Editions Syllepse, 2002), 468–74. Fallaize is also the author of a study of Beauvoir's fiction, *The Novels of Simone de Beauvoir* (London and New York: Routledge, 1988).

[4] To my knowledge, there are six other essays partly or wholly concerned with Beauvoir and translation, but only Simons and Fallaize have original things to say about the translation of *The Second Sex*. Anna Alexander, 'The Eclipse of Gender: Simone de Beauvoir and the *différance* of Translation', *Philosophy Today*, 41/1 (1997), 112–22, discusses reasons why Beauvoir has been neglected and includes a brief account of Simons's paper. Terry Keefe analyzes the translation of Beauvoir's interview with Alice Schwartzer included in Elaine Marks and Isabelle de Courtivron's much used anthology *New French Feminisms* in Terry

One might think that once the sorry state of the translation was brought to the attention of Beauvoir's publishers they would be eager to rectify it. Not so. Thanks to Margaret Simons's efforts, Knopf (the original hardback publishers) and Vintage (responsible for the paperback) have known about the problems with the English text since the early 1980s. They have repeatedly refused to do anything at all. (Knopf and Vintage are imprints of Random House.) To be sure, the translator, H. M. Parshley (1884–1953), must share responsibility for the state of the text. But whatever Parshley's linguistic and philosophical shortcomings may have been, he is not responsible for the fact that Knopf/ Vintage still refuse to commission a new translation or to let some other publisher try its hand at the task.

Beauvoir's text first entered the US best-seller lists in the spring of 1953. In the intervening years the paperback edition of the English translation has sold well over a million copies.[5] It remains politically urgent to continue to draw attention to the deplorable state of the English text. Perhaps it may even help to persuade Knopf/Vintage to relent. But I am not writing for the publishers. They already know all they need to know about the state of the text. The main purpose of this essay is to alert contemporary readers of Beauvoir to the shortcomings of the existing translation of *The Second Sex*. While we wait

---

Keefe, 'Another 'Silencing of Beauvoir'? Guess What's Missing This Time', *French Studies Bulletin*, 50 (1994), 18–20. Anne D. Cordero has written an excellent paper on the translation of *Memoirs of a Dutiful Daughter* and another on the translation of the short story 'The Woman Destroyed' (Anne D. Cordero, 'Gender Terminology in Simone de Beauvoir and her Translators', *The Platte Valley Review*, 23/2 (1995) 51–61; Anne D. Cordero, 'Simone de Beauvoir Twice Removed', *Simone de Beauvoir Studies*, 7 (1990), 49–56). Sheryl A. Englund, 'A Dignified Success: Knopf's Translation and Promotion of *The Second Sex*', *Publishing Research Quarterly*, 10/2 (1994), 5–18, is not in fact about the translation itself but about the correspondence between Knopf and H. M. Parshley, and the marketing and promotion of the book. The essay quotes documentary evidence from Knopf archives and is of some historical interest, although Englund appears to be unaware of Simons's pioneering work: 'There has been no thorough study of the specific alterations that Parshley made in the translation of *Le Deuxième sexe*', Englund writes (17). Finally, H. M. Parshley's correspondence with Knopf is presented in Yolanda A. Patterson, 'H. M. Parshley et son combat contre l'amputation de la version américaine', in *Cinquantenaire du Deuxième Sexe*, ed. Christine Delphy and Sylvie Chaperon, with assistance from Kate and Edward Fullbrook (Paris: Editions Syllepse, 2002), 475–81.

[5] 'Paperback sales of the American edition of "The Second Sex" reportedly have passed the million mark', Richard Gillman wrote in 1988 ('The Man Behind the Feminist Bible', *New York Times Book Review*, 22 May 1988, 40).

for a new translation we need to be able to teach and read Beauvoir's epochal essay without being trapped by Parshley's mistakes.

Drawing on the work of Simons and Fallaize, I shall first discuss Parshley's cuts and omissions. Then I shall go on to show that the philosophical incompetence of the translation produces a text that is damaging to Beauvoir's intellectual reputation in particular and to the reputation of feminist philosophy in general, and that the translation at times makes it difficult to discover what Beauvoir actually thought about important feminist issues. My example here will be Beauvoir's discussion of motherhood. Finally, in the last section of the article I shall discuss the story behind the text: the publishing history, the translator's role, and what the chances are of getting a new translation and edition in the near future. I hope that this paper will be useful to anyone reading the English text of *The Second Sex*. Given that the introduction to *The Second Sex* is particularly widely used in interdisciplinary feminist contexts, I have paid special attention to this part of the book, but I also provide a wide range of new examples and analyses from the rest of the text. Throughout I stress the philosophical and theoretical consequences of Parshley's misunderstandings of the text.[6]

Simone de Beauvoir died in 1986. Her works will not enter the public domain until 2056. I sincerely hope that we won't have to wait until then before we can read her epochal essay in a decent English translation. While we wait, I offer this essay as a stopgap measure. Read alongside Beauvoir's text it should help English-language readers of *The Second Sex* to deal with the shortcomings of a text they are still obliged to use.

A SORRY MESS: CUTS AND OMISSIONS

In an admiring essay on H. M. Parshley, written partly in response to Margaret Simons's 1983 critique, Richard Gillman states: 'In his correspondence with Alfred Knopf and others at the New York publishing house, Parshley refers specifically to cutting or condensing the equiva-

---

[6] The difference between this article and Margaret Simons's pioneering paper is that she pays more attention to the cuts in the text and I pay more attention to the philosophical and theoretical inadequacies of the English text. Nevertheless I too shall speak of cuts, and, although she only spends one densely printed page documenting philosophical mistranslations, Simons was the first to draw attention to some of the most egregious philosophical errors in the English text. Fallaize provides a full and sensitive discussion of the effects of the severe cuts in the 'Married Woman' chapter and relates these to the lack of recognition of Beauvoir's analysis of housework in the work of Betty Friedan and Anne Oakley.

lent of 145 pages from the original two-volume, 972-page French edition.[7] I own the original edition and can certify that it is indeed 972
pages long. If Parshley did what he said he was doing, then he cut 15
per cent of Beauvoir's text, even more than the 10 per cent that Simons
estimated to have been deleted.

These cuts are not signalled in the text. The only trace of them is
the one line on the title page that proclaims that the book is 'translated and edited' by H. M. Parshley. The acknowledgment that some
'editing' had been going on was, incidentally, missing in the original
1953 edition.[8] Simons has shown that the women's history section is
hard hit. Here Parshley cut seventy-eight women's names and eradicated just about every reference to socialist feminism.[9] Within the
history section the chapter on the Middle Ages has fared the worst: it
is reduced to a third of the original length.[10] According to Simons,
Parshley also cut descriptions of women's anger and women's oppression, while keeping intact references to men's feelings. 'Parshley apparently found evidence of woman's oppression, and genuine struggle
between the sexes irritating, [and] systematically deleted misogynist
diatribes and feminist arguments', she writes.[11] I can attest to this. As
an example, I offer one of my own favourite 'Parshleyisms', from the
introduction:

BEAUVOIR: La légende qui prétend que les Sabines ravies ont opposé à leurs
ravisseurs une stérilité obstinée, raconte aussi qu'en les frappant de lanières
de cuir les hommes ont eu magiquement raison de leur résistance... (*DS*
1986, i. 20)

LITERAL TRANSLATION: The legend that claims that the ravished Sabine women
opposed their ravishers with stubborn sterility, also tells us that the men
magically overcame their resistance by beating them with leather straps...

PARSHLEY: In the legend of the Sabine women, the latter soon abandoned their
plan of remaining sterile to punish their ravishers... (*SS* 1989, p. xxvi)

[7] Gillman, 'Feminist Bible', 40. Although Gillman's rhetorical strategy is deplorable (he
seems to believe that in order to defend Parshley he has to attack feminists in general and
Margaret Simons in particular), his essay is a goldmine of information about Parshley, and I
have found it very useful in writing this essay.

[8] Although the copyright page gives 1952 as the date of the edition, the American
translation of *The Second Sex* was published on 24 February 1953. Parshley finished his
translation on 7 August 1951 (see Gillman, 'Feminist Bible', 41).

[9] Simons, 'Silencing', 560, 562.

[10] I have this figure from the table of cuts in *The Second Sex* included as an appendix on
page 9 in the manuscript version of Fallaize, 'The Housewife's Destiny'.

[11] Simons, 'Silencing', 562.

Simons was also the first to point out that almost half the chapter (about 35 pages) on 'The Married Woman' was cut by Parshley. Included in the cuts are entire pages from Beauvoir's ground-breaking, Bachelard-inspired analysis of housework.[12] In the 'Married Woman' chapter Parshley 'drastically cuts much of [Beauvoir's] supporting evidence', Fallaize writes.[13] According to Fallaize, Parshley routinely expurgates quotations from French sources while occasionally expanding Beauvoir's references to American sources. He also eliminates her copious literary references and has little time for psychological or psychoanalytical evidence. (Although Fallaize writes only about the 'Married Woman' chapter, all this is true for the rest of the book as well.) Moreover, Fallaize shows, Beauvoir's brilliant analysis of the Manichean battle between good and evil enacted in a housewife's everyday struggle against dirt is reduced to incomprehensible jumble in Parshley's attempt to turn eleven pages in French (*DS* 1986, ii. 260–71) into five pages in English (*SS* 1989, 448–52): 'Whole pages consist of a mishmash of half sentences and summaries cobbled together in a mess which cannot be dignified with the name of translation.'[14]

In general, Fallaize demonstrates that Parshley's cuts hit hard Beauvoir's extensive documentation of women's lived experience. Her lively quotes from women's diaries, novels, and letters, from male novelists describing women, and from psychoanalytical case studies disappear without trace. 'There is a loss of anecdote told from women's point of view, making the text seem less rooted in women's experience', Fallaize writes. The text comes across as 'Beauvoir's personal opinion', she concludes, rather than as well-supported analysis of a specific historical and cultural situation.[15]

Here's a small example to help bring out the importance of Fallaize's conclusion. 'A text by Virginia Woolf shows how reality is concentrated in the house, while the space outside collapses', Beauvoir writes (*DS* 1986, ii. 262; my translation).[16] This sentence is followed by six lines by Woolf making precisely this point. Parshley, on the other hand, writes:

---

[12] Simons, 'Silencing', 562. One example can be found in *SS* 1989, 451, where Parshley in six and a half lines summarizes three full pages in Beauvoir's original (see *DS* 1986, ii. 263–6).
[13] Fallaize, 'The Housewife's Destiny', 3.
[14] Ibid. 4.
[15] Both quotations in this paragraph come from Fallaize, 'The Housewife's Destiny', 4.
[16] 'Un texte de V. Woolf nous montre la réalité se concentrant dans la maison, tandis que l'espace du dehors s'effondre' (*DS* 1986, ii. 262).

'Reality is concentrated inside the house, while outer space seems to collapse' (*SS* 1989, 450), before briskly moving on to the next paragraph. There is no trace of Woolf here. The sentence is no longer a commentary foregrounding the powers of observation of an admired woman writer but a dogmatic proclamation of dubious validity.

Such cuts are not ideologically innocent. According to Fallaize, they impoverish Beauvoir's text by depriving us of the rich variety of women's voices that make up the French text. In my view they also make it particularly easy for hostile critics of Beauvoir to claim that she was uninterested in women, and therefore 'male-identified', yet even the most cursory reading of the French text shows that this accusation could not be more unfair.[17]

One of the conclusions one can draw from reading Fallaize's suggestive essay is that whereas in French *The Second Sex* provides an intimate view of French culture in the mid-twentieth century, in English it does not. Inspired by Fallaize, I took a closer look at the eleven pages on housework that Parshley cut to five. In these eleven pages Beauvoir's French text quotes Colette, Colette Audry, Madeleine Bourdhouxe, Gaston Bachelard, Marcel Jouhandeau, Violette Leduc, and Francis Ponge. She even includes a brief quotation from James Agee's *Let Us Now Praise Famous Men*.[18] In English they have all disappeared. Saved from the general hecatomb, however, is a passage in which Rilke tells Lou Andreas-Salomé that Rodin had absolutely no interest in house and home (see *SS* 1989, 449; *DS* 1986, ii. 261). What could possibly justify such editing?

Parshley constantly covers up the syntactical gaps left by his own cuts by rewriting Beauvoir's text. Often he adds a brief summary of the content of the quote he has just axed. The result is often bizarre. At one point Beauvoir discusses Hegel's analysis of marriage. Here is Parshley's translation:

---

[17] See also Moi, *What Is a Woman?*, 181–7, for evidence of Beauvoir's close reading of women's texts in *The Second Sex*.

[18] This is simply a list of authors included in *DS* 1986, ii. 260–71 but omitted from *SS* 1989, 448–52. It is not intended to be a list of writers who influenced Beauvoir. Fallaize writes about the whole chapter that 'examples from women writers such as Violette Leduc, Colette Audry, or Virginia Woolf are gone' ('The Housewife's Destiny', 4). Simons writes, more generally, that the 'massive cuts from Book II obscure the influence on Beauvoir of writers such as Hegel, Kierkegaard, Colette, Virginia Woolf, Colette Audry, Bachelard, and Violette Leduc' (Simons, 'Silencing', 563).

I have heard a pious mother of a family inform her daughters that 'love is a coarse sentiment reserved for men and unknown to women of propriety.' In naive form this is the very doctrine enunciated by Hegel when he maintains that woman's relations as mother and wife are basically general and not individual. He maintains, therefore, that for her it is not a question of *this husband* but of *a husband* in general, of children in general. Her relations are not based on her individual feeling but on a universal; and thus for her, unlike man, individualized desire renders her ethic impure. (*SS* 1989, 435)

In this passage everything from 'when he maintains that' to 'renders her ethic impure' is Parshley's attempt at summarizing a quotation from Hegel's *Phenomenology of Spirit*, which covers over half a page in Beauvoir's text (see *DS* 1986, ii. 235). Beauvoir did not write this, and neither did Hegel. In French there is something magnificent about Beauvoir's juxtaposition of a sexist maxim from a conservative French mother and a long, verbatim quotation from the equally conservative Hegel. In precisely such moments we see in action Beauvoir's unique power to see the philosophy in women's most practical and everyday concerns. Presented as Beauvoir's own words, Parshley's potted summary loses the contrast between Beauvoir's presentation, the mother's voice, and Hegel's voice, and also gives the impression that Beauvoir is something less than a stellar reader of Hegel.[19] This is not an isolated example: such cuts and cover-ups abound.

Finally, there are Parshley's silent deletions of sentences or parts of sentences. Such brief cuts are ubiquitous. Unless one reads the French and the English texts side by side and line by line they are hard to detect, yet they are utterly damaging to the integrity of Beauvoir's analysis. We have already seen what happened to the Sabine women's resistance in English. Here's another crucial omission from the introduction:

BEAUVOIR: Il est clair qu'aucune femme ne peut prétendre sans mauvaise foi se situer par-delà son sexe ... (*DS* 1986, i. 13)
LITERAL TRANSLATION: Clearly, no woman can without bad faith claim to be situated beyond her sex ...
PARSHLEY: [Omits the sentence on *SS* 1989, p. xx]

The sentence disappears from a particularly important juncture in the text; namely, the moment where Beauvoir is discussing the hopeless 'choice' between having to claim that women are essentially different

[19] There are innumerable examples of this kind. For more, curious readers can consult the next few pages (*SS* 1989, 435–7), which are an extremely abbreviated rendition of *DS* 1986, ii. 235–43.

from men, or that they are simply human beings, just like men.[20] This sentence is the first step towards Beauvoir's radical reformulation of the question of women's difference. In general, Parshley's translation makes it very difficult to see that Beauvoir has a coherent and deeply original philosophy of sexed subjectivity, one that never degenerates into a general theory of 'femininity' or 'difference'. The English text therefore makes it all too easy to accuse Beauvoir of 'wanting women to become like men'.[21]

At this stage readers with a smattering of French may be heading for the nearest bookstore or library to pick up the first available copy of the French text. Before rushing out the door, they should consider a few facts. The best existing French edition is the first, 1949, edition, the so-called *édition blanche*.[22] It is still in print. French paperbacks are traditionally liable to change without warning. As far as I know (but I have not carried out a systematic comparison), the currently available *Folio* pocket edition—the one that has *premier dépôt légal 1986* on the back page—is a fairly correct reprint of the original *édition blanche*.[23] Because so many readers have it, this is the one I quote from in this essay.

[20] I discuss this dilemma in Moi, *What Is a Woman?*, 200–7.

[21] 'Beauvoir's final message is that sexual difference should be eradicated and women must become like men', Tina Chanter writes in *Ethics of Eros: Irigaray's Rewriting of the Philosophers* (New York: Routledge, 1995), 76.

[22] I have found one hilarious misprint in the *édition blanche*, carried over to the *Folio* edition; namely, a passage where both editions make Hegel speak of the *foyer érotique* rather than *éthique*. Both editions print: 'Dans le foyer du règne **érotique**, il ne s'agit pas de *ce mari-ci* mais *d'un mari* en general, des enfants en général' (*DS* 1986, ii. 235). For the same misquote in the *édition blanche* see *DS* 1949, ii. 207. What Hegel actually writes in §457 of the *Phenomenology of Spirit* is this: 'In the **ethical** household, it is not a question of *this* particular husband, *this* particular child, but simply of husband and children generally' (G. W. F. Hegel, *Phenomenology of Spirit*, trans. A. V. Miller, (Oxford: Oxford University Press, 1977), 274). As we have just seen, however, this misprint does not affect English-language readers, since Parshley, true to form, leaves out this long quote, replacing it with a three-line summary of his own making (see *SS* 1989, 435).

[23] New misprints have crept into the *Folio* edition. All versions of the *Folio* edition print: 'elle se découvre et se choisit dans un monde où les hommes lui imposent de s'assumer **contre** l'Autre' (*DS* 1986, i. 31). This introduces a severe contradiction with Beauvoir's earlier claim; namely, that women have *not* posited themselves as subjects, that they haven't organized in a unit which would gain identity from their opposition to other units (see *DS* 1986, i. 19; *SS* 1989, xxv). The 1949 *édition blanche* prints the correct version; namely: 'elle se découvre et se choisit dans un monde où les hommes lui imposent de s'assumer **comme** l'Autre' (i. 31). For once Parshley, who translated from the *édition blanche*, gets it right: 'she finds herself living in a world where men compel her to assume the status of the Other' (*SS* 1989, xxxv).

Owners of older French paperback versions should be very careful. For a long time Gallimard published a *Collection Idées* version of *Le Deuxième Sexe* (available until the *Folio* edition came on the market). In this edition, inexplicably, the whole of the second chapter of the 'Myths' section—seventy-five pages containing analyses of Montherlant, D. H. Lawrence, Claudel, Breton, and Stendhal—is nowhere to be found. When Gallimard published the book in the *Folio* edition, the missing chapter was restored. But readers should also know that the *Folio* edition marked *dépôt légal 1979* is seriously defective. The biology chapter is missing two-thirds of its pages, including every reference to the fact that biology is not immutable and unchangeable.[24] The 1986 edition restores the missing pages, but as a result page references to the first volume of the *Folio* edition vary considerably in scholarly works.

TRADUCED BY TRANSLATION: PARSHLEY AND PHILOSOPHY

Intellectual women have always struggled to be taken seriously as intellectuals. In the eighteenth century they were called bluestockings and compared to dogs walking on their hind legs. In the nineteenth century they were told that their ovaries would atrophy if they kept diverting their precious vital energy to the brain. Women philosophers, in particular, have had enormous difficulties in gaining respect for their work, even when they were working on ostensibly 'universal' questions. And women philosophers working on questions of special interest to women have always had even less of a chance of being taken seriously than other intellectual women. In my experience, the problem has not disappeared in the first years of the twenty-first century (just ask women literary critics about the 'theory boy' syndrome in contemporary graduate schools). This is why, in my view, the philosophical inadequacies of Parshley's translation of *The Second Sex* have more pernicious ideological effects than similar linguistic inadequacies in translations of male philosophers.

The most striking thing about existentialist vocabulary is that it often uses words that also have a perfectly ordinary everyday meaning. It is therefore easy to overlook the philosophical implications of Beauvoir's language. *Authentique*, for example, is a common French word,

[24] For further examples see Astrid Deuber-Mankowsky and Ursula Konnertz, 'Einleitung', *Die Philosophin*, 20 (1999), 10.

which usually can be translated as genuine, real, original, or authentic, according to context (an 'authentic' Louis XVI chair, a 'genuine' signature, etc.). But in Beauvoir and Sartre's vocabulary, an 'authentic' act is one that is carried out in good faith; that is to say, one that does not try to deny freedom and the responsibility that comes with freedom. To be 'inauthentic' is to be in bad faith, which means trying to escape the awareness of choice, responsibility, and freedom.

These terms, then, have to do with subjects who either assert themselves as subjects (they 'assume' or 'shoulder' their freedom, Beauvoir would say) or seek to deny their status as agents responsible for their actions. Given that much of Beauvoir's essay is taken up with a searching analysis of the ways in which a sexist society encourages women to take up positions of bad faith—that is to say, to hide their freedom, their status as subjects, from themselves—the word *authentique* is crucial to *The Second Sex*. When Parshley freely transforms Beauvoir's 'authentic' into 'real', 'genuine', and 'true' he turns her questions about women's freedom into moralizing sentimentality:

BEAUVOIR: Car le dévouement maternel peut être vécu dans une parfaite authenticité; mais en fait, c'est rarement le cas...(DS 1986, ii. 372)

LITERAL TRANSLATION: For maternal devotion can be lived in perfect authenticity; but in fact this is rarely the case...

PARSHLEY: For while maternal devotion may be perfectly genuine, this, in fact, is rarely the case...(SS 1989, 513)

Parshley here turns Beauvoir's recognition of the possibility of freely chosen, good-faith motherhood into an insinuation that most mothers engage in false displays of 'maternal devotion'. One does not need to believe that H. M. Parshley was the ringleader of a sinister sexist plot to find this translation inadequate. What vitiates Parshley's work, quite simply, is his inability to recognize a philosophical term when he sees one.

Examples of Parshley's philosophically deaf ear abound. I shall draw attention to just four important types of mistakes. There are many more, but I hope that this will be enough to convince most readers of the gravity and extent of the problem. I shall now briefly back up the following claims: (1) Parshley turns terms for existence into terms for essence. (2) Parshley tends to take words for subjectivity (*sujet, subjectivité*) to mean 'unsystematic', 'personal', or 'not objective'. (3) Parshley completely fails to recognize Beauvoir's pervasive references to Hegel. (4) Finally, a brief variation on this last point: Parshley has no idea that Beauvoir's central concept of 'alienation' (*aliénation*) is a philosophical term taken from Hegel and Lacan, and he therefore makes her important theory of the production of women's subjectivity under patriarchy invisible in English.

Beauvoir's existence, Parshley's essence

Beauvoir was an existentialist. She believed that 'existence precedes essence', which is another way of saying that women are made, not born. Nowhere in the French text does she deviate from this fundamental philosophical position. Parshley's text, however, introduces, from time to time, references to human or female nature. Nothing could clash more completely with Beauvoir's existentialist philosophy, and nothing could make her look more self-contradictory. Here's a simple example from the introduction:

> BEAUVOIR: La femme a des ovaires, un utérus; voilà des conditions singulières qui l'enferment dans sa subjectivité...(DS 1986, i. 14)
>
> LITERAL TRANSLATION: Woman has ovaries, a uterus; there we have the particular circumstances that imprison her in her subjectivity...
>
> PARSHLEY: Woman has ovaries, a uterus; these peculiarities imprison her in her subjectivity, circumscribe her within the limits of her own nature...(SS 1989, p. xxi)

Although this quote comes from a passage describing sexist attitudes, Parshley's explanatory addition about the 'limits of her own nature' is bound to produce misunderstandings. This is simply not the kind of vocabulary Beauvoir would use.

The existentialist term *pour-soi* is usually translated as 'for-itself'. This conveys Sartre's understanding of consciousness as a lack of being, as negation of any particular being, as ceaseless negativity. The opposite of being-for-itself is being-in-itself (*être-en-soi*). This is the mode of being of things, of nonconscious phenomena. It is probably the most fundamental distinction in French existentialist philosophy. Margaret Simons first drew attention to the following example of Parshley's art:

> BEAUVOIR: La femme se connaît et se choisit non en tant qu'elle existe pour soi mais telle que l'homme la définit...(DS 1986, i. 233–4)
>
> LITERAL TRANSLATION: Woman knows and chooses herself not as she exists for herself, but as man defines her....
>
> PARSHLEY: Woman sees herself and makes her choices not in accordance with her true nature in itself but as man defines her...(SS 1989, 137–8)[25]

---

[25] See also Simons, 'Silencing', 563.

Here are some more examples in the same vein:

BEAUVOIR: leur attitude ontologique . . . (*DS* 1986, i. 76)
LITERAL TRANSLATION: their ontological attitude . . .
PARSHLEY: their essential nature . . . (*SS* 1989, 36)

BEAUVOIR: savoir comment en elle [la femme] la nature a été reprise au cours
de l'histoire . . . (*DS* 1986, i. 77)
LITERAL TRANSLATION: know how nature has been taken up (transformed) in
her [woman] in the course of history . . .
PARSHLEY: discover how the nature of woman has been affected throughout
the course of history . . . (*SS* 1989, 37)

Eva Gothlin has shown that Henri Corbin introduced the term *réalité humaine* for Heidegger's *Dasein* in 1938.[26] Readers of Sartre and Beauvoir need to recognize the term. *Dasein* could be translated as 'human existence', 'being-in-the-world', or even 'for-itself', and Corbin's *réalité humaine* should therefore be translated in the same way. Alternatively, one could use 'human-reality' and signal its specific meaning in a separate note and glossary, as Hazel Barnes does in *Being and Nothingness*.[27] To do what Parshley does, however, is to turn Beauvoir's philosophy into a travesty of itself. Again, Simons was the first to cite the following example:

BEAUVOIR: réalité humaine (*DS* 1986, i. 40)
LITERAL TRANSLATION: 'human reality' or 'human existence'
PARSHLEY : 'the real nature of man' (*SS* 1989, 7)[28]

All this is fairly elementary, in the sense that we are dealing with obvious errors of translation. Here's a more subtle example, one that arises in a context where Beauvoir starts pushing the philosophical terms of her male colleagues in a new direction, to accommodate her revolutionary analysis of women's existence. To understand this example, we need to realize that when Beauvoir writes *réalité féminine* and puts it in quotation marks, she is first of all alluding to Corbin's *réalité humaine* and, second, introducing a subtle understanding of sexed existence in a concept Sartre and Heidegger thought of as uni-

[26] Eva Gothlin, 'Reading Simone de Beauvoir with Martin Heidegger', in *The Cambridge Companion to the Philosophy of Simone de Beauvoir*, ed. Claudia Card (Cambridge: Cambridge University Press, 2003) 43–65, at 48.
[27] Jean-Paul Sartre, *Being and Nothingness*, trans. Hazel E. Barnes (New York: Washington Square Press, 1992).
[28] See also Simons, 'Silencing', 563. There is an allusion to the same example in Alexander, 'The Eclipse of Gender', 114.

versal. At the end of the introduction to *The Second Sex* Beauvoir gives a brief overview of the book she is about to write. First she will investigate how woman is understood by biology, psychoanalysis, and historical materialism, she writes. Then she will (the reference here is to the rest of volume I in French) go on to show:

BEAUVOIR: positivement comment la 'réalité féminine' s'est constituée, pourquoi la femme a été définie comme l'Autre et quelles en ont été les conséquences du point de vue des hommes. Alors nous décrirons du point de vue des femmes le monde tel qu'il leur est proposé . . . (DS 1986, i. 32)[29]

LITERAL TRANSLATION: positively how women's being-in-the-world has been constituted, why woman has been defined as Other and what the consequences have been from men's point of view. Then I shall describe, from women's point of view, the world such as it is offered to them . . .

PARSHLEY: exactly how the concept of the 'truly feminine' has been fashioned—why woman has been defined as the Other—and what have been the consequences from man's point of view. Then from woman's point of view I shall describe the world in which women must live . . . (SS 1989, p. xxxv)

One might say that this is not too grievous an error. Since Parshley puts 'truly feminine' in quotation marks, the reader gets the (correct) impression that Beauvoir is critical toward such a concept. But to a philosopher the difference is immense. Parshley's translation indicates, and rightly so, that *The Second Sex* is going to be an investigation of ideology, but it entirely obscures the radical philosophical project that is also under way; namely, a transformation of a universal theory of *la réalité humaine* or *Dasein* into an analysis of situated, sexed existence.

Subjectivity

In Parshley's version *sujet* is only occasionally rendered as 'subject'. This makes it difficult to see that Beauvoir actually has a sophisticated theory of female subjectivity.

[29] After *proposé* there is a footnote, which states that this will be the purpose of a second volume. What Beauvoir is doing here, then, is to specify that the first volume will be devoted to an examination of women's situation as the other *from the point of view of men*, whereas the second volume ('Lived Experience') will be devoted to women's experience of their situation. This is a distinction often overlooked by readers of Beauvoir. Thus the pioneering feminist historian Gerda Lerner accuses Beauvoir of identifying with the 'patriarchal world view': 'De Beauvoir assumes the patriarchal world view and thinks from within it; thus, she never sharply distinguishes between patriarchal myth about women and the actuality of women's lives' (Gerda Lerner, 'Women and History', in *Critical Essays on Simone de Beauvoir*, ed. Elaine Marks (Boston: G. K. Hall, 1987), 154–68, at 158). But Lerner only quotes from the first volume of *The Second Sex*, namely the 'History' section.

BEAUVOIR: s'affirmer comme sujet (DS 1986, i. 21)
LITERAL TRANSLATION: to affirm/assert oneself as a subject
PARSHLEY: affirm his subjective existence (SS 1989, p. xxvii)

BEAUVOIR: elles ne se posent pas authentiquement comme Sujet (DS 1986, i. 19)
LITERAL TRANSLATION: they do not authentically posit themselves as subjects
PARSHLEY: They do not authentically assume a subjective attitude (SS 1989, p. xxv).

Confronted with the previous example, readers may well wonder why women can't just be objective. The same problem arises with another Parshley gem. In certain situations, Beauvoir writes, sexism obliges her to 'remove her subjectivity' from her claims. Her words are: 'éliminant par là ma subjectivité' (DS 1986, i. 14). Parshley writes: 'thereby removing my subjective self' (SS 1989, p. xxi).[30]

Here's a final example, where Parshley shows that, for him, subject is pretty much the same thing as 'ego' and 'self'. This example can also serve as a transition to the next section, in which I shall discuss Parshley's translation of se poser.

BEAUVOIR: Le drame de la femme, c'est ce conflit entre la revendication fondamentale de tout sujet qui se pose toujours comme l'essentiel et les exigences d'une situation qui la constitue comme inessentielle... (DS 1986, i. 31)
LITERAL TRANSLATION: The drama of woman is the conflict between the fundamental claim of every subject, which always posits itself as essential, and the demands of a situation that constitutes her as inessential...
PARSHLEY: The drama of woman lies in this conflict between the fundamental aspirations of every subject (ego)—who always regards the self as the essential—and the compulsions of a situation in which she is the inessential... (SS 1989, p. xxxv)

Hiding Hegel

Even more disastrous from a philosophical point of view is the fact that Parshley seems unaware of the pervasive references to Hegel in Beauvoir's text. In the introduction she uses the verb poser, which is the French translation of Hegel's German setzen. Problems arise because this verb is also a perfectly ordinary French verb meaning 'to place' or 'to put'. Parshley is clearly thrown for a loop by Beauvoir, who uses it in contexts where she speaks of the subject (either a person or a

[30] The important distinction between having to eliminate one's sexed subjectivity and being imprisoned in it is almost impossible to spot in English. I discuss it in Moi, What Is a Woman?, 204–19.

group) 'positing itself'—coming to consciousness of itself as a subject—through opposition to some other person or group.

There is here a transparent allusion to Hegel's account of the development of self-conscious subjectivity in the master–slave dialectic. For
Beauvoir, the verb *poser* indicates that the subject has a mediated or
self-conscious relationship to what it posits: itself, reciprocity with the
other, or whatever it is. For her the verb indicates self-conscious subjectivity, agency, and conflict. Every time this verb turns up the Hegelian overtones are there. When it disappears, the text loses the dynamic
understanding of female subjectivity and agency and the alienation that
threatens it, which is so characteristic of Beauvoir's thought. I shall
now show exactly how this happens.

The expressions *poser* and *se poser* are used well over a dozen times
in the introduction alone. Parshley translates them variously as 'pose',
'stand face to face with', 'regards', 'assume', 'make a point of', 'readily
volunteer to become', 'plays his part as such', 'postulate', or he simply
does not translate the French phrase at all. No reader of the English
text could guess that there is some philosophical rigor behind all this.
It is quite obvious that Parshley never realized that *poser* was a philosophical term for Beauvoir. Here are some examples:

BEAUVOIR: elles n'ont pas les moyens concrets de se rassembler en une unité
qui se poserait en s'opposant... (*DS* 1986, i. 19)

LITERAL TRANSLATION: they lack concrete means for organizing themselves
into a unit which could posit itself (as a subject) through opposition...

PARSHLEY: Women lack concrete means for organizing themselves into a unit
which can stand face to face with the correlative unit... (*SS* 1989, p. xxv)

BEAUVOIR: C'est que dans le rapport du maître à l'esclave, le maître ne *pose* pas
le besoin qu'il a de l'autre... (*DS* 1986, i. 20)

LITERAL TRANSLATION: This is because in the relation of master to slave, the
master does not *posit* the need he has for the other...

PARSHLEY: In the relation of master to slave the master does not make a point
of the need that he has for the other... (*SS* 1989, p. xxvi)

BEAUVOIR: Aucun sujet ne se pose d'emblée et spontanément comme l'inessen-
tiel... (*DS* 1986, i. 17)

LITERAL TRANSLATION: No subject posits itself spontaneously and right away as
the inessential...

PARSHLEY: No subject will readily volunteer to become the object, the inessential... (*SS* 1989, p xxiv)

BEAUVOIR: Tout sujet se pose concrètement à travers des projets comme une
transcendance... (*DS* 1986, i. 31)

LITERAL TRANSLATION: Every subject posits itself as a transcendence concretely
through projects...

PARSHLEY: Every subject plays his part as such specifically through exploits or
projects that serve as a mode of transcendence... (*SS* 1989, p. xxxiv)

BEAUVOIR: elle éprouve le lien nécessaire qui la rattache à l'homme sans en
poser la réciprocité... (*DS* 1986, i. 21–2)

LITERAL TRANSLATION: she feels the necessary tie that connects her to man
without positing the reciprocity of it...

PARSHLEY: she feels the necessary bond that ties her to man regardless of
reciprocity... (*SS* 1989, xxvii)

BEAUVOIR: ils ne *posent* pas la femme comme une inférieure... (*DS* 1986, i. 27)

LITERAL TRANSLATION: They do not *posit* woman as inferior...

PARSHLEY: They do not *postulate* woman as inferior... (*SS* 1989, p. xxxi)

These examples also show that Parshley adds entities that have nothing
to do with Beauvoir's understanding of consciousness, such as 'ego'
and 'self', that his formulations tend to deprive women of agency, and,
of course, that the translation completely obscures Beauvoir's appropriation of Hegel for her own radical purposes.

Alienation Alienated

Finally, I will take a quick look at the term *aliénation*.[31] This term has
quite specific meanings in philosophy (Marx, Hegel) and psychoanalysis
(Lacan). Beauvoir uses it correctly and rigorously with specific reference
to both Lacan and Hegel. Her understanding of the formation of
women's sexed subjectivity, in particular, is influenced by Lacan's understanding of alienation in the mirror stage. Parshley, as one might expect,
never realizes that this is a philosophical concept. From time to time he
does translate it as 'alienation'. But at other times he has other ideas:

BEAUVOIR: Il [l'enfant] essaie de compenser cette catastrophe en aliénant son
existence dans une image dont autrui fondera la réalité et la valeur. Il
semble que ce soit à partir du moment où il saisit son reflet dans les
glaces—moment qui coïncide avec celui du sevrage—qu'il commence à
affirmer son idéntité:[32] son moi se confond avec ce reflet si bien qu'il ne se
forme qu'en s'aliénant... (*DS* 1986, ii. 15)

---

[31] Various examples of Parshley's mistranslation of *aliénation* can be found in Simons,
'Silencing', 563, and in Moi, *Simone de Beauvoir*, 156–64.

[32] Here Beauvoir's text has a footnote referring to Lacan's *Les Complexes familiaux dans la
formation de l'individu*, a text first published in 1938. For a modern reprint see Jacques
Lacan, *Les Complexes familaux dans la formation de l'individu: Essai d'analyse d'une fonction en
psychologie* (Paris: Navarin, 1984).

LITERAL TRANSLATION: He [the child] tries to compensate for this catastrophe by alienating his existence in an image whose reality and value will be established by others. It appears that it is at the time when he recognizes his reflection in a mirror—a time which coincides with that of weaning—that he starts to affirm his identity. His I [ego][33] merges with this reflection to the extent that it is only formed through its own alienation.

PARSHLEY: He [the child] endeavors to compensate for this catastrophe by projecting his existence into an image, the reality and value of which others will establish. It appears that he may begin to affirm his identity at the time when he recognizes his reflection in a mirror—a time that coincides with that of weaning: his ego becomes so fully identified with this reflected image that it is formed only in being projected (*SS* 1989, 269).

This is one of Beauvoir's most Lacanian moments, but anyone who reads the English text (which does contain a footnote referring to Lacan) would have to wonder how well she had understood Lacan. How could *anyone* take 'alienation' to mean 'projection'? But there is more:

BEAUVOIR: la fillette sera encouragée à s'aliéner dans sa personne tout entière, et à considérer celle-ci comme un donné inerte... (*DS* 1986, ii. 27)

LITERAL TRANSLATION: the little girl will be encouraged to alienate herself in her whole body, and to consider it as an inert given...

PARSHLEY: the little girl will be led to identify her whole person [*sic*!] and to regard this as an inert given object... (*SS* 1989, 278–9)

BEAUVOIR: Plus profondément aliénée que l'homme... (*DS* 1986, ii. 183).

LITERAL TRANSLATION: Being more profoundly alienated than the man...

PARSHLEY: Being more profoundly beside herself than is man... (*SS* 1984, 397).

Most of the examples of philosophical incompetence that I have provided here come from the first thirty pages of the French text. Imagine the cumulative effect of reading such a corrupt text for almost a thousand pages. Imagine the effect on philosophers looking for clarity of thought and consistency of concepts. How could they escape the thought that in spite of her brilliance Beauvoir must be a careless and inconsistent thinker?

---

[33] The French *moi* translates Freud's *Ich*, which James Strachey translates as 'ego' in *The Standard Edition*, but this is a translation that many writers consider quite misleading (Sigmund Freud, *The Standard Edition of the Complete Psychological Works*, ed. and trans. James Strachey, 24 vols. (London: The Hogarth Press, 1953–74)).

Traduced by Translation

The translation is not only bad in itself, it also frequently leads anglophone readers astray. In my classes, for example, my students are usually upset at Beauvoir's failure to appreciate the situation of transgendered people:

BEAUVOIR: En refusant des attributs féminins, on n'acquiert pas des attributs virils; même la travestie ne réussit pas à faire d'elle-même un homme: c'est une travestie . . . (*DS* 1986, ii. 601)

LITERAL TRANSLATION: One does not acquire virile attributes by rejecting female [feminine] attributes; even a transvestite doesn't manage to turn herself into a man—she remains a transvestite . . .

PARSHLEY: One does not acquire virile attributes by rejecting feminine attributes; even the transvestite fails to make a man of herself—she is a travesty . . . (*SS* 1989, 682–3)

Feminist philosophers face more serious obstacles. Here's just one important example, concerning Beauvoir's understanding of the body:

BEAUVOIR: Cependent, dira-t-on, dans la perspective que j'adopte—celle de Heidegger, de Sartre, de Merleau-Ponty—si le corps n'est pas une *chose*, il est une situation: c'est notre prise sur le monde et l'esquisse de nos projets . . . (*DS* 1986, i. 73).

LITERAL TRANSLATION: Nevertheless, one will say, in the perspective I am adopting—that of Heidegger, Sartre, Merleau-Ponty—if the body isn't a *thing*, it is a situation: it is our grasp of the world, and a sketch [outline] of our projects . . .

PARSHLEY: Nevertheless it will be said that if the body is not a *thing*, it is a situation, as viewed in the perspective I am adopting—that of Heidegger, Sartre, and Merleau-Ponty: it is the instrument of our grasp upon the world, a limiting factor for our projects . . . (*SS* 1989, 34)

On the grounds of this sentence, Beauvoir has been taken to task by many thinkers for getting Merleau-Ponty wrong, and for being a Cartesian believer in the body–mind split. Judith Butler, for example, writes that 'Beauvoir insists that the body can be the instrument and situation of freedom'.[34] She also speaks of Beauvoir's 'normative ideal of the body as both a "situation" and an "instrumentality" '.[35] Apart from the fact that I can't quite see why it's normative to say that the

---

[34] Judith Butler, *Gender Trouble: Feminism and the Subversion of Identity* (New York: Routledge, 1990), 153 n. 21.

[35] Ibid. 152 n. 20.

body is a situation, the 'instrumentality' invoked by Butler is clearly Parshley's. Parshley may think of the body as an instrument and as a limiting factor for some inner spirit, but Beauvoir doesn't. She thinks of the shape of the human body as showing us in outline the kind of projects human beings can have. This is more like Wittgenstein's 'The human body is the best picture of the human soul' than it is like Descartes's mechanistic picture of body and soul.[36]

In the same way, the Australian philosopher Penelope Deutscher uses Parshley's Cartesianism against Beauvoir: 'Beauvoir's account of feminine embodiment is disturbing not only because of its negativity, but also because it takes for granted that female embodiment simply is a limitation. Beauvoir presents these facts with the explanation that she is adopting the perspective "of Heidegger, Sartre and Merleau-Ponty," for whom the body is "a limiting factor for our projects." This is an extremely contentious representation of Heidegger, Sartre and Merleau-Ponty.'[37] Like Butler, Deutscher is reading Parshley, not Beauvoir. Completely betraying Beauvoir's thought, the English text leads anglophone feminist philosophers into error. The effect is to diminish the feminist intellectual enterprise as a whole.[38]

THE TRANSLATION OF MOTHERHOOD

We have seen that the cuts and omissions in *The Second Sex* place serious obstacles in the way of readers who want to find out what Beauvoir's feminism is like. I have also shown that Parshley's translation of *The Second Sex* is not doing philosophers any favors. But there is more. It is widely believed, for example, that *The Second Sex* polemi-

[36] Ludwig Wittgenstein, *Philosophical Investigations*, trans. G. E. M. Anscombe, 3rd edn. (New York: Macmillan, 1968), 178.

[37] Penelope Deutscher, *Yielding Gender: Feminism, Deconstruction and the History of Philosophy* (London and New York: Routledge, 1997), 177.

[38] Since the 1970s the introduction of the word 'gender' in everyday English has further complicated the task of translating Beauvoir's 1940s French, in which the sex/gender distinction does not appear. A new translation of *The Second Sex* would have to take the utmost care with words such as *femme, féminin, femelle, homme, masculin, mâle,* and *sexe*. The misleading implications of Parshley's translation of various expressions of sex and gender differences probably have more to do with the ways in which usage in the 1950s differed from contemporary usage than with any specific shortcoming of Parshley's. He nevertheless tends to impose 'femininity' on women in a way that is foreign to Beauvoir's thought. Thus he routinely speaks of 'feminine behavior' where Beauvoir means 'women's behavior', and he will say 'feminine legs' where Beauvoir actually speaks of a 'woman's legs' (*jambes de femme*).

cizes against motherhood. A typical example of this attitude can be found in Drucilla Cornell's original and thoughtful *At the Heart of Freedom: Feminism, Sex and Equality.*[39] Given its title and its impassioned plea for a feminism based on freedom—one toward which I feel very sympathetic—one might have expected *The Second Sex* to be a central point of reference for Cornell. It is not. There are surely all kinds of reasons for this, but the one Cornell explicitly states is that Beauvoir 'urged' or 'advocated' the avoidance of motherhood in the name of freedom:

> To argue that one has to give up mothering, as many of our own symbolic mothers in the feminist movement have urged us to do, as the only way to make ourselves an end in ourselves, is an enforced sexual choice.[*] Part of our struggle is to explode the barriers of such enforced sexual choices. Mothering has meant enslavement to many women, but that is because women have been forced to take on a particular persona only because they are mothers.[40]

I have marked with [*] the point where there is a footnote in Cornell's text. The footnote reads as follows: 'De Beauvoir, *The Second Sex*. She writes, "There is one feminine function that it is actually almost impossible to perform in complete liberty. It is maternity." '[41] Elsewhere in the book Cornell repeats this claim, invoking the same passage in support.[42] But, of course, Cornell is quoting Parshley, not Beauvoir:

> BEAUVOIR: Il y a une fonction féminine qu'il est actuellement presque impossible d'assumer en toute liberté, c'est la maternité . . . (DS 1986, ii. 618)
> LITERAL TRANSLATION: There is one female function which it is almost impossible to undertake in complete freedom today, namely motherhood . . .
> PARSHLEY: There is one feminine function that it is actually almost impossible to perform in complete liberty. It is maternity . . . (SS 1989, 696)

Parshley has made an elementary French mistake. *Actuellement* doesn't mean 'actually', 'as a matter of fact', or 'really'; it means 'now', 'today',

---

[39] Drucilla Cornell, *At the Heart of Freedom: Feminism, Sex and Equality* (Princeton, NJ: Princeton University Press, 1998).

[40] Ibid. 27.

[41] Ibid. 199 n. 65. Cornell's page reference is to page 774 in the 1974 Vintage edition of *The Second Sex*, which corresponds to page 696 in the 1989 Vintage edition that I am using in this essay.

[42] 'Less extreme feminists like Simone de Beauvoir simply advocated the avoidance of motherhood in the name of freedom', Cornell writes (*Heart of Freedom*, 130). At this point there is a footnote. The footnote refers to the very same passage in *The Second Sex* (see Cornell, *Heart of Freedom*, 221 n. 43).

'nowadays'. Parshley turns Beauvoir's reference to the circumstances prevailing in France in 1949 into a general, universalizing claim. (The sentence comes from the last section of *The Second Sex*, entitled 'Towards Liberation', which explicitly deals with the situation of 'independent women' in France at the time.) Beauvoir's point, in fact, is precisely the same as Cornell's, namely that current concrete conditions prevent women from freely choosing motherhood.

But Cornell's claim appears to be overstated even in relation to Parshley's mistaken rendering of Beauvoir's point. (I still can't see any 'urging' in Parshley's sentence.) Like so many other feminists, Cornell probably doesn't ground her claim about Beauvoir's attitude towards motherhood on one single sentence but on a more general and widespread impression that *The Second Sex* is hostile to motherhood. Once I took a closer look at the translation of the passages concerning mothers and motherhood in *The Second Sex*, I realized that Parshley's translation techniques have a lot to do with this.[43] In the paragraph from which Cornell's citation is taken, for example, he goes on to produce a simply astounding *contresens*:

BEAUVOIR: Il faut ajouter que faute de crèches, de jardins d'enfants convenablement organisés, il suffit d'un enfant pour paralyser entièrement l'activité de la femme ... (DS 1986, ii. 618)

LITERAL TRANSLATION: I should add that given the lack of appropriately organized day nurseries and kindergartens, having a child is enough to paralyze a woman's activity entirely...

PARSHLEY: It must be said in addition that in spite of convenient day nurseries and kindergartens, having a child is enough to paralyze a woman's activity entirely... (SS 1989, 696–7).

To translate *actuellement* as 'actually', *faute de* as 'in spite of' (and *convenable* as 'convenient') in the very same paragraph, is quite a feat. As a result of Parshley's dismayingly elementary mistakes, Beauvoir sounds as if she thinks children are always going to be a paralyzing burden for women regardless of how many excellent nursery schools and crèches there are. This is the exact opposite of what she is actually saying in the paragraph we are dealing with here, which I shall now quote in its entirety:

---

[43] There are other reasons why feminists persist in misunderstanding Beauvoir's views on motherhood, but in this paper I shall only discuss matters of translation.

There is one female function which it is almost impossible to undertake in complete freedom today. It is motherhood. In England and America and some other countries a woman can at least decline maternity at will, thanks to contraceptive techniques. We have seen that in France she is often driven to painful and costly abortion; or she frequently finds herself responsible for an unwanted child that can ruin her professional life. *If this is a heavy charge, it is because, inversely, custom does not allow a woman to procreate when she pleases.* The unwed mother is a scandal to the community, and illegitimate birth is a stain on the child; only rarely is it possible to become a mother without accepting the chains of marriage or losing caste. If the idea of artificial insemination interests many women, it is not because they wish to avoid intercourse with a male; *it is because they hope that freedom of maternity is going to be accepted by society at last.* I should add that given the lack of appropriately organized day nurseries and kindergartens, having a child is enough to paralyze a woman's activity entirely; she can go on working only if she abandons it to relatives, friends, or servants. *She is forced to choose between sterility, which is often felt as a painful frustration, and burdens hardly compatible with a career. (SS* 1989, 696–97; *DS* 1986, ii. 618; emphases mine; translation amended)

I can't find any advocacy of childlessness in this passage. What I do find, however, is strong plea for true freedom of choice, an explicit recognition that it can be a 'painful frustration' for a woman to be forced not to have children, and that the reason why an unwanted child can be such a disaster in 1949 is that society does not allow a woman to procreate when it suits her. Beauvoir's ideal is *la maternité libre*, not childlessness. Her point, obviously, is that in 1949 this ideal was nowhere near realization.

Here's a quote that a lot of people devoutly believe is not to be found in *The Second Sex*—and for once Parshley gets it more or less right:

'Woman is lost. Where are the women? The women of today are not women at all!' We have seen what these mysterious slogans mean. In men's eyes—and for the legion of women who see through men's eyes—it is not enough to have a woman's body nor to assume the female function as mistress or mother in order to be a 'true woman.' *In sexuality and maternity the subject can claim her autonomy*; the 'true woman' is one who accepts herself as Other. *(SS* 1989, 262; emphasis mine; translation slightly amended)[44]

Beauvoir does believe, then, that a woman's sexuality and her procreative function can be freely chosen, 'authentic' projects. Yet they don't

---

[44] See *DS* 1986, i. 406 for the original French text.

have to be. They can also be carried out in the deepest alienation. Beauvoir refuses to essentialize motherhood: the meaning of mother-hood will depend on the woman's attitude and total social and per-sonal situation. Both here and elsewhere, Beauvoir explicitly says that to have a child can be a project, an exercise of freedom, autonomy, and choice:

BEAUVOIR: Enfanter, c'est prendre un engagement... (DS 1986, ii. 386)
LITERAL TRANSLATION: To have a child is to undertake a commitment...
PARSHLEY: To have a child is to undertake a solemn obligation... (SS 1989, 522)

The translation obliterates the emphasis on *engagement* ('commit-ment'). When that word disappears, the connotations with freedom, project, authenticity, and good faith that the word *engagement* carries for French existentialists disappear with it. Instead we get sentimental pieties about 'solemn obligations'. Traduced by translation, indeed.

Finally, some readers may think that I have chosen atypical passages to exemplify Beauvoir's views. Does she not start the chapter entitled 'The Mother' with an impassioned plea for abortion rights? Yes, she does. Doesn't that prove that she is more interested in abortions than babies? Not at all. Beauvoir began writing *The Second Sex* in 1946. Marie-Jeanne Latour, the last woman to be guillotined in France, was executed in 1943. Her crime? She had performed abortions.[45] Why did she have so many customers? Because during the Vichy regime contra-ception, including the act of spreading information about contracep-tion ('contraceptive propaganda'), was illegal.[46] 'Contraception and legal abortion would permit woman to undertake her maternities in freedom', Beauvoir writes (SS 1989, 492; DS 1986, ii. 343).

What this shows is that Beauvoir believes (and I agree) that we will never have freedom of choice unless the choice *not* to have children is understood as a choice that can be as affirming and positive for women as the choice to *have* children. Unless we manage to undo the sexist and

---

[45] This horrific story is told in Claude Chabrol's 1988 film *Une affaire de femmes* (distrib-uted in the US as *A Story of Women*) with Isabelle Huppert as Marie-Jeanne Latour.
[46] This was during the Vichy regime. But contraception and 'propaganda' about contra-ception were first outlawed in France in 1920 and did not become legal until the so-called *loi Neuwirth* was passed in 1967. Abortion, also outlawed in 1920, remained illegal until 1974. For a brilliant account of French legislation on these issues see Claire Duchen, *Women's Rights and Women's Lives in France 1944–1968* (London: Routledge, 1994), particu-larly ch. 4.

heterosexist ideology that posits that motherhood is every woman's destiny, that only a mother is a real woman, and that women's true nature can be found in mothering, women will never be able genuinely to choose whether to have children or not. As women in the early twenty-first century struggle with the harsh reality of trying to combine work and motherhood, as we worry about losing the race against the biological clock, as we strive to resist pressure to have children, we measure again how radical Beauvoir's analysis of motherhood really is.

'IT'S A VERY SUCCESSFUL BOOK': SOME NOTES ON THE PUBLISHING HISTORY AND THE CURRENT SITUATION

In the mid-1980s Margaret Simons asked Knopf to publish a new, full translation of *The Second Sex*. Knopf turned the proposal down. Here's *The New York Times Book Review* account of the story in 1988: 'Ms. Simons felt so strongly about the deletions she tried to persuade Knopf to publish an expanded, fully translated version of the volume. Knopf turned her down because, as Ashbel Green, the firm's vice president and senior editor, says: "Our feeling is that the impact of de Beauvoir's thesis is in no way diluted by the abridgment." '[47] In the publishers' version the problems with Parshley's text have been reduced to one of 'deletions', although Simons also documented philosophical inaccuracies. *The New York Times Book Review* continues: 'Knopf also said no to Ms. Simons' request that the rights to reprint the book be given to another publisher for republication purposes. Mr. Green explains: "It's a very successful book that we want to continue publishing." '[48]

This is still Knopf's (or Knopf/Vintage's) position. On 21 December 1999 I sent an express letter to Knopf/Vintage, proposing that they commission a new translation and edition. In putting together the letter I was much helped by Elizabeth Fallaize, Emily Grosholz, and Margaret Simons. The letter emphasized the potential for substantial new sales of the new translation. I also wrote that I thought that it would be possible to raise money from various foundations and other philanthropic sources to fund the work required to produce a transla-

---

[47] Gillman, 'Feminist Bible', 40.
[48] Ibid.

tion and an edition that would satisfy scholars as well as general readers. I then summarized the problems with the Parshley translation as follows:

- about 10 per cent of the text is missing[49]
- philosophical terms are horrendously mistranslated or simply not recognized as philosophical throughout the text
- sentences are edited or rewritten in misleading ways
- there are elementary mistranslations of French.

With the letter I enclosed a copy of Margaret Simons's 1983 essay, a copy of Elizabeth Fallaize's forthcoming essay on the 'Married Woman' chapter, a condensed overview of the examples in this article and a draft of the first three sections of this article. I also sent a copy of all this paperwork to Anne-Solange Noble, Foreign Rights Director of Gallimard, Beauvoir's French publisher.

For a very long time I heard nothing. After various attempts to extricate a reply I finally got two, one e-mail from Luann Walther at Vintage dated 17 March 2000, and a letter from Judith Jones at Knopf dated 18 March, 2000. Together the two responses made five general points:

1. Everyone associated with the book back in the 1950s had the best of intentions; in particular, there was no intention of trying to minimize Beauvoir's feminist positions or to make her look like an incoherent thinker.
2. Beauvoir agreed to the translation and the cuts Blanche Knopf and H. M. Parshley made, so there is a strong case for leaving things as they are.
3. The cutting of the English version was not the result of a sexist plot but simply an attempt to make the book less daunting in length, and so more accessible to the American reader; a new full translation would make the book monumental.
4. Translations are always subjective; translators always leave traces of themselves in their texts, which is why translations date so often.
5. Knopf and Vintage feel that there would not be enough of an audience to make it worthwhile to retranslate and publish the full text. When they decide to let the current edition go out of print, another publisher, perhaps a university press, might want to do a new edi-

[49] As mentioned above, the figure is actually more likely to be 15 per cent.

tion. Until then, however, interested readers will have to consult the French original to find out what Beauvoir actually wrote.

There are three different kinds of considerations here: the intentions and wishes of the parties involved back in the early 1950s; the nature of translation; and, finally, the commercial considerations.

The question of what one can expect from a translation is always interesting. The publishers' argument seems to be that if we agree that all translations are subjective then there is no reason to find fault with Parshley's particular efforts. This amounts to saying that since no translation can ever be a perfect rendering of all the nuances of the original (which is true enough), then all other criteria for quality are moot. Or, in other words: since the ideal translation can't be had, since all translations are subjective, it really doesn't matter whether we are given an excellent or a deplorable subjective translation. Beauvoir would surely have called this a bad-faith argument.

As for the question of the intentions of Blanche Knopf and H. M. Parshley in the early 1950s, it's a red herring. I don't have to prove criminal intent to show that a new text is badly needed; all I need to do is to prove that the current text is bad. Parshley had never translated French before. He 'knew the language solely from Boston Latin School and his undergraduate years at Harvard', Gillman writes.[50] He had no training in philosophy, and knew nothing of the then brand-new form of philosophy called existentialism. Hazel Barnes's brilliant translation of Sartre's *Being and Nothingness*, which contains a glossary of existentialist terms, did not appear until 1956. Given his limited qualifications, Parshley must have found the task of translating *The Second Sex* daunting indeed.

Parshley was probably chosen for the job of translating *The Second Sex* for two reasons: his strong advocacy of the text and his reputation as an expert on sexuality. 'He wrote the script for and also co-starred in the 1931 Universal Pictures film "The Mystery of Life," which traced the history of evolution', Gillman writes. 'His co-star was . . . the famed Scopes "monkey trial" lawyer Clarence Darrow.'[51] He also, Gillman tells us, published a book entitled *The Science of Human Reproduction: Biological Aspects of Sex* (1933) and was a regular reviewer of books on sex for *The New York Herald Tribune* until his death in 1953. And he was a great admirer of Beauvoir's essay. When Knopf asked him

---

[50] Gillman, 'Feminist Bible', 40.   [51] Ibid.

whether the book should be published in America, Parshley replied that he found it 'a profound and unique analysis of woman's nature and position, eminently reasonable and witty, and it surely should be translated'.[52] It is quite likely that Parshley would not have cut Beauvoir's text if Knopf hadn't required him to do so. The cuts were implemented on the publishers' orders, to save money and to make the book less expensive.[53]

Parshley, who was born in 1884, started work on the translation in November 1949. He suffered a heart attack in April 1950, but he continued work from his hospital bed. In August 1951 he sent the finished manuscript to Knopf. The book was finally published on 24 February 1953. Parshley lived just long enough to see the book enter the best-seller lists and to hear that Beauvoir had written to Blanche Knopf to say: 'I find the book superb. The translation seems excellent.'[54] He died suddenly in May 1953, from another heart attack.

Parshley's personal commitment to the book is not in doubt. His intentions were noble, although Beauvoir's biographer Deirdre Bair goes too far when she claims that Parshley was 'a kind of hero'.[55] But none of this changes the fact that the translation produced by the heroic Parshley fails to convey Beauvoir's philosophical subtlety and depth. We can celebrate Parshley's personal courage and good will without concluding that his translation must be preserved for all eternity. New generations of readers deserve to experience the pleasures and insights of a new text.

In his apology for Parshley, Richard Gillman writes:

[Parshley] has become a controversial figure among de Beauvoir scholars, some of whom consider his translation sexist. It is an arresting paradox in view of the fact that Parshley was not only the translator and editor of *The Second Sex*, but probably the book's most important proponent this side of the Atlantic. He figured heavily in the Knopf decision to publish an American edition, and then struggled to keep the translation essentially true to the original.[56]

There is no paradox here. My argument is not that Parshley set out to undermine *The Second Sex*, but that his translation is unsatisfactory in

[52] Letter from Parshley to Knopf, quoted in Gillman, 'Feminist Bible', 40.

[53] See Gillman's account of his interview with William Koshland, a former chairman of the board of Knopf (Gillman, 'Feminist Bible', 40).

[54] Quoted in Gillman, 'Feminist Bible', 41.

[55] Quoted ibid. 40.   [56] Gillman, 'Feminist Bible', 1.

many ways. Most importantly, it is philosophically incompetent, and therefore makes Beauvoir look like the fuzzy thinker sexists believe women in general and feminists in particular actually are. We should, in other words, distinguish between sexist intentions and sexist effects. The latter may well be unintentional, but that does not necessarily make them less damaging.

For all his good intentions, however, Parshley (like so many other academics in the 1950s) was not untouched by sexist ideology. 'Mlle de Beauvoir's book is, after all, on woman, not on philosophy', he writes in his introduction to the text (*SS* 1989, p. xxxviii). As if women and philosophy were mutually exclusive! But there is more: 'A serious, all-inclusive, and uninhibited work on woman by a woman of wit and learning! What, I had often thought, could be more desirable and yet less to be expected? When I was asked . . . to read Mlle Simone de Beauvoir's *Le Deuxième Sexe* . . . I was not long in realizing that the unexpected had happened' (*SS* 1953, p. xxxvii). This reminds me irresistibly of Mary Ellmann's send-up of backhanded praise by sexist reviewers: '[The critic] had despaired of ever seeing a birdhouse built by a woman; now *here* is a birdhouse built by a woman. Pleasure may mount even to an admission of male envy of the work examined: an exceptionally sturdy birdhouse at that!'[57]

Finally, there is the question of Beauvoir's attitude to the translation. Her remark in the letter to Blanche Knopf is probably mere politesse. Even Deirdre Bair calls it 'a white lie'.[58] When Beauvoir learned about the problems with the translation she was dismayed. Margaret Simons, who sent her essay on Parshley's translation to Beauvoir in the early 1980s, writes: 'That Beauvoir did not realize the dimensions of the problems in the English translation until recently is evident from a letter she wrote me in response to this article: "I was dismayed to learn the extent to which Mr. Parshley misrepresented me. I wish with all my heart that you will be able to publish a new translation of it" '[59] (Simons 1983, 564).

Ultimately, then, the answer to the question of why we can't get a new, complete translation of *The Second Sex* doesn't come down to the finer points of translation theory, or to Beauvoir's or Parshley's intentions: it comes down to publishing policy, and so, ultimately, to money.

---

[57] Mary Ellmann, *Thinking About Women* (New York: Harcourt, 1968), 31.
[58] Quoted in Gillman, 'Feminist Bible', 41.   [59] Simons, 'Silencing', 564.

In their letters to me Knopf/Vintage imply that it will cost too much to do a new translation, let alone a proper scholarly edition. There just isn't a market for that kind of investment, they say. Yet they do not say that the current text is selling so badly that it is on the point of going out of print. It is obviously selling well enough to make the idea of letting another publisher do a proper edition look unattractive. According to Knopf/Vintage, we're in a double bind: the book sells too well to go out of print but not well enough to warrant a new edition. The status quo can be prolonged forever; interested readers will just have to learn French.

This is not the attitude of publishers in other countries. In May 2000 the small publishing house Pax in Oslo published a new complete edition of Le Deuxième Sexe, to replace their own highly defective edition from the late 1960s. Public interest was remarkable. In a country with a population of 4.5 million, the 800-page tome freshly translated by Bente Christensen sold 20,000 copies in just a few months. In Sweden (9 million inhabitants) Åsa Moberg, with philosophical assistance from Eva Gothlin, is just finishing her new, complete translation. Apparently, then, small Scandinavian publishers can afford to retranslate Le Deuxième Sexe, whereas the giant Random House, with exclusive rights to the huge, worldwide English-language market, cannot.[60]

My understanding is that Gallimard, Beauvoir's French publishers, want a new English translation.[61] Unfortunately it appears unlikely that they have the necessary legal grounds on which to challenge Knopf. In May 2000 Continuum/Athlone in London asked Gallimard for rights to do an academic edition of The Second Sex. In March 2001 The Modern Library (another division of Random House) in New York inquired about rights for a new translation. Neither publisher received a reply.[62] At the moment, then, there simply is no way around Knopf and Vintage. Although they have full knowledge of all the evidence to the contrary, editors at both imprints continue to insist that there really is no need for a new translation. There is no need to

[60] Moreover, the defective English text also has negative influence in other countries. The new Chinese translation published in Taiwan only a few years ago, for example, appears to be a translation of Parshley, not of Beauvoir.

[61] E-mail from Anne-Solange Noble to me, 15 January 2001.

[62] E-mail from M. J. Devaney (Modern Library) to me, 5 March 2001, and e-mail from Tristan Palmer (Continuum, formerly Athlone) to me, 2 April 2001.

elaborate on what this tells us about the state of commercial publishing in America.

What is needed, of course, is a new scholarly *edition*, not just a translation. English-language readers need a new text, but they also need enough information to understand Beauvoir's exceptionally wide range of references to people, authors, texts, political events, and social phenomena. In the introduction alone, for example, we are expected to know something about the political affiliations and intellectual status in France in 1949 of Claude Mauriac, François Mauriac, Julien Benda, Emmanuel Lévinas, Claude Lévi-Strauss, and Henri de Montherlant. We must also be able to place politically and socially two ephemeral magazines, *Franchise* and *Hebdo-Latin*. In addition to such explicit references, there are oblique allusions to Colette and Colette Audry, quite invisible to the non-specialist. And who on earth is Madeleine Bourdhouxe? (see page 43 above). Moreover, like so many other French essay writers, Simone de Beauvoir frequently either omits references or garbles the names, dates, and titles that she does supply.[63] Succinct, unobtrusive notes explaining such matters would make the text far more accessible to contemporary readers.

A new edition of a fresh, complete, and correct translation would decisively advance the study of Beauvoir, of feminist theory and philosophy, and of French post-war culture all over the English-speaking world. It would sell well too. Sadly, it looks as if there is little chance of getting a new text any time soon, let alone in time for the centenary of Beauvoir's birth on 9 January 2008.[64] Yet Simone de Beauvoir deserves nothing less. Feminism deserves nothing less.

ACKNOWLEDGEMENTS

A first version of this essay was presented at the 'Legacies of Simone de Beauvoir' conference at Pennsylvania State University in November 1999, on

---

[63] A reference to Dorothy Parker in the introduction is wrong. Beauvoir also gets the title of Ferdinand Lundberg and Marynia L. Foot Farnham, *Modern Woman: The Lost Sex* (New York: Harper and Brothers, 1947) slightly wrong, and in fact never bothers to supply the names of the authors. See Moi, *What Is a Woman?*, 181–4 for a discussion of the effect of such inaccuracies.

[64] In November 2001 I sent an e-mail to Gallimard asking if there had been any development on the English-rights front. I received no reply.

the kind invitation of Emily Grosholz. A different version was presented at a panel on 'The Most Underrated Masterpiece of the French Twentieth Century', organized by Jeffrey Mehlman at the MLA Convention in Chicago in December 1999. The essay was originally published in *Signs: Journal of Women in Culture and Society,* 17/4 (2002), 1005–35. I want to thank my research assistant Erin Post for finding books and articles for me, and Li Li Hsieh and Eva Gothlin for providing last-minute references. I also owe thanks to Anne-Solange Noble, Foreign Rights Director at Gallimard in Paris, for supplying information about the rights situation for *The Second Sex.* Finally, I want to thank Elizabeth Fallaize and Nancy Bauer for their advice and support.

PART II
PHILOSOPHICAL
CONTEXT

4

Complicity and Slavery in *The Second Sex*

Susan James

In the Introduction to *The Second Sex* Simone de Beauvoir characterizes the category of the other as primordial (*SS* 1972, 16; *DS* 1986, i. 16). To understand the relations between social groups, including men and women, we must start from Hegel's insight that there is 'in consciousness itself a fundamental hostility to every other consciousness; the subject can be posed only in being opposed—he sets himself up as the essential, as opposed to the other, the inessential, the object' (*SS* 1972, 17; *DS* 1986, i. 17). Here Beauvoir presents a framework for explaining the relations between the sexes which makes them continuous with other human relationships. That man should subjugate woman is not in itself unexpected, since it exemplifies a universal disposition also manifested in the behaviour of nations and races, and even in that of three travellers who share a train compartment and make vaguely hostile 'others' out of the passengers surrounding them (*SS* 1972, 17; *DS* 1986, i. 16). What is surprising, however, is the extent of man's success; for while domination is usually an unstable and temporary achievement upset by war, potlatch, trade, or treaties, woman has been subordinate to man throughout history, and the sheer persistence of this state of affairs therefore needs to be accounted for. The difference Beauvoir sets out to examine is thus one of degree rather than kind. Among the social relations that express the primordial dynamic between subject and other, man's subjugation of woman is an extreme case. It lies at one end of a spectrum of more or less constant forms of domination (though its immutability makes it appear ahistorical), and its persistence is what renders it puzzling. Why, we are encouraged to wonder, is the relation between man and woman not more volatile and changeable, and thus more like the relations between other groups of people? Or, as Beauvoir puts it, whence comes this submissiveness in the case of woman (*SS* 1972, 18; *DS* 1986, i. 17)?

Although she initially poses the problem in these terms, Beauvoir does not always stick to a comparative approach and sometimes presents a view of woman's domination to which struggles between men are irrelevant. Man, as this strand of her narrative portrays him, is unremittingly transcendent in all aspects of his life. In addition to dominating woman, he belongs to the social spheres of work, politics, and intellectual life, where he exists as one transcendent being alongside others, and where his subject position is unequivocally affirmed. In representing the broader social world as a region where men confront one another as active agents, Beauvoir draws a veil over the struggles for domination that occur within it. The invincibly transcendent creature who figures in her more highflown descriptions of masculinity is worlds away from those men who find themselves in the position of the other, whether by virtue of their beliefs, class, or colour, with the result that their experience of immanence sometimes goes unacknowledged.

This portrayal of man as transcendent, which appears to suggest that the domination of woman is a unique and unparalleled problem, crops up at various points in *The Second Sex*, but it is outweighed by Beauvoir's insistence that members of both sexes suffer subjection, and also that men's experience of domination can shape their behaviour towards women. In dominating his wife, she argues, a husband makes up for 'all the resentments accumulated during his childhood and his later life, those accumulated daily among other men whose existence means that he is browbeaten and injured—all this is purged from him at home as he lets loose his authority upon his wife (*SS* 1972, 483; *DS* 1986, ii. 297). He looks to her to be his double and to repair his self-esteem 'after a hard day of struggle with his equals, of yielding to his superiors' (*SS* 1972, 483; *DS* 1986, ii. 296), and where her admiration is not enough enacts his power by resorting to tyranny and violence. Here we are allowed to glimpse the complexity of the male world, which reveals itself not simply as a realm of transcendent subjects, but as one where men, like women, can be rendered immanent. Between men, as well as between men and women, the struggle that Beauvoir compares with that between Hegel's master and slave continues, and in both types of relationship some individuals are confined to otherness. The crucial difference between them is not that the public realm contains uniformly transcendent men while the private one contains both transcendent men and immanent women, since transcendence and immanence are to be found in each. However, whereas a man who is subordinated in the public realm can dominate a woman in the private one and can thus occupy both subject and object positions, woman does not have the same latitude. With the important exception of women who assert their transcendence by dominating their children (*SS* 1972, 527; *DS* 1986, ii. 370), there is no social arena where woman can achieve recognition as a subject.

This strand of Beauvoir's argument develops out of the comparative approach from which she begins, and returns her to the question it raises: If men are not invincibly transcendent, and if, as she asserts, 'the temptation to dominate is the most truly universal, the most irresistible one there is' (*SS* 1972, 483; *DS* 1986, ii. 297), what prevents women from becoming subjects, either by objectifying other women or by objectifying men? Beauvoir answers with two interconnected arguments, one broadly social and psychological, the other more abstractly philosophical. The first charts the cultural images of masculinity and femininity in the light of which men and women (or at any rate men and women of the mid-twentieth century whose culture is European in origin) understand themselves, together with the possibilities and obstacles that their self-understandings contain. The second appeals to the master–slave dialectic discussed in Hegel's *Phenomenology.*[1]

Through the use of this latter argument Beauvoir places her work in a Hegelian framework and encourages her readers to understand it in Hegelian terms. However, it is difficult to see exactly what light the relationship between master and slave is meant to cast on that between man and woman. As several commentators have pointed out, Beauvoir does not regard woman's position as exactly analogous to the slave's; she herself notes that, unlike the slave, woman has not risked her life in a battle for recognition. Moreover, since her relationship with man is not shaped by a life and death struggle, there is at least one significant

---

[1] G. F. W. Hegel, *Phaenomenologie des Geistes*, trans. A. V. Miller as *Phenomenology of Spirit* (Oxford: Oxford University Press, 1977), paras. 178–96. Kojève lectured on the *Phenomenology* in Paris during the 1930s and although Beauvoir did not attend his lectures she read the work in 1940 (see Eva Lundgren-Gothlin, *Sex and Existence: Simone de Beauvoir's Second Sex*, trans. Linda Schenck (Hanover, NH: Wesleyan University Press, 1996), 56–67; Nancy Bauer, *Simone de Beauvoir, Philosophy, and Feminism* (New York: Columbia University Press, 2001), 86–7).

respect in which the position of man diverges from that of master; namely, that his supremacy is not founded on a fight.[2] These disanalogies are crucial to Beauvoir's argument, since it is precisely the fact that man and woman fail to fit Hegel's account of the struggle between master and slave that makes their relationship problematic. By placing her work in a Hegelian context, Beauvoir is able to present woman's submissiveness as anomalous, and thus to pose the question around which *The Second Sex* is organized.

Does Beauvoir also draw more deeply on the master–slave dialectic? Here recent commentators are divided. Following up her observation that Hegel's definition of the slave seems to apply particularly well to woman (*SS* 1972, 96; *DS* 1986, i. 114), Eva Gothlin claims that Beauvoir's analysis of the relationship between man and woman is modelled on the very first phase of the dialectic 'where the master has proved himself as pure self-consciousness by not having set life up as supreme, and where the slave is apparently the party for whom the significant value is sheer survival, life'.[3] For ultimately biological reasons, woman does not embark on the struggle for recognition but remains closer to the animal, committed to maintaining her existence.[4] According to this view, Beauvoir finds inspiration in a particular part of Hegel's account and applies it to the case in hand. However, Lundgren-Gothlin's interpretation has been challenged by Nancy Bauer, partly on the grounds that it underestimates Beauvoir's originality. Rather than simply taking over a section of the dialectic, Bauer argues, Beauvoir transcends Hegel by developing possibilities that he ignores. While he assumes that a subjectively self-certain being will struggle to be recognized as a subject, Beauvoir identifies an alternative response: that of trying to get the other to confirm one as an object, of attempting 'to seduce others into allowing you to alienate yourself in their gaze'.[5] In *The Second Sex* Beauvoir shows how boys are taught to achieve this alienation by getting women to reflect back to them their own image

---

[2] For recent discussions of this point see, in addition to the authors cited in the previous footnote, Tina Chanter, *Ethics of Eros: Irigaray's Reading of the Philosophers* (London: Routledge, 1995), 65; Catriona Mackenzie, 'A Certain Lack of Symmetry: Beauvoir on Autonomous Agency and Women's Embodiment', in Ruth Evans (ed.), *Simone de Beauvoir's* The Second Sex: *New Interdisciplinary Essays* (Manchester: Manchester University Press, 1998), 123–4; Debra B. Bergoffen, *The Philosophy of Simone de Beauvoir: Gendered Phenomenologies, Erotic Generosities* (Albany, NY: State University of New York, 1997), 155–60, 170–1.

[3] Lundgren-Gothlin, *Sex and Existence*, 74.　　　　[4] Ibid. 75–9.

[5] Nancy Bauer, *Simone de Beauvoir*, 211.

of themselves as independent beings, and girls learn to do it by turning themselves into mirrors and being rewarded for their passivity and the approbation they give to men. For both, their relationship with the other satisfies a fundamental need for confirmation. So Beauvoir departs from Hegel by constructing a more comprehensive account of human relationships than the one contained in the master–slave dialectic. Although Hegelian demands for recognition do occur, they are unable to explain man's domination of woman, which rests on the willingness of each to alienate themselves as objects.[6]

Despite the substantial differences between their interpretations, Gothlin and Bauer share the view that Beauvoir uses the Hegelian dialectic to articulate her central problem: Why is it that 'the males find in woman more complicity than the oppressor usually finds in the oppressed' (*SS* 1972, 731; *DS* 1986, ii. 649)? Addressing it, she enters a territory into which the *Phenomenology* does not venture, and develops a ground-breaking analysis of woman as Absolute Other. However, once this much is agreed, we encounter a further question about Beauvoir's place in the history of philosophy. If her work goes beyond the Hegelian legacy, how should we position it? Several impressive studies have convincingly overturned what was for a while the received wisdom that *The Second Sex* is based solely on Sartre's existentialism and contains nothing of its own.[7] But this makes the question all the more pressing. Should we read this work as indebted to Merleau-Ponty? As shaped by Nietzsche? As completely novel?

I shall offer a reading of *The Second Sex* which places it in the context of an older tradition of philosophical enquiry into the character of social hierarchy and the passions that create and sustain it. Since this tradition is a long one, I shall only attempt to discuss a part of it, although it is a part with which Beauvoir was undoubtedly familiar. In French philosophy of the late seventeenth century, I shall show, hierarchical social relations are widely held to depend on the affects of

---

[6] Ibid. 211–24.

[7] On the evolving debate about the connections between the philosophies of Sartre and Beauvoir see Kate Soper, *Humanism and Anti-humanism* (London: Hutchinson, 1986); Sonia Kruks, *Situation and Human Existence: Freedom, Subjectivity and Society* (London: Unwin Hyman, 1990); Michèle le Doeuff, 'Simone de Beauvoir: Falling into (Ambiguous) Line', in Margaret Simons (ed.), *Feminist Interpretations of Simone de Beauvoir* (University Park, Pa.: Pennsylvania State University Press, 1995), 59–78; Debra Bergoffen, *The Philosophy Of Simone de Beauvoir*. Part of this discussion is usefully summarized by Nancy Bauer (*Simone De Beauvoir*, 136–41).

admiration and contempt, which are understood to operate on and through the body. In the resulting economy of the passions, people are construed as complicitous in their domination, in a sense that comes very close to the one articulated by Beauvoir. At the same time, writers of this period are aware that being dominated can amount to servitude and, like Beauvoir, are sensitive to the mechanisms by which people become effectively enslaved. In early-modern discussions of social hierarchy we therefore find a collection of interrelated themes which recur in Beauvoir's work and illuminate some aspects of it more clearly than the Hegelian context in which it is usually set. My argument will consequently draw attention to a strand of discussion which has largely been neglected, but which may help us to understand the preoccupations of both Beauvoir and some of her philosophical contemporaries.

Beauvoir's analysis of the relations between man and woman assumes that all human beings desire esteem or admiration, and that they can only gain it from other human beings. This view is deeply embedded in seventeenth-century moral psychology, where it is dramatized by Arnauld and Nicole in a thought-experiment designed to uncover the limitations of *l'homme machine*.[8] Imagine a world in which there is only one person, and in which every other apparently human creature is in fact a mechanical statue. The lone person knows perfectly well that the statues are entirely devoid of reason and thought. Nevertheless, he is able to control their movements and can make them behave in a thoroughly human fashion. He may therefore amuse himself by getting them to display admiration for him; but their outward shows of respect will never nourish his self-esteem because more than mere behaviour is needed to arouse this passion. What is required are the passionate responses of other humans capable of conscious thought. This example concentrates attention on three pertinent themes. First, Arnauld and Nicole are concerned with the role of subjectivity in social relations; although they do not use the language of transcendence and immanence, they share Beauvoir's (and Hegel's) conviction that the desire for an other can only be satisfied by a human being. Secondly, they recognize the importance of *passionate* interactions between people. Finally, they focus on the passions of

---

[8] Antoine Arnauld and Pierre Nicole, *Logic or the Art of Thinking*, trans. and ed. Jill Vance Buroker (Cambridge: Cambridge University Press, 1996), 55.

admiration and self-esteem which, as I shall show, also play an important part in Beauvoir's argument.

Among seventeenth-century philosophers the passions are widely regarded as manifestations of a natural and functional sensitivity to the harms and advantages that people, objects, and states of affairs may bring us. To fear something, for instance, is to perceive it as potentially damaging. Moreover, unlike sensory perceptions, our passions prompt us to act, and it is thus by virtue of our fears, hopes, and loves that we respond to the world.[9] In the classifications of the affects to which early modern philosophers are so attached a central position is often given both to esteem or admiration and to contempt or disdain.[10] These passions are evoked by aspects of the world that we perceive as possessing *grandeur* and *petitesse*, both thickly descriptive terms which can apply to things by virtue of their size, brilliance, birth, age, wisdom, and so on. Malebranche, for example, explains that we are inclined to admire things that strike us as large, such as the night sky or monumental buildings, and to disdain things that are small, such as insects. Equally, we are inclined to feel admiration or esteem for people whose power or rank exceeds our own, and contempt for those below us on the social scale.[11] Admiration and contempt can thus be excited by both people and objects; but because only people can return passion for passion, the most elaborate and consequential analyses of them deal with human relationships. In a particularly rich portrayal, Malebranche explains that our passions are simultaneously mental and physical. Fear, for example, is constituted both by a feeling and by a configuration of the body, a constellation of facial expressions, gestures, and postures which allows the passion to be read and evokes answering passions in those who read it. In some cases such transmissions of feeling are roughly mimetic; for example, if I perceive that someone is

[9] These assumptions are shared by a wide range of seventeenth-century authors. For further discussion see Susan James, *Passion and Action: The Emotions in Seventeenth-Century Philosophy* (Oxford: Clarendon Press, 1997).

[10] For example, Descartes describes them as species of *wonder* that, in his classification, is the first of all the passions. (See René Descartes, *Les Passions de l'Ame*, ed. G. Rodis Lewis (Paris, 1988), ii. 54, trans. as *The Passions of the Soul* in *The Philosophical Writings of Descartes*, ed. J. G. Cottingham, R. Stoothoff, and D. Murdoch, 2 vols. (Cambridge: Cambridge University Press, 1984–5), ii. 328–404.

[11] Nicolas Malebranche, *De la recherche de la vérité*, ed. G. Rodis Lewis, 3 vols., in *Oeuvres Complètes*, ed. A. Robinet, 2nd. edn. (Paris, 1972), i. 91; ii. 127 (hereafter RV), trans. Thomas M. Lennon and Paul J. Oldscamp as *The Search after Truth* (Columbus, Ohio: Ohio State University Press, 1980), 31, 382 (hereafter LO).

desperate, I too may become distressed (*RV* ii. 92–3; *LO* 351). In other cases, however, including the exchange of scorn and esteem, the process is more complex.

Malebranche offers a full account of the effects of these particular passions, which can be most easily conveyed through an invented example.[12] Imagine a petitioner who comes before a prince. When the petitioner perceives that the prince's *grandeur* is superior to his own, he feels himself to be base, and experiences a kind of humility. He also gives his passions bodily expression, manifesting his *petitesse* in his supplicating stance, his bent head and respectful countenance. These changes have an effect on the prince, who feels contempt for the petitioner's *petitesse*, but at the same time recognizes his submissive air as a response to his own *grandeur*. The petitioner's countenance and bearing provide the prince with sensible evidence of his comparative greatness, and upon perceiving this he feels pride and self-esteem, passions which he in turn expresses by drawing himself up to his full height, staring at the space above the petitioner's head, or swelling out his chest. Finally, these changes have a further effect on the petitioner, who feels, alongside the baseness we have already noted, a kind of self-esteem. Some of the prince's *grandeur* rubs off on him, so to speak, and his connection with a person greater than himself increases his sense of his own worth. As he leaves the court, he holds his head a little higher and stands a little straighter.

Malebranche emphasizes that this self-reinforcing dialogue is mechanical, by which he means roughly that our bodies are structured in such a way that we express our passions and are moved by those of others without having to think about it (*RV* ii. 121–2; *LO* 343). To some extent, we can learn to control and modify these reactions, but the mutual dependence bred by our disposition to admire people for their *grandeur* and scorn them for their lack of it is one of the chief mechanisms that bind us together into hierarchical communities where each stratum feeds off those above and below it, and depends on them for its sense of worth. It is easy to be reminded of the dependence of Hegel's master on his slave when one reads Malebranche's claim that 'the general of an army depends on all his soldiers because they hold him in regard. It is often this slavery which produces his *générosité*, and the wish to be esteemed by all those who see him frequently causes

---

[12] The example distils Malebranche's discussion at *RV* ii, 120 ff; *LO* 377–8.

him to sacrifice other desires that are more pressing and more rational' (RV ii. 84; LO 343, translation modified). But whereas Hegel presents the master's dependence as an unwanted consequence of his subjugation of the slave, Malebranche sees it as an aspect of a functional and divinely ordained social order. He is concerned with hierarchical relations between men—princes, courtiers, magistrates, peasants, philosophers—who need to be admired, and are highly sensitive to the esteem and contempt that others feel for them. Their sensitivity consists in an attunedness to the ways in which these passions are embodied, together with a natural disposition to embody the changing levels of their own self-esteem and self-contempt. Their ability to act is shaped by the passions directed towards them, and they are thus bound into a system of exchange which makes them vulnerable, but is at the same time potentially empowering.

The central features of this seventeenth-century discussion all recur in Beauvoir, who allots an important place to admiration in her analysis of the hierarchical relations between man and woman. In her role as Absolute Other, woman sustains man's self-esteem by reflecting back to him an image of himself; but the image must be an admiring one. Men 'seek to find in two living eyes their image haloed with admiration and gratitude, deified' (SS 1972, 217; DS 1986, i. 302). The look or gaze so central to Beauvoir's account is significant. Man searches for his image in two human eyes, he looks to woman's facial expression for confirmation of his worth, and it is through her body that she makes her admiration manifest. This passion may have many objects, some of them coinciding with the forms of grandeur that interest philosophers such as Malebranche; for example, woman may admire man for his strength, power, wealth, munificence, or learning. Thus the relation between man and woman resembles that between man and man in so far as it is a relation between haves and have-nots. (A man's wealth may win him the esteem of a man who is poor, and an educated man may be esteemed by one who lacks learning.) Because the woman Beauvoir portrays is excluded from the public realm, she lacks the valued qualities it can supply. Ill educated and financially dependent, her admiration for males who possess these qualities is a form of a passionate exchange that also occurs between men. At the same time, however, there are forms of admiration that man gains specifically from woman, forms of grandeur to which only woman is responsive. Some of man's qualities, and among others his vital qualities, can interest woman only; he is virile, charming, seductive, tender and cruel only in reference to her. If he sets a high value on these more secret virtues, he has an absolute need of her; through her he will experience the miracle of seeming to himself to be another, another who is also his profoundest ego. (*SS* 1972, 216–17; *DS* 1986, i. 301–2)

Man's need to be esteemed for his sexual and erotic powers lies at the heart of his relation with woman, and here, too, as Beauvoir illustrates throughout *The Second Sex*, woman is called on to admire what she herself lacks. The activity and independence of the male body and of masculine sexuality, as contrasted with the passivity and immanence of woman, set the terms of a relationship in which woman finds traits to admire in man that he cannot admire in her. *Grandeur*, as Beauvoir constructs it, is explicitly masculine; it is available only to the transcendent, and thus denied to woman. 'How could one expect her to show audacity, ardour, disinterestedness, grandeur? These qualities appear only when a free being strikes forward through an open future, emerging far beyond all given actuality (*SS* 1972, 616; *DS* 1986, ii. 493). Woman's life, devoted to cooking and washing diapers, is 'no way to acquire a sense of grandeur' (*SS* 1972, 615; *DS* 1986, ii. 492).

If woman creates man's self-esteem by admiring him, how does he respond to her? While Beauvoir allows that men sometimes sustain their sense of their own value by disdaining women (she cites Montherlant as an author who needs to render women abject so that he can feel contempt for them (*SS* 1972, 238; *DS* 1986, i. 331)), she is alive to the fact that the admiration of a thoroughly degraded person is usually unsatisfying; hence, 'man aspires to clothe in his own dignity whatever he conquers and possesses' (*SS* 1972, 113; *DS* 1986, i. 136). Drawing on a wide range of sources, she enumerates the qualities that can make woman's esteem worth having and arouse an answering passion in man. He may esteem her for her willingness to satisfy his demands, and for the many ways in which she makes herself useful to him (*SS* 1972, 660; *DS* 1986, ii. 557); for her ability to give him erotic pleasure; for her beauty; for her ability to understand him and enter into his projects (*SS* 1972, 637; *DS* 1986, ii. 520); for her ability to enlarge the realm of his experience; for her willingness to argue with him and yet be defeated; and so on. It is helpful here to return for a moment to Malebranche, who identifies two kinds of exchange of esteem. In some situations people esteem one another for different reasons, as when a nobleman esteems a philosopher for his wisdom and the philosopher esteems the nobleman for his rank. The forms of *grandeur* that are in play may not be equally valued (Malebranche complains that social rank is regarded as more impressive than the wisdom of philosophers), but each is recognized as admirable. In other situations esteem is non-reciprocal; a prince may find nothing to esteem in a servant, although his recognition of the servant's esteem for him may evoke a different passion such as a feeling of mild benevolence. Even here, however, Malebranche argues that the servant may derive some self-esteem from his relation with the prince if it allows him to perceive himself as sharing the prince's *grandeur.* Thus the lesser members of a household, a court, a guild, or a profession may acquire self-esteem by association with the great.

Beauvoir takes it that both kinds of exchange occur between man and woman. Because the sexual and social forms of *grandeur* to which the highest value attaches belong to man (either by virtue of his masculinity or by virtue of woman's exclusion from the public realm), woman has comparatively little to give and is particularly dependent on association for her self-esteem. A woman gains her social status, wealth, and connections from her relationship with a man; and at the same time she admires him for one set of qualities and is admired by him for another. Beauvoir's discussion of this form of exchange departs from the framework supplied by early-modern authors such as Malebranche who inhabit a world where the comparative values of different kinds of *grandeur* are hotly contested—where the claims of virtue are regularly played off against those of status, and true wisdom competes with false philosophy. By contrast, the forms of *grandeur* available to man and woman are, as Beauvoir articulates them, mono-lithic, and because the most valuable are stacked firmly on the mascu-line side, the admiration of man for woman is not qualified by any challenge to his social or sexual superiority. Beauvoir here draws atten-tion to an aspect of hierarchy which early-modern writers overlook. In their anxiety to vindicate a society organized around widely differing degrees of power, Malebranche and many of his contemporaries con-ceive esteem and contempt as passions which pass smoothly up and down the vertical scale running from *petitesse* to *grandeur* and serve to unite the members of different social ranks into a relatively harmonious social whole. They are therefore untroubled by the possibility that there may be points at which the standards of *grandeur* and *petitesse* alter in such a way as to make mutuality of esteem impossible. Such blockages can occur in the relations between men, as Beauvoir points out in her remarks about race (*SS* 1972, 289; *DS* 1986, i. 403), but she is of course most interested in the divide between man and woman.

Beauvoir's insights into the multifarious ways in which this division is constructed have been widely discussed, and we need only note some of the principal strategies she identifies. Contrasting understandings of man as active (and thus as transcendent and in control of himself) and of woman as passive (and thus as immanent and out of control) are rooted in their bodily differences. The softness of woman's body, the secretions that flow from it, the doubling and blurring of boundaries that occur during pregnancy, the uncontrollability of conception, her penetration during sexual intercourse, and the diffuseness of her sexual pleasure are all understood to make her, by comparison with man, inert and passive. By the same token, the comparative hardness and containedness of man's body, the neatness and visibility of his sexual organs, his well-defined erotic climax, and his role in intercourse contribute to the association of masculinity and activity. Each sex understands and evaluates itself with reference to the other, and the superiority and inferiority of the self-images that man and woman internalize are heightened by a range of further interpretative devices. First, bodily differences that are a matter of degree are imagined as oppositions; for example, although man is prey to uncontrollable bodily secretions these are obliterated in the contrast with flows of menstrual blood or amniotic fluid, so that woman alone emerges as leaky and unbounded. Secondly, 'the categories in which men think of the world are established from their point of view, as absolute'; for example, although bodily differences render each sex mysterious to the other, mystery attaches only to woman. 'A mystery for man, woman is considered to be mysterious in essence' (*SS* 1972, 286; *DS* 1986, i. 399–400). Finally, the indefeasibility of bodily differences serves to naturalize them, so that the superiority of man and inferiority of woman appear inevitable. While a colonial administrator or a general could escape from the unjust hierarchical relations in which they are involved by giving up their jobs, 'a man could not prevent himself from being a man. So there he is, culpable in spite of himself and labouring under the effects of a fault he did not himself commit; and here she is, victim and shrew in spite of herself' (*SS* 1972, 732; *DS* 1986, ii. 652–3). Society inculcates in individual men and women a normative understanding of their own bodily and above all sexual powers; moreover, because these are affirmative for men and diminishing for women, the scene is set for admiration and contempt.

As we have seen, Beauvoir's emphasis on embodiment works with an understanding of the self that had already been central to French philosophy in the seventeenth century. Like writers of this period, Beauvoir takes it that our properties and powers are emotional, and that our passions are both constituted by and manifested in our bodily states and abilities. In the hierarchical social order discussed by Malebranche, people's self-esteem is expressed in their habitual postures, movements or tones of voice, and in their responses to those they encounter. Moreover, these traits shape what they can do, and also what they can be. Analogously, Beauvoir articulates an account of the way man's and woman's experiences of themselves as embodied human beings constitute their passions and capacities. As passive, woman admires man and suffers feelings of humiliation and self-disgust, and her identity also shapes and limits her actions.

In each of these accounts we find two complementary interpretations of the complicity of people at the bottom of the heap in the power of those above them. First and most important, the acceptance of social subordination is to be explained by the ways in which differences of power are embodied, and therefore shape the way we understand ourselves, the way others understand us, and what we can do. Just as a man of low rank who tried to behave like a prince would be regarded as vainglorious rather than estimable, so women who try to act like men are viewed as outlandish (*SS* 1972, 692; *DS* 1986, ii. 601). To this extent—and here *The Second Sex* implicitly departs from Sartre's account of bad faith—complicity is not a matter of choice. As Beauvoir summarizes her argument, 'all the main features of [woman's] training combine to bar her from the roads of revolt and adventure' (*SS* 1972, 730; *DS* 1986, ii. 649). At the same time, the psychic benefits that go along with social subordination produce a further knot of affects and interpretations. Rather as the *grandeur* of a prince rubs off on a petitioner, woman 'may fail to lay claim to the status of subject because she lacks definite resources, because she feels the necessary bond that ties her to man regardless of reciprocity, and because she is often very well pleased with her role as the Other' (*SS* 1972, 21; *DS* 1986, i. 21–2). The self-esteem gained from associating with those who possess *grandeur* is still self-esteem, but this way of getting it depends on psychological strategies which have their own costs. Since woman is 'doomed to dependence, she will prefer to serve a god rather than obey tyrants' (*SS* 1972, 653; *DS* 1986, ii. 547) and will therefore project her desires on to her relationship with man; 'she is quick to see genius in the man who satisfies her desires' (*SS* 1972, 628; *DS* 1986, ii. 509); she 'judges her judge, and she denies him his liberty so that he may deserve to remain her master' (*SS* 1972, 665; *DS* 1986, ii. 563). At the same time, her sense of her sexual abasement reinforces her need for esteem; 'nothing but high admiration can compensate for the humiliation of an act she considers a defeat' (*SS* 1972, 658; *DS* 1986, ii. 554). Beauvoir here explores woman's *ressentiment* in Nietzschean terms, but also echoes her early-modern predecessors who are equally familiar with the link between our desire for self-esteem and our disposition to project. As Malebranche remarks:

dependence on the great, the desire to share in their greatness and the perceptible glamour surrounding them, often cause men to render divine honours to mere mortals... If God gives authority to princes, men give them infallibility, an infallibility that is neither limited to particular subjects or occasions nor confined to particular ceremonies. The great know everything by nature; they are always right even when they pronounce on matters about which they are completely ignorant. Anyone who pauses to question their views does not know how to live. To doubt them is to lack respect and to condemn them is to rebel, or at least to exhibit oneself as foolish, extravagant and ridiculous (*RV* i. 333; *LO* 168, translation modified).

Hierarchical relations, whether or not they are between man and woman, thus provide the subordinate with a motive for forming illusory beliefs about their superiors. Yet this illusion is never complete, and is in perpetual conflict with the more realistic recognition that the great have their weaknesses.

Beauvoir vividly portrays this split, and the suffering to which it gives rise. Woman is locked into the subordinate position described so far, but at the same time distanced from it, so that, confronting man, she

is always play-acting; she lies when she makes believe that she accepts her status as the inessential other, she lies when she presents to him an imaginary personage through mimicry, costumery, studied phrases. These histrionics require a constant tension; when with her husband or with her lover, every woman is more or less conscious of the thought: 'I am not being myself' (*SS* 1972, 557; *DS* 1986, ii. 411).

As she simultaneously lives and acts out her existence as other, woman is hypocritical, abject, resistant, and servile by turns, and experiences an associated range of passions. She is deceitful and hypocritical towards man, who demands that she gives herself over to him and sincerely recognizes the superiority of his merits.

She lies to hold the man who provides her daily bread; there are scenes and tears, transports of love, crises of nerves—all false—and she lies also to escape from the tyranny she accepts through self-interest. He encourages her in make-believe that flatters his lordliness and his vanity; and she uses against him in turn her powers of dissimulation. (*SS* 1972, 626; *DS* 1986, ii. 506)

She is humiliated by sex and rendered abject by her lover's judgemental gaze. 'It is not given to woman to alter her flesh at will: when she no longer hides it, she yields it up without defence . . . and is unable to take arrogant pride in her body unless male approval has confirmed her youthful vanity' (*SS* 1972, 402; *DS* 1986, ii. 159–60). Her knowledge of her disadvantage makes her cruel and spiteful, and 'she will even be very happy if she has occasion to show her resentment to a lover who has not been able to satisfy all her demands: since he does not give her enough, she takes savage delight in taking back everything from him' (*SS* 1972, 732; *DS*, 1986, ii. 652). Finally, she is servile.

Woman wears herself out in haughty scenes, and in the end gathers up the crumbs that the male cares to toss to her. But what can be done without masculine support by a woman for whom man is at once the sole means and the sole reason for living? She is bound to suffer every humiliation; a slave cannot have the sense of human dignity; it is enough if a slave gets out of it with a whole skin (*SS* 1972, 615; *DS* 1986, ii. 492).

This dispiriting catalogue of female stratagems is strikingly continuous with early-modern interpretations of the corrosive effects of subordination. Seventeenth-century analysts of esteem recognize perfectly well that its role in a harmonious social hierarchy can be undermined by contrary passions, and believe that one way to hold these at bay is to maintain a certain distance between ranks. People who only glimpse a monarch on ceremonial occasions may carry away an undisturbed image of his *grandeur*.[13] But—and this is a particularly acute problem in relation to servants and courtiers—esteem is easily destroyed by intim-

---

[13] La Bruyère, *Les Caractères*, ed. R. Garapon (Paris: Classiques Garnier, 1980), p.222 (6) (hereafter *C*), trans. as *Characters* by Henri Van Laun (Oxford: Oxford University Press, 1963), p.116 (6) (hereafter *Ch.*).

acy. A courtier who observes the illnesses, weaknesses, and tyrannies of a prince is unlikely to view him with unadulterated esteem, and in fact writers regularly portray the courtier as trapped in a position comparable to that of Beauvoir's woman. In the same way that woman is overwhelmingly dependent upon man, the courtier's self-esteem depends to an unusual extent on the *grandeur* of the prince; in this respect he is no more than a glorified version of the *valet-de-chambre* who, as La Bruyère tartly points out, judges himself by the fortunes of the people he serves (*C* 264.33; *Ch.* 148.33). In the same way that the hierarchical relation between man and woman appears ineluctable to them both, courts set store by differences of rank that assure the supremacy of the prince, so that the courtier's subordination cannot be overcome. In the same way that woman admires man while appreciating the gap between the image she esteems and the reality, so it is with the courtier. His investment in the prince's grandeur may make him 'render divine honours to mere mortals' (*RV* i. *333*; *LO* 168), but his simultaneous knowledge of, and contempt for, the prince's weaknesses gives rise to the very range of stratagems that Beauvoir attributes to woman. The courtier is hypocritical; he subscribes to all the opinions of the prince regardless of how quickly they change (*RV* i. 366; *LO* 169–70), he dissimulates constantly (*C* 224.18; *Ch.* 118.18), and he is an inveterate flatterer (*C* 224.18; *Ch.* 118.18). Abject before the prince, he compensates himself for his own abasement by dominating others, and, like woman, he is servile. 'Men are willing to be slaves in one place if they can only lord it in another. It seems that at court a proud, imperious and commanding mien is delivered wholesale to the great for them to retail in the country; they do exactly what is done to them and are the true apes of royalty (*C* 22–3.12; *Ch.* 117.12).

Seventeenth-century accounts of the courtier's habitual vices illuminate two connected aspects of his servitude. First, he is dependent on the arbitrary will and accompanying passions of the prince for the outward aspects of his social status and his self-esteem. This dependence makes him deferential so that he follows the prince's opinions and tastes rather than developing or standing by any of his own. Secondly, while he invests in the *grandeur* of the prince he is also aware of its limitations, and consequently finds himself split between a range of passions that are self-deceiving, such as excessive admiration, and a range that are demeaning, such as self-contempt. How, though, do these traits make the courtier a slave? According to a neo-Roman tradition of republican thought that is important in seventeenth-century politics, one is enslaved if one is subject to the arbitrary will of another, for instance if one is subject to a king who possesses discretionary powers. The fact that such a king has the power to impose arbitrary restrictions on one, regardless of whether he does so, is enough to remove one's liberty, which can therefore be realized only in a republic of free citizens.[14] The early-modern writers I have been discussing are not, of course, republicans; Malebranche, for example, argues that, as well as head and heart, the body politic must have hands and feet, 'small people as well as great, people who obey as well as those who command' (*RV* ii. 72; *LO* 333). Nevertheless, they share with this republican tradition a conception of, and disdain for, the vices that monarchies and comparable constitutions engender. As they see it, courtiers suffer an extreme form of dependence which tends to undermine their virtue and makes them incapable of the straightforwardness, courage, or proper pride that are among the qualities of an *honnête homme*. Even though the courtier is not in their view deprived of *political* freedom, he is nevertheless socially and psychically unfree, and this is why it is appropriate to describe him as a slave.

Beauvoir's insistence that the relations between the sexes are unlike other forms of oppression hinges on her claim that woman is subordinated by virtue of a bodily difference from which she cannot escape. The barrier that prevents a courtier from becoming a prince is a social one, but the fact that woman's inferiority is written on her body creates a form of subordination qualitatively unlike any other. Moreover, whereas there are various forms of *grandeur* to which a courtier may aspire, such as elegance or wit, none is available to woman. The seventeenth-century philosophers I have discussed outline a position that implicitly challenges both Beauvoir's claims, and is at the same time conformable with a divergent strand of argument to be found in *The Second Sex*. According to this view some forms of *grandeur* are more ineluctable than others; for example, while a courtier may reasonably aspire to become a little wiser, there is nothing he can do about his lack of royal blood. He inhabits a milieu where this deficiency is an inescapable and defining mark of inferiority that shapes his passions and his body, so that he is as much formed by his domination

---

[14] On this conception of liberty see Quentin Skinner, *Liberty before Liberalism* (Cambridge: Cambridge University Press, 1988); Philip Pettit, *Republicanism: A Theory of Freedom and Government* (Oxford: Oxford University Press, 1987).

as is woman. Beauvoir might respond by insisting that the courtier can retire to the country while woman cannot retire from womanhood (SS 1972, 732–3; DS 1986, ii. 652–3), but this stance has to be balanced against her belief that our passionate evaluations of our bodies are socially constructed and susceptible to change.[15] Striving to accommodate both this conviction and the need to explain why women have always been dominated, she sometimes represents the bodily differences between man and woman as discontinuous with those between men (and for that matter with those between women). However, as she also acknowledges,[16] there is little in her overall position to warrant such a divide. Men's *grandeur* and *petitesse* are written on their bodies, and the same is true of women; moreover, bodily differences of various kinds—between races, nationalities, sexes, or classes—may contribute to interpretations of inferiority or superiority, and thus to oppression or subordination. Finally, oppression can amount to slavery, and men as well as women sometimes find themselves enslaved.

For a number of seventeenth-century philosophers, as much as for Beauvoir, slavery is defined by a range of psychological and social traits organized around the passions of esteem and contempt. To this extent, they draw on a common and deeply embedded understanding of servitude. There is nevertheless a vital difference between them. An author such as Malebranche is tolerant of domination; although he condemns the extreme deference of the courtier, he regards the existence of social hierarchy as both inevitable and proper (RV ii. 122; LO 377). Nor does he see it as altogether extinguishing freedom. Beauvoir, however, takes a quite different line, arguing that freedom can only exist where reciprocal recognition is achieved, where each views himself and the other simultaneously as object and as subject (SS 1972, 172; DS 1986, i. 238). Taking something from Hegel's account of the instability of the relationship between master and slave, she concludes that, despite its persistence, the domination of woman by man is not unavoidable and can be overcome.

---

[15] See Judith Butler, 'Sex and Gender in Simone de Beauvoir's "The Second Sex"', in *Yale French Studies*, 72 (1986), 35–49; Toril Moi, *What is a Woman? And Other Essays* (Oxford: Oxford University Press, 1999); Lundgren-Gothlin, *Sex and Existence*, ch. 14; Bergoffen, *The Philosophy of Simone de Beauvoir*, 146–55; Kristiana Arp, 'Beauvoir's Conception of Bodily Alienation', in Simons (ed.), *Feminist Interpretations of Simone de Beauvoir*, 161–77; Julie K. Ward, 'Beauvoir's Two Senses of Body in *The Second Sex*', in Simons (ed.), *Feminist Interpretations of Simone de Beauvoir*, 223–42.

[16] See e.g. SS 1972, 288; DS 1986, i. 402.

Much of the fascination of *The Second Sex* lies in its analysis of the self-images available to woman and the psychic bind they create. Divided between admiration and contempt for man and for herself, she struggles for forms of self-respect that are precarious and liable to be self-defeating. Like the courtier who strives to be witty or elegant, the forms of *grandeur* available to her are systematically inferior to the ones from which she is excluded; and, like the courtier, equality of esteem is beyond her reach. Beauvoir's conception of what it is to be dominated is thus continuous with one to be found in seventeenth-century discussions of social hierarchy. Like her, early-modern philosophers are deeply interested in the ways that subordination is maintained and in the complicity that it involves; like her, they explain complicity as a set of embodied and affective attitudes which contribute to our identities; and, like her, they regard esteem and contempt as passions central to our struggles for power. Their analysis provides a framework for considering Beauvoir's account of the character of woman's submissiveness which is, I believe, more fruitful than the Hegelian dialectic to which she directs attention. It is therefore helpful to see *The Second Sex* in a longer historical context, as extending to woman an existing interpretation of servitude, with dramatic and revolutionary effect.

ACKNOWLEDGEMENTS

A version of this article was published in Claudia Card (ed.), *The Cambridge Companion to Simone de Beauvoir* (Cambridge: Cambridge University Press, 2003). In revising it I have been greatly helped by the comments of the Oxford University Press's anonymous referees.

5

Simone de Beauvoir and Human Dignity

Catherine Wilson

Is human dignity a feature that is detected or one that is postulated? If it is detected, how reliably is it detected, and if errors are common are they more likely to be errors of over-attribution or of under-attribution? If dignity is postulated, is it postulated universally? Can one lose the feature by behaving in certain ways, or lose the entitlement to have it postulated in oneself? What are the social consequences of possessing or lacking human dignity?

The answers to these questions are not obvious. An important contribution of *The Second Sex* to moral philosophy is its treatment of human dignity as a relational concept pertaining to our estimation of others and, at the same time, as a concept distinct from mere social prestige. A deficiency in the possession of human dignity, Simone de Beauvoir believed, was an objective deprivation experienced by most, if not all, women. Women's inferior moral/social dignity was neither a delusory negative attribution of patriarchal society, nor an irrelevancy about which no right-thinking person should care. Yet her understanding of the conditions and manifestations of dignity has placed her at odds with later theorists who adduce numerous citations to show that Beauvoir was objectionably essentialist in her thinking and that her values were too much shaped by the philosophical tradition—a masculine tradition.[1]

The general form of the accusation is that Beauvoir is too ready to exalt the virtues of autonomy and self-sufficiency and that her conceptual equations are unconvincing. Her prescriptions for a dignified life

---

[1] For a summary of the critical literature up to 1995, see Karen Vintges, 'The Second Sex and Philosophy', in Margaret Simons (ed.), *Feminist Interpretations of Beauvoir* (University Park, Pa.: Pennsylvania State University Press, 1995), 45–58, at 50–1.

seem to set women up for failure, in so far as men's comparative independence from the demands of child-bearing and child-raising enables them to meet more easily the postulated conditions of human dignity. Beauvoir's insistence that dignity is tied to the performance of paid labour seems naive in light of subsequent experience; women have found the role of employee to expose them to new oversights and insults. It also seems disconnected from her preference for intellectual labour above all other forms. Intellectual paid labour that confers dignity on women is clearly a good thing for the small number who enjoy it, but is there a credible theory of emancipation behind this matter-of-fact observation?

This essay will try to answer that question in the affirmative. This is not to say that Beauvoir's theory is flawless or complete: she did not, for example, deal adequately with the question of the independent woman and her children or, more generally, with the question of morally acceptable forms of emotional dependency. But her view of the relation of women's economic status to moral status is one of the strongest aspects of the theory of emancipation in *The Second Sex*. Beauvoir believed that dignity depended both on the manner in which one was regarded by others and on one's relations to the material and the intellectual world. She believed that the activities that would make women the objects of social regard would also give their lives objective value. Productive and creative activities requiring intensive training and application, she thought, were valuable not solely because they were the traditional activities of men and because women were discouraged or prevented from engaging in them. They were intrinsically valuable because they offered the possibility of transcendence of the mundane. In taking part in them, one experienced and expressed one's freedom through the resistance of the material upon which one labored and the possibility of transforming it in accord with human preferences.

Both Beauvoir and her predecessor Kant, in the importance they attach to the term 'dignity', stand somewhat apart from the mainstream of contemporary moral-political discourse, where references to human dignity have largely been supplanted by references to human rights. Rights are considered in political theory to be possessed in virtue of species membership. They need not be earned by meritorious performances of any sort and cannot be withheld or withdrawn from subsets of the species. But the price of getting them, so to speak, for free, in theory (in reality they can be very costly to acquire), is that one does not get much: the right not to be tortured, imprisoned without trial, or murdered, and perhaps the right to vote or to receive an elementary education. The acquisition of these rights is a substantial gain, if one does not have them to start with. But their possession is not sufficient for living a decent human life; it is not even sufficient for the *opportunity* to live a decent human life. The richer notion of dignity offers more in this regard. Someone who can experience her own dignity as a person and whose personal dignity is acknowledged by others either meets the conditions of having a decent human life or is well on her way to doing so. But the price of taking dignity to be a central normative concept, measured in terms of liability to philosophical contestation, is correspondingly higher than the price of taking on rights.

This chapter is divided into three sections. The first provides some motivation for taking Beauvoir's elision of human dignity and social dignity seriously, by showing how the Kantian approach to moral philosophy left the relationship of moral to social status in a confused state. The second draws on Beauvoir's discussions of the relationship between work and human dignity to present an argument for specialized labor as the condition for obtaining the latter. The third discusses some objections to Beauvoir's conception of the role of the independent woman.

1. The comparative social status of men and women in a particular milieu can be measured by looking at who controls the disposition of the household income, who can come and go from the family dwelling more freely, whose infidelities are punished more severely, who is most likely to suffer a fatal mishap in infancy, who is better nourished, and who comes into contact with garbage and excrement.

In wealthy societies most of these indicators are still highly relevant. It is only recently and in some parts of the world that women's nutritional status and life expectancy has come to exceed that of men. Women are not, by and large, self-indulgent purchasers of other persons' hard-won incomes. Especially in poor countries, women tend to spend less on themselves, more on their households and children, than men do, and men in every culture spend more than women do on personal items and services and intoxicants. Nearly all the maintenance work of human life, food-gathering, feeding, the tending of children and animals, making, repairing and laundering garments, and the cleaning of dwelling places, is accomplished by women, whether or not they earn an income. Women have always dealt with the detritus of settlement, seeing to it that what wore out, ran out, or broke was replenished and restored, biological life included.

Women's lower status is not a function of their greater indolence. Their capacity for hard physical labour is taken for granted cross-culturally, and extends to mining and road works in some areas of the world. In many agricultural societies 'women do the most exhausting and boring tasks, while the performance of the men is sometimes limited simply to being present to supervise the work of the women'.[2] As Partha Dasgupta remarks: 'Poor women in poor countries are always working women... Their choice of occupation is dictated by an almost universally inflexible role they must assume, of being at once mother, wife, and housekeeper. Out of necessity they seek jobs that require little or no education. All this implies low financial returns.'[3] Not only do women choose, under constrained circumstances, the kinds of work that pay poorly and enter the most lucrative and visible professions at a lower rate, in wealthy countries men are paid approximately 25 per cent more than women for the same work.[4]

Women enjoy less social prestige than men in the most superficial and even venal sense. They control personally only a fraction of the world's wealth, they possess little executive power, and they win fewer awards and prizes. Women sit less often in the first-class sections of airplanes, and dine less often in expensive restaurants. Adult men in North America are routinely addressed by waiters, taxi drivers, conductors, clerks, and other service personnel as 'Sir', while adult women are commonly addressed directly without an honorific. There are fewer buildings, libraries, bridges, and expressways named after women. Historically, women have more often been the subjects of derogatory discourse and they are more often depicted in art and literature as grieving, ruined, punished, abandoned, etc.

---

[2] Anne Oakley, *Housework* (London: Allen Lane, 1974), 173, cited from Esther Boesrup, *Women's Role in Economic Development* (London, 1970).

[3] Partha Dasgupta, *An Inquiry into Well-Being and Destitution* (Oxford: Clarendon Press, 1993), 308–9.

[4] Heather Joshi and Pieralla Paci, *Unequal Pay for Women and Men: Evidence from the British Cohort Study* (Cambridge, Mass.: MIT Press, 1998), 18–19.

In short, women's social status is objectively low even in the modern world, and not just where tradition rules or in hard-scrabble backwaters where people are believed not to know any better. Women's deficiencies with respect to objective social dignity are consistent with their being loved by fathers and husbands, admired by brothers, and so on. Women are often powerful at home, where one deals with them as known individuals. Yet their social dignity is vulnerable once they leave the house—or the sphere of womanly activities: marketing and beauty culture—and once they are placed in situations in which they are in direct competition with men.

We have been taught, meanwhile, that moral dignity and moral worth are different from social distinction and pecuniary rewards. We 'know' that a person can possess inner human dignity, whether or not he or she is outwardly impoverished or exploited, through his or her possession of fortitude and self-respect. We believe that there is an invisible property, moral dignity, which all humans possess, with the possible exception of those who are seriously depraved victims of their appetites. Moral dignity is supposed to be recognized in the award of rights, and, except in the most benighted regions of the world, the law upholds these basic rights, and so moral dignity. So all seems well, or reasonably well, on that score. We also 'know' that there is another, visible feature, social prestige, that not all humans possess, but only those who behave in certain ways and exhibit certain characteristics. It is beyond the reach of law. No one who fails to behave in a certain way and exhibit certain characteristics can complain that they are harmed when they are not regarded as possessing social prestige. So all seems well on that score too.

At least since Kant, in other words, most philosophers have tried to distinguish between intrinsic worth as a human being, which confers certain entitlements, and social prestige, which can perhaps entail a large income or cause waiters to fawn, but that has no moral significance. Kant contrasts, in the *Doctrine of the Virtues*, pathological love and respect with moral love and respect. Pathological love and pathological respect are felt towards particular persons in virtue of their qualities and are contingent, while moral benevolence and respect are generalized and obligatory. The respect one feels towards a parent or a teacher, or the respect an inferior feels towards a superior, is different, he says, from the moral respect one ought to feel towards all other rational beings.[5] If human dignity is taken to demand moral, not pathological, respect, dignity does not need to be earned. The failure can only be on the side of the one who fails to posit the other's dignity and to respect it. Conversely, if I do not receive social respect I have only myself, or no one, to blame. I am simply not what the Germans term a *Respektsperson*. This is morally irrelevant.

It is understandable why Kant saw matters this way. He was offended by the elision in the ancient moral philosophers between the notion of an excellent human being and the notion of being regarded in a certain way, and tried to correct it. But the reader doesn't have to endorse Kant's view that rationality, rather than some other characteristic, prompts the attribution of moral dignity to find the following questions interesting: How can we tell, when a person does not possess the contingent qualities that draw forth pathological respect from others in a way to which she and others can attest by pointing to visible marks of attention and deference, that she is an object of purely moral respect? How can an observer tell whether the morally required posit has actually been made, by someone else towards him, or even by himself towards himself? Perhaps it is sufficient, one might venture, to establish that his rights are respected and that he is not treated merely as a means to some end. But this does not seem to be quite right. Our not treating another merely as a means is supposed to follow from our recognition of his dignity, not to exhaust the concept of dignity. My not making X, Y, and Z into my slaves may be a necessary condition of my positing them as dignified, but it is hardly a sufficient condition.

All Kant can tell us in this connection—here, or elsewhere, for that matter—is that where love orders us to be concerned with the welfare of others their dignity directs us to keep a distance.[6] The dignity attribution is the attribution of a property of an efficacious off-putting force: Kant even likens the simultaneous operation of benevolence and respect to the simultaneous operation of attractive and repulsive forces in physics.[7] So we should be able to see whether A_1 has in fact posited moral dignity in A_2 by looking to see whether A_1 treats A_2 as though A_2 emanated something analogous to an off-putting force, a quality of *noli me tangere*. On this model, dignity is relational. If A_2 seems to A_1 to emanate something of the sort, and A_1 responds accordingly, A_2 has

---

[5] Kant, *Elements of Ethics*, in *Ethical Philosophy*, trans. J. W. Ellington (Indianapolis, Ind.: Hackett, 1983), A 449.
[6] Ibid.   [7] Ibid.

been invested with moral dignity. To say that A_2 has in fact moral dignity though A_1 fails to recognize it is to say that A_2 is regarded (by us) as emanating an off-putting force, though A_1 appears insensitive to it.

This is all very elegant, but now that we are down to metaphysical bedrock the notion of moral respect still seems to be limited in content and application. We have not been told what the attribution of something like an off-putting force entails when it comes to the question how A_1 can behave towards A_2, or how A_3 can allow A_1 to behave towards A_2 without protesting and intervening, or how A_2, on her own behalf, can allow A_1 to behave towards her.

One might suppose that this vague metaphysical concept—the dignity postulated as belonging to every human being—distracts attention from the problems of concrete inequality and should be exposed as an ideological stand-in, ridiculed, and abandoned. But now imagine a world in which philosophers all agree that social prestige is the only real kind of dignity. If you have it, others are more or less deterred from taking hold of you, physically, instrumentally, symbolically. If you don't—there are no limits (except for basic human rights)! It is not obvious that there would be more drive in such a world to equalize social prestige than there is in our world. 'Abstract' metaphysical notions anchor moral ideals. So it is worth pursuing the question of the difference between pathological and moral dignity in Kant's system to see whether it makes sense to consider a kind of social dignity, distinct from the kind of prestige that, by definition, cannot be possessed universally, as a moral requirement.

Kant insists that it is inconsonant with human dignity to behave in a servile manner. Thus Kant:

Do not become the vassals of men. Do not suffer your rights to be trampled underfoot by others with impunity. Incur no debts for which you cannot provide full security. Accept no favors that you might do without. Do not be parasites or beggars... Complaining and whimpering, even merely crying out in bodily pain are unworthy of you, and most of all when you are aware that you deserve pain.[8]

Kant thinks of affronts to human dignity as a kind of *lèse-majesté*, the criminal breach of manners involved in touching the sovereign. This conception of human dignity holds some promise. The obligation to

---

[8] Kant, *Elements of Ethics*, A 436.

observe distance can be taken to imply that we must not 'take hold of' other rational—or whatever you like—creatures physically, instrumentally, or symbolically, or allow them to take hold of us. A_1 cannot, at one and the same time, regard A_2 as invested with moral dignity, experience A_2's boundaries as a person, and take hold of A_2 in certain ways.

Of course A_1 can swing A_2 around at a square dance, and it would be a lengthy business to try to give exact criteria for acceptable and unacceptable kinds of 'taking hold'. Nevertheless, when stronger A_1 beats weaker A_2, or dominant A_1 gets subordinate A_2 to perform menial services for him on a non-reciprocal basis, or clever, greedy A_1 induces vain, ambitious A_2 to remove her clothes and model for him, A_1 has failed to posit an efficacious off-putting force in A_2. With only a little conceptual stretching, we might argue that dignity is violated in certain situations when A_1 does not listen to what A_2 says, or when A_1 fails to ask A_2's opinion. For, when A_1 neither listens nor asks, he betrays his assumption that his conception of things completely encloses that of A_2. A_1 does not behave as though A_2 is a true conversational partner and at the same time a repository of different truths currently unthought by A_1.

But there is still a problem with this manner of conceiving moral dignity. Suppose there is a creature of human shape that incurs what appear to be large social debts for certain vulnerabilities and liabilities that exists in a condition of vassalage, and that cries. Does this creature have human dignity? Yes and no. For it would seemingly be a moral fault in us were we to fail to make the required posit and fail to treat this creature as radiating a force making us conscious of its boundaries and its integrity, making it do our will, or using it for our amusement, or failing to listen to it. Yet Kant sometimes suggests that because the creature does not ascribe dignity to itself it has forfeited the right to our consideration. Through its servile behaviour it has negated the obligation on our part to respect it, though we must still observe some minimal restraint in dealing with it. Kant says nothing about the impropriety of maintaining others in a servile relationship. He does not tell us: 'Do not hold vassals!'; 'Do not create conditions that enforce dependency!'; 'Do not bring tears to others' eyes and cries to their lips!'.

We are stuck in the following paradox. If the possession of human dignity is universal but carries no determinate implications for what can be done to X beyond some minimal set of restraints, it is adequate only to an account of morality according to which we can do anything to people, so long as we do not violate their basic human rights. If, on the other hand, the required posit carries richer implications, then we have to conclude that many humans lack some degree of human dignity and that the morally obligatory posit is not made of them. Yet the beholder does not seem to be at fault. For the beholder sees that the requisites of human dignity have not been satisfied at all in the abject person, or have not been fully satisfied in intermediate cases, and quite properly refuses to postulate dignity, or full dignity.

This problem can be made more concrete with the help of Thomas Hill's article 'Servility and Self-Respect',[9] a close reading and interpretation of the passages from Kant just discussed. Hill is convinced the notion of human dignity is consequential in terms of behavior and interpersonal relations and is not a useless abstraction or one suited only to the rudiments of political philosophy. He portrays a Deferential Wife:

This is a woman who is utterly devoted to serving her husband. She buys the clothes *he* prefers, invites the guests *he* wants to entertain... She willingly moves to a new city in order for him to have a more attractive job... [S]he tends not to form her own interests, values, and ideals; and when she does she counts them as less important than her husband's.[10]

What should our attitude towards the Deferential Wife be? Of course we will not be inclined to feel pathological respect for her, in so far as she is manifestly not an important or charismatic person. At the same time, we will not suppose that her passivity would excuse violations of her rights by murdering or assaulting her, or locking her up, or making her a slave. But since we should not admire moral failures or even regard them neutrally, it seems that we do not owe her moral respect. Hill argues that while one may work to make others happy without possessing the Kantian vice of servility, Deferential Wife is a moral failure where a key duty to oneself is concerned. Her demeanour reveals a defect in her, the failure 'to understand and acknowledge one's own moral rights'.[11] Hill distinguishes between servility that reflects, as he puts it, a misunderstanding of one's rights and servility that reflects the low value one places on them; only the latter is morally culpable.[12]

---

[9] Thomas E. Hill, Jr., 'Servility and Self-Respect', *Monist* (1973), 87–104.
[10] Ibid. 89.   [11] Ibid. 93.   [12] Ibid. 96–7.

Though Hill's attention to the phenomenon of marital capitulation is welcome, this conclusion should make us uneasy. Surely Hill is right to detect something morally wrong in this situation that needs remediation, but is he right to fix the entire moral fault on Deferential Wife?[13] Why shouldn't we regard Deferential Wife with the same moral respect as we regard non-deferential wives in view of her essential humanity and rationality and simply admit that we are not impressed 'pathologically' by her force of personality and accomplishments? And can't it be at least partially someone else's fault if I do not sufficiently value my 'rights'? Why doesn't Complacent Husband bear some moral responsibility? Is it really plausible, finally, to suppose that this example actually concerns rights?

As we consider the imaginary case further, we may come to wonder why a person who positively radiates an aura of *noli me tangere* and by whom we might be pathologically impressed should be entitled to greater moral regard. Contrast the case of Deferential Wife with that of Autonomous Wife, who buys clothes that *she* likes, refuses to entertain her husband's friends, and whose interests, values, and ideals are formed quite independently from her husband. It is not clear that Autonomous Wife has more human dignity than Deferential Wife does. Clearly, human dignity is compatible with *some* degree of accommodation to the desires of others, perhaps even with a profound degree of accommodation to the desires of others, and independence in all matters of taste and choice is not a sufficient condition of dignity. The notion of human dignity rationally posited and unsupported by pathological impressions, i.e. distinct from the notion of contingent social prestige, is not useless. But Kant's struggle to represent moral dignity as a higher image of prestige, and, at the same time, as strictly opposed to prestige supported by pathological impressions is incoherent.

Beauvoir brings clarity to the issue by treating dignity as social dignity and by showing why social dignity reflects objective values. Social dignity, in her system, is more than an attribution anchoring rudimentary rights. But it is different from prestige, which, as is well understood, can only be obtained at the expense of others and reflects

---

[13] The habit of 'blaming the victim' is analyzed by J. Harvey in chapter 5, 'Reversing the Charges', of *Civilized Oppression* (Lanham, Md.: Rowman and Littlefield, 1999), 79–99. The overall intention of Hill's 1973 article was arguably *not* to blame the victim but to provide a form of philosophical legitimation for the suggestion that women (and blacks, who also figure in the essay,) did not need to be as deferential as they ordinarily were in that era.

what may be temporary or irrational preferences, rather than values. We are not obliged merely and confusingly to postulate moral dignity in others and to withhold the attribution for such social failures as choosing one's clothes in accord with someone else's tastes. Rather, we are obliged to cultivate the material conditions under which social dignity is universally attainable. This is not to deny that some persons will fail to make something of themselves, to live lives that are worthwhile, because they are too concerned with what others think of them and whether they are sufficiently liked and accepted. But such failures should be individual; there should be no excess liability attached to being a woman in this respect. In a well-ordered world the moral fault of servility will not turn out to be a sex-linked character defect.

Though she does not resist the temptation to exhibit women as the antitypes of dignified humanity, Beauvoir is clear that dignity is a relational concept. If a group does not possess it or is not ascribed it, this can only be because they see themselves in a certain way and are seen by others in a certain way, whatever the basis of these perceptions in the group's social performances may be. Though the English translation of the introduction to *The Second Sex* misleadingly suggests that women are consigned to a lower sphere of existence and do not have full membership in the human race,[14] the sense of the original is different:

We will try to show concretely how 'feminine reality' is constructed, why women have been, from the perspective of men, defined as the Other, and what the consequences have been. And then we will describe, from the perspective of women, the world as it appears to be given to them; and we will be able to understand the difficulties into which they stumble when, in trying to escape the sphere in which they have up to now been confined, they try to take part in the human social world [au *Mitsein* humain]. (*DS* 1949, i. 32; my translation)

Lack of social dignity, contrary to what Kant maintains, affects one's very personhood.[15] Not having a bridge named after you does not entail that you have less human dignity than someone who does have a bridge named after him, that your life is worth less, or that your dignity is

---

[14] Cf. Parshley's somewhat distorted translation: 'I shall try to show exactly how the concept of the "truly feminine" has been fashioned . . . and what have been the consequences from man's point of view. Then, from women's point of view, I shall describe the world in which women must live; and thus we shall be able to envisage the difficulties in their way as . . . they aspire to full membership in the human race' (*SS*, p. xxxiv).

[15] See Harvey's discussion of the inadequacy of certain prevalent philosophical conceptions of 'harm' in *Civilized Oppression*, 19 ff.

injured or violated because there are no bridges named after you. But if you are a member of a group one of whom it would be unthinkable to name a bridge after, it is likely that you are estimated by your society as having less importance as a person. This may be because members of your society constantly and inexplicably fail to detect that feature in you, which you really possess, or because they neglect to postulate it: there is little epistemological difference there. If you are a member of the sex that is more frequently aborted, or that is known to be easy to persuade en masse to sell sexual favours for money, or whose mobility is restrained, you are in a position to argue that your human dignity has been in-jured—that something has been taken away—or that others are failing to acknowledge something in you.

As startling as the thought may seem, Beauvoir's view is that women's lesser social status makes it difficult for them to take part in the human world—not simply the world constructed by men and erroneously stipulated to be human—but the world of culture and manufacture to which women paradoxically both belong and do not belong.

2. Before going further, a potential misconception needs clearing up. Beauvoir did not claim that women exist in a state of degradation, without honor, excluded from human *Mitsein*. Consider the following passage from the introduction to *The Second Sex*:

In the bosom of the family, the female appears to the child and the young man to be clothed in the same social dignity as the adult males. Later on, the young man, desiring and loving, has experienced the resistance, the independence, of the woman desired and loved; in marriage, he respects in his wife the spouse, the mother, and in the concrete events of conjugal life she affirms herself before him as a free being. He can therefore persuade himself that the social hierarchy between the sexes is a thing of the past and that, generally speaking, apart from some differences, woman is an equal. (*SS* 1952, p. xxxii; *DS*, i. 27, my translation)

She continues:

Yet as he acknowledges certain inferiorities—of which the most important is the fact that she cannot do professional work—he supposes the reasons to lie in her nature. When he is required to adopt an attitude of collaboration and care, he can thematize their situation in terms of abstract equality, and the concrete inequality that he recognizes does not enter the picture. As soon as he finds himself in conflict with her, however, the situation is reversed. Now, he thema-tizes her concrete inequality, and her abstract equality is denied. (Ibid.)

Her point can be put in this way. Face to face with an individual woman whom he knows well, and with whom he is involved in an affective or productive project, the individual man can regard her with the same respect and deference—social and moral—that he would another man. A man is likely to respect his own mother, sister, and aunts, whom he knows to be self-aware, intentional beings and agents, whose decisions and actions make his lived experience very different from what it would otherwise have been. The individual wife is regarded as a *pour-soi* and as a source of happenings in the world of a meaningful nature by her family, even if wives rarely enjoy the veneration accorded to mothers. But men do not regard unknown or distant women as sources of happenings in the world to which they must respond. Rarely are the enterprises or decisions of an unknown woman or women understood to influence the prospects of a man, though men may feel that women's overall way of being has a significant impact on the character and quality of their lives. Women are more or less conscious, by contrast, of how the enterprises and decisions of men they do not know personally, through cultural and military action, legislation, and policing, give social experience its general shape.

It is often alleged that Beauvoir is a gender essentialist who regards historically male enterprises and accomplishments as paradigmatic of worthwhile human activity. This is thought to be an especially unproductive combination of views.[16] She is certainly critical of women's behaviour and gender mannerisms. Many of her characterizations seem to derive from the tradition of French physiological anthropology, which rests on the nineteenth-century premiss that there exists a series of rapports between the physical characteristics observed or assumed of others and their psychological, intellectual, and moral characteristics. 'I have shown', Beauvoir writes, 'how her muscular weakness disposes her to passivity' (*SS* 1952, 792; *DS* ii. 556). Women *as a class* are, in her view, too focused on their individual subsistence to rise either to abstract and transcendent thought or to structured and coherent group action. *They* are unable to sustain real friendships (*SS* 1952, 604; *DS* ii. 363). *They* are narcissistic, idle, superstitious,[17] and

[16] Accusations of 'phallocentrism' and 'ventriloquism' are levied by Celine T. Léon, 'Beauvoir's Women: Eunuch or Male?' in Simons (ed.), *Feminist Interpretations of Simone de Beauvoir*, 152–3.
[17] 'Women's mentality [*sic*] perpetuates that of agricultural civilizations which worshipped the magic power of the land' (*SS* 1952, 665; *DS*, ii. 424).

negative. *Their* lack of generosity towards those they perceive as sexual competitors leads to their failure as teachers (*SS* 1952, 657–8; *DS* ii. 416). When women try to band together for collective action, *they* rarely succeed. Women factory workers did not know how to defend themselves from abuse or to unionize for better wages; *they* expressed a 'resigned inertia' and remained in unproductive competition with one another (*SS* 1952, 130; *DS* i. 195). Much of what women had endured historically, she implied, was *their* own fault.[18] From women's political incompetence to the sexual abjection of the aging maiden, it often seems that there is nothing unreconstructed women can do or be in Beauvoir's eyes that is admirable or even acceptable. Even women's writing is derisory, for 'literature assumes sense and dignity when it makes its appeal to persons engaged in projects' (*SS* 1952, 660; *DS* ii. 419), and women manifestly have no projects. They cannot be Kafkas or Van Goghs:

The men we call great are those who—in one way or another—have taken the weight of the world upon their shoulders; they have done better or worse, they have succeeded in re-creating it, or they have gone down; but first they have assumed that enormous burden. This is what no woman has ever done, what none has been *able* to do. To regard the universe as one's own, to consider oneself to blame for its faults and to glory in its progress, one must belong to the caste of the privileged; it is for those alone who are in command to justify the universe by changing it, by thinking about it, by revealing it; they alone can recognize themselves in it and make their mark upon it. It is in man not in woman that it has hitherto been possible for Man to be incarnated. (*SS* 1952, 793; *DS* ii. 557)

Yet the fact that in Beauvoir's view 'for women to become truly human they must aspire to masculine qualities'[19] needs some context-ualization. Women were supposed to aspire to what she considered to be exemplary human qualities, but the means of production of those qualities, as she saw it, was in the hands of men, who reserved them for their exclusive use. Women had been handed over the means to produce 'feminine reality', and the 800 or so pages of *The Second Sex* can be understood not as condemnation of the victim but as a study of

---

[18] Michèle Le Doeuff points out the frequent recourse to an analogy between oppression and moral fault in *Hipparchia's Choice*, trans. Trista Selous (Oxford: Blackwell, 1991), 58; cf. p. 130.

[19] Moira Gatens, *Feminism and Philosophy: Perspectives on Difference and Equality* (Cambridge: Polity Press, 1991), 46.

how the manufacture of 'feminine reality' was the adaptation of thinking, aware human creatures to the outer world, construed as a set of
economic and biological circumstances. Once this was understood, the
workings of this mental-material *machine infernale* that churned out
feminine reality could be halted. And this implied for her that women
had to start behaving differently; more, indeed, like men. The contor-
tions they had to put themselves through and the adjustments they
had to make in order to conform to feminine reality were distortions
of their humanity.

Still, it is fair to say that Beauvoir did not entertain the possibility
that women were in exclusive control of the means of production of
some exemplary human qualities and ought to give over some propor-
tion of their ownership.[20] Women, in her view, produced along with
men, ideational 'feminine reality', while attending to material needs.
They did not otherwise produce significant ideational constructions of
plain reality.

According to Beauvoir, men arrogated human dignity to themselves,
and acquired with it certain forms of liberty and utility that women do
not enjoy, because they were able to create value. They were able to
create value because they became the users of tools and so mastered
the techniques of craft and construction. Beauvoir's admiration for
homo faber really is unlimited: 'The stick and the club with which he
armed himself to knock down fruits and to slaughter animals became
forthwith his instruments for enlarging his grasp upon the world . . .
he put his power to the test . . . he burst out of the present, he opened
the future' (SS 1952, 71; DS i. 110–11). The male, she says, digs canals,
irrigates, lays out roads, builds temples, 'creates a new world', and he
makes laws and institutions as well (SS 1952, 87–8; DS i. 128).[21] Meanwhile, '[g]iving birth and suckling are not *activities*; they are natural
functions' (SS 1952, 71; DS i. 110). Women remain as a result mired in
immanent existence; they have no more human dignity than the nest-
building birds.

Transcendence of natural functions and the initiation of world-
building activities, Beauvoir thought, is simply better in the absolute

---

[20] Beauvoir's somewhat contradictory attitudes towards what Léon calls 'feminine spe-
cificity' are explored in 'Beauvoir's Woman: Eunuch or Male?', 149 ff.

[21] Cf. SS 1952, 147: 'The true control of the world has never been in the hands of
women; they have not brought their influence to bear on technique or economy, they have
not made and unmade states, they have not discovered new worlds' (DS, i. 219–20).

scale of values than immanence. They have a higher value, as it were, by default, in so far as there is no value in inert nature. But she did not reach this conclusion merely by taking Sartre's word for it. Rather she fused the materialism she absorbed from Marx and Engels, with its inherited conception of the economic value-adding power of human labor, with the Sartrean notion of the moral value-adding power of consciousness. If values are made, then making has value. And values are pre-eminently made, economists and moralists have always stressed, by human counter-natural, or nature-surpassing activity. Men, she concluded, have had 'moral prestige along with physical strength from the start; they created values, mores, religions; never have women disputed this empire with them' (*SS* 1952, 144; *DS* i. 221).

Given this analysis, the solution to the problem seemed—in some of its dimensions—obvious to her. Women's labour was the key. Instead of being other people's instruments, for the performance of domestic labour, they needed to employ tools, intermediary instruments, that would enable them to build and fashion the world, both materially and intellectually. In doing so they would release themselves from economic dependency and experience the pride of standing on their own two feet. They would contribute to world making and be honored for it, and they would experience the personal satisfactions that come when one takes part in innovation and creation:

It is through gainful employment that woman has traversed most of the distance that separated her from the male; it is employment alone that guarantees her a concrete freedom. Once she ceases to be a parasite, the system based on her dependence crumbles; between her and the universe there is no longer any need for a masculine mediator... When she is productive, active, she reconquers her transcendence; in her projects, she concretely affirms herself as a subject; in connection with the aim she pursues, with the money and rights she takes possession of, she tests and experiences her responsibility. (*SS* 1952, 755–6; *DS* ii. 521, translation modified)[22]

There are several problems with this analysis.

First, the stress on labour seems to be somewhat misplaced. Not all kinds of labour are conducive to human dignity under its relational aspect. Some labour is exploitative and simply degrades the worker.

---

[22] Parshley writes 'aims' for the singular 'aim'.

Few forms of labour enable the married woman to escape the status of client to her higher-earning husband.

But these points do not weigh heavily against Beauvoir's claim that labour is a necessary condition of dignity. She acknowledged that women in agricultural societies work far harder than men do, and that 'for the most part, rural labour reduces woman to the condition of a beast of burden'(SS 1952, 151; DS i. 224). But she believed at the same time that even unpaid work conferred moral/social dignity. The Corsican peasant woman, she insisted, although subject to unremitting demands on her time, 'shares the man's responsibilities, interests, and property; she is respected and often is in effective control . . . She often has more moral prestige than her husband' (SS 1952, 150–1; DS i. 224–5). Even modern factory work, she argued, was not intrinsically demeaning. Gainful labour—defined roughly as the transformation of the material world receiving monetary as opposed to purely emotional reward—offered women the chance 'to integrate themselves into a world that would be their world, in the elaboration of which they would participate with joy and pride' (SS 1952, 756; DS ii. 522). What (unpaid) agricultural work and (paid) factory work have in common, and what differentiates them from housework, and even the secretarial and retail positions she considered inferior, is their visibility, communality, and visible communality.

Second, Beauvoir's emphasis on tools might seem misplaced. That early humans fed themselves mainly by knocking and clubbing rather than gathering and grinding is doubtful, and the idea that women did not invent and avail themselves of tools for extending their range of activities instead of doing everything with bare hands is absurd. Scraping tools, needles, the loom, the shuttle, the potters' wheel, grindstones, egg-beaters, churns, sewing machines, are the tools principally of women. Writing instruments such as pens, pencils, and even typewriters have been available to women for a long time. Nowadays women use computers in their work as call-centre operators and all manner of tools as low-paid assemblers of television sets. It has not advanced their status. So tool use per se does not explain much.

Nevertheless, there have been certain tools that women have not been permitted to use or have been discouraged from using. High-tech laboratory equipment, artists' materials, film-production apparatus, the intellectual tools acquired through advanced education, the tools of influence provided by command of news media and other publications, and other such tools that contribute to the formation of consciousness and social reality were reserved for the use of men. But why should access to such tools be considered relevant to the possession of human dignity and not merely to the acquisition of the social prestige that we can agree is not identical to it?

Beauvoir recognized that the Corsican peasant woman's status was in some respects lower than that of her comparatively idle husband who wiled away his hours playing cards, drinking, and socializing in cafés. And her endorsement of factory work was in a way provisional. She had her eye the whole time, as she freely admits in her chapter 'The Independent Woman', on 'the fairly large number of privileged women who find in their profession economic and social autonomy. They are the ones *"met en cause"* when one considers woman's possibilities and her future' (*SS* 1952, 757; *DS* ii. 523). Michèle Le Doeuff expresses her intentions most appropriately: '*The Second Sex* seems to be saying that once a crack has opened in the wall, it is the duty of the woman who benefits from it, to use it to the maximum to establish herself at last as a subject condemned to be free.'[23] For Beauvoir did not in the end think that value arises simply from mastering nature through tools, but by bringing into the world new 'objects' that transcend biological needs. Value is associated not with the necessities of maintenance, but—here she agreed with the majority of great philosophers—with the free productions of leisure.

Every subject poses himself as transcendence with respect to his projects concretely; he achieves his liberty only through a continual surpassing towards other liberties. There is no justification for present existence other than its expansion into an indefinitely open future. Every time transcendence falls back into immanence, there is a degradation of existence into the *en-soi*, from freedom into facticity; this fall is a moral delict if it is consented to by the subject; if it is inflicted upon him, it takes on the form of frustration and oppression. In either case, it is an absolute evil. (*SS* 1952, p. xxxiii; *DS* i. 31, translation modified)

Because Beauvoir's thought and language in this connection has proved so contentious, it might be helpful to try to explicate it by turning the discussion aside for a moment to the historical hypothesis articulated by the social historian Elise Boulding.

[23] Le Doeuff, *Hipparchia's Choice*, 131.

Surveying the history of civilizations, Boulding became convinced that women had once possessed social equality with men, and that with urbanization and the rise of militaristic nation states and government by bureaucracy their status had diminished. In present-day nomadic cultures, she observed, women retain their social equality to a surprising degree. In such societies males and females co-operate in the difficult business of keeping life going, and, although there is some division of labor, a spirit of egalitarianism and mutual trust and gratitude prevails. Nomadic women are scornful of their village and urban sisters and seem aware that settlement would entail a loss in their freedom and dignity.[24] Why did the rise of civilization bring with it claustration, special laws against women, and the gradual exclusion—by a series of small, cunning acts, none of them individually amounting to very much, but cumulatively enormous in their effects— of women from positions of authority and influence? Boulding's answer is consonant with Beauvoir's: women did the wrong kind of work.

After the neolithic age, according to Boulding, men became specialists when the opportunity arose, and women remained generalists, so that the burden of maintenance activities fell to them. The work they perform varies from culture to culture, but in all human societies women perform a greater number of separate tasks than men do.[25] Although in some possible world the more valued sex might be the one that performed more separate activities, and that performed activities that were perceived as more closely related to biological survival, with humans—both male and female—it is the other way around. Our praise literature is directed towards the specialist, the one who is pre-eminent, and who does fewer kinds of things. There is a sentimental undercurrent of praise for 'all the things mothers do', and, as private persons, individuals may admire the way a household is run by other individuals, but high honours are reserved for him who does one, comparatively useless, thing—the priest, the scholar, the administrator.

Diversification works against social honour. Beauvoir implicitly recognizes this fact in regarding the factory worker on the assembly line

---

[24] Elise Boulding, 'Nomadism, Mobility and the Status of Women', in *Women in the Twentieth Century World* (New York and London: Sage, 1977), 33 ff.

[25] Elise Boulding, *The Underside of History* (Newbury Park, Calif.: Sage, 1992), 122.

as superior to the clerk or secretary. The clerk and secretary express their vassalage in the multiple services they provide and their constant adaptation to the moment-by-moment needs of the one they serve. (A slave or serf in ancient and medieval times was sometimes described as one who did not know what he was going to be doing next.[26]) But even the housewife, who is not explicitly commanded in her tasks, who can decide in what order they are to be done, and who will readily express her preference to live in a clean and tidy house, is a low-status generalist. For the housewife is a weak imitator of the experts: she is an amateur chef, confectioner, courtesan, contractor, teacher, decorator, and hostess.[27] Beauvoir lives up to her reputation of not liking women by quoting with approval Philip Wylie's attack on the meddlesome and ignorant American mom and her good-works activities in the community: ' "Knowing nothing about medicine, art, science, religion, law, sanitation...she seldom has any special interest in *what*, exactly she is doing as a member of any of these endless organizations, so long as it is *something*." '[28] The effort of women is not, she continues, 'integrated in a coherent and constructive plan, it does not aim at objective goals; it tends only to make their tastes and interests imperiously clear...Not being specialists in politics, or in economics, or in any technical branch, [women] have no concrete grasp upon society' (*SS* 1952, 660; *DS* ii. 479):

They issue prohibitions instead of trying to discover avenues of progress; they do not try positively to create new conditions. They attack what does exist in order to eliminate evils. This explains why they always unite against something: alcohol, prostitution, pornography...As long as woman remains a parasite, she cannot take part effectively in making a better world. (*SS* 1952, 661; *DS* ii. 480)

Only rarely does it happen that women 'are entirely committed to some enterprise and become truly effective' (ibid.).

---

[26] David Brion Davis, *The Problem of Slavery in Western Culture* (Ithaca, NY: Cornell University Press, 1966), 97.

[27] The Stewartist philosophy of housewifery, propounded by the disgraced financier Martha Stewart, publisher of *Living* magazine, cannot rescue the housewife from the condition of semi-competent, multitasking generalist. On why housework is not an eligible existential choice see Donald L. Hatcher, 'Existential Ethics and Why it's Immoral to be a Housewife', *Journal of Value Inquiry*, 23 (1989) 59–68.

[28] The quotation is from Wylie's *A Generation of Vipers*, published in 1942 (*SS* 1952, 661; *DS*, ii. 480).

True specialization involves the consumption of extra resources, extra time, and extra assistance, as well as concentration and privileged access. To specialize is to do work that only a fraction of a given population can do and that offers scope for individual innovation. Being a specialist is to be distinguished from having a specialty. In a society like Plato's, in which scribes, doctors, and confectioners are slaves, they are not specialists, and in a society in which there are distinct castes of potters, tanners, and soldiers, not all specializations confer dignity, as the work does not need to be defended against intruders. But where investment and study are required as well as personal devotion and talent, and where access is controlled and one may defect from the profession but not enter it at will, work is specialized and confers status. When a group holds antecedent low status, it will not be encouraged to specialize and it may be prevented from doing so. To be sure, the average man digging up the roadway is no more expressing his transcendence through specialist labour with tools than the average woman standing on the assembly line. But the woman who stands on the assembly line has broken free of the household. She has entered the realm of the sex that specializes. And this was an essential step, in Beauvoir's mind, for women's attainment of a social dignity not dependent on the moody, fluctuating gaze of the intimates of her household.

If not simply labour, or labour with tools, but specialist labour is a necessary and also sufficient condition of the possession of social dignity for women, it will not be necessary for them to adopt the habits, postures, and interests of men. To the extent that women have looked for what Le Doeuff calls 'cracks in the wall' and have wriggled through them, consuming time and social resources, they have contributed to the social dignity of their sex. But Beauvoir's analysis contains an implicit warning. Even in the most exalted professions, women may be accustomed to spreading their energies more widely and hence more thinly than men. Focused concentration on a single, well-defined task may not feel right to many women, and the tendency to dilettantism in a man may be apprehended and countered by his instructors, who do not trouble themselves in the case of a woman. Further, women can anticipate that their efforts to specialize will not be facilitated to the same extent as men's efforts, even if they are not denied all use of the tools and instruments required.

3. Several reasonable objections might be made at this point.

First, it might be argued that Beauvoir misdiagnosed the problem and its solution. Women in our society, it might be argued, do not lack moral/social dignity. If they are not ascribed it, it is not they who ought to change their behaviour and adjust their preferences. Rather, the perceptions of the wider society need adjusting. The worth of unpaid labour, and of breadth and flexibility in all forms of labour, should be recognized and appropriately valued.

There are several responses that need to be made. First, there is little to be gained by insisting that women *in our world* are in full possession of moral/social dignity, though they are misperceived as lacking it. That they are not perceived as possessing moral/social dignity equivalent to men's is evident from the conditions under which they very frequently work, live, fall ill, and die, and from the way in which, even in egalitarian societies, they are portrayed, written about, and spoken to. But dignity is an intrinsically relational concept. To possess it simply *is* to be perceived in a certain way—as Kant tried to express with his analogy between dignity and an efficacious off-putting force.

Second, the dichotomy posed—Should women change or should beliefs about women change?—is a false one. As Beauvoir expresses it: 'what-in-men's-eyes-she-seems-to-be is one of the essential factors in her concrete situation' (*SS* 1952, 155; *DS* i. 228). The actions of individual women constitute performances to which the social world responds by changing its perceptions and by either facilitating or impeding those performances. Specialization is not the only performance that can improve the conditions under which women live, but it is an important one. And the influx of women into such technical disciplines as economics and anthropology, as well as into philosophy, since the publication of *The Second Sex*, quite apart from its role in altering the social knowledge that women's opportunities are limited and that they are less competent than men, has had important repercussions on social policy.

A second objection is that specialization is intrinsically an elitist notion and that Beauvoir was only addressing and taking into account a privileged few in *The Second Sex*. Her solution to the problem of women's absent social dignity accordingly lacks general application. The notion that women should develop expertise and consume surplus social resources can be meaningful only for well-off women in well-off countries. In so far as Beauvoir was recommending to French house-wives that they seek an education and a career rather than marrying young and producing a brood of children, her advice was in order. But where it is a question of just getting by, or where children weigh heavily in the equation, this advice is not particularly wise and will not be particularly welcome. Specialization is not the answer to the prob-lems faced by single mothers in the inner city or village women in India and Africa.

We can concede the justice of this criticism in the short run. But while Beauvoir's capacious curiosity extended to the lives of shop girls and courtesans alike, her particular interest in an intellectual elite is admitted and explained; it is not an unconscious bias. Highly edu-cated women were, in her view, those on whom the burden of con-structing a new manner of life-in-the-world-and-with-others would fall. For these women, she thought, on account of their expertise and their greater level of exposure, had more resources at their disposal and greater social power. In any case, to suggest that no one should be encouraged to specialize on the grounds that not everyone, every-where is able to specialize, or that we do not yet understand how to make specialization possible even for many middle-class women, is illogical.

As noted earlier, Beauvoir did not give any sustained attention to the conflict between the conditions of specialization and women's affection for and sense of responsibility towards children. What she had to say on the subject of motherhood is not, however, insensitive or uninteresting. (*SS* 1952, 586 ff.; *DS* ii. 386 ff.).

A third objection is that the term 'transcendence', as Beauvoir wields it, is one with too much baggage. Its semantic field embraces such terms as 'exploit', 'project', 'conquest', the 'infinitely open future' and suggests colonial incursions and the long discredited doctrine of Manifest Destiny. It is properly wondered how the adoption of expan-sive projects by that half of the human race that until now has tried to repair, maintain, and attend to personal needs can be the occasion of moral renewal. The 'free and autonomous being like all other crea-tures' which woman is said to be essentially seems to be the all-too-familiar Kantian subject, enlarging his boundaries by the expression of his will. Indeed, talk about values and the creation of values seems to reflect the concern with accumulating and hoarding that characterizes historically male economic activities. The notion that human action is the source of all value does not even seem to be philosophically coherent. Once human action has come into play, unimproved nature can be construed as brutish and degraded by contrast with the perfections of art. But it cannot be brutish and degraded at the original moment, as it would need to be if human activity were to have an absolute value. Why must the drive to change the material contours of the world, to get it dug up, built taller, fenced, spanned, written down, proved, doctrinalized, and so forth, be taken as normative for humanity in general?

One response to this line of argument is that it is simply wrong to recommend that women renounce their aspirations to invent and create—and to pile up goods, should they desire to do so. But this response does not take us very far. After all, a society in which everyone occupies an expert niche and strives for advancement amidst other experts, and in which the generalist activities of the former homemaker are parcelled out to an array of food-preparation services, cleaners, drivers, and tutors, meets no one's ideal of graciousness and familial identity and requires, anyway, generalist co-ordination. At issue is the possibility that women's social dignity might be elevated if the discrepancy between male and female levels of specialization were simply reduced. This could be effected by limiting men's opportunities for specialized labour, relative to their present exaggerated levels.

We have few philosophical precedents that could assist us in attaching immanent activities to available notions of human dignity in such a way as to make such reductions immediately appealing to those who must endure them. In so far as dignity in most philosophers from Aristotle to Kant to Beauvoir is associated with independence and freedom from mundane tasks, the prospects for such a mapping seem at first remote. No one is in a position simply to decide that non-specialist activities are of great value, are henceforth to be regarded as such and to be enjoyed by both sexes, and to make a stipulation to that effect. But perhaps we can begin to imagine that a reciprocal movement to Beauvoir's, offering a less restrictive notion of human dignity, emerges as we go. The existence of such a movement would not refute her, not at all, for such a movement could only come about as women took their places amongst the specialists and the privileged. It would require intellectuals to theorize much as

Beauvoir did about the sources of value, and to articulate new philosophical conceptions of work and leisure, in which the notions of
repair, maintenance, and restoration played as central a role as de-
struction and wreckage and magical creation *ex nihilo* seem to play in
the old schemes of values.

6

Must We Read Simone de Beauvoir?

Nancy Bauer

Given that daughters tend to have ambivalent relationships with their mothers, it should come as no surprise that fifty years down the road feminist academics still don't know quite what to do with *The Second Sex*. When Simone de Beauvoir's landmark work on women appeared in English in 1953 there weren't feminist scholars around to love it or hate it. Feminist theory would not invent itself for another couple of decades; once it did, it took its intellectual nourishment, at least initially, primarily from Marxism rather than from Beauvoir. By the time feminist theory began to take off, Betty Friedan's *The Feminist Mystique* (1963) and Kate Millett's *Sexual Politics* (1971) had superceded *The Second Sex* as rallying cries for women's liberation. Anyone who reads the Friedan or the Millett against *The Second Sex* will see Beauvoir's influence, albeit sometimes refracted in unusual ways, on pretty much every page—despite the paucity of references to her work. Like *The Second Sex* in its day, these books stunned the general populace and provided women with new ways to construe and articulate their experience. But feminist theorists understandably took little professional notice of the Millett and the Friedan: both were long on description and short on philosophy. And the typical attitude toward *The Second Sex* was that its descriptions of women's lives were at least as old hat as the dribs and drabs of warmed-over existentialism that Beauvoir, notoriously Jean-Paul Sartre's life-long partner, had evidently felt obliged to recycle.

Still, feminist theorists have always had some knowledge, however repressed, of the debt we owe to Beauvoir. *The Second Sex* is universally acknowledged as the founding text of contemporary feminism. This acknowledgment usually comes out not in feminists' scholarly writing but in their course syllabuses: as I've put the point elsewhere, assigning the 'Introduction' and maybe another chapter or two of *The Second Sex* in your introductory feminist theory class is equivalent to genuflecting on your way into the family pew.[1] As with any ritual that one performs mindlessly, teaching little chunks of *The Second Sex* year after year hardly tends to stir the soul, either the teacher's or the students'. So most of us go on assigning 'The Woman in Love' or 'Biology' as though Beauvoir's writing were theoretically passé and of purely historical interest. It's no wonder that—despite Beauvoir's absolutely explicit words to the contrary, even in the defective English translation of *The Second Sex*—we continue to teach that Beauvoir was a biological essentialist (or, alternatively, the founder of anti-essentialism), that she thought women's bodies doom them to 'immanence' and thus make women hopelessly inferior to men, that she was completely opposed to motherhood, and that she considered herself exempt from the condition of being a woman—in effect, a man *manqué*. None of this is in *The Second Sex*. But since it's unfashionable actually to read the book these days, most feminists who teach it—most feminists, that means—look upon it as a flawed artifact and would never imagine that Beauvoir has anything to teach us today.

In the opinion of a growing number of feminist philosophers and literary scholars, the widespread neglect of Beauvoir is a loss to both feminist theory and philosophy in general.[2] My own view is even stronger: I see this neglect at the heart of various stalemates that continuously paralyze academic feminists in our attempts to improve the lot of women. While women suffer, we take sides in various hopeless theoretical battles: equality vs. difference, essentialism vs. anti-essentialism, sex vs. gender. Our theory has unmoored itself from women's everyday lives. And yet we ignore the fact that *The Second Sex* shows us how to find our way back to the real world.

It might be claimed that theory's unmooring of itself is a necessary stage in a feminist division of labor: we intellectuals, at this relatively early stage of the game, are arguably still figuring out how what we do in our studies dovetails with struggles in the real world. But it seems to me

---

[1] See my *Simone de Beauvoir, Philosophy, and Feminism* (New York: Columbia University Press, 2001), 172, where I characterize the ubiquitous quoting of the famous line that opens book II of *The Second Sex*—'One is not born, but rather becomes, a woman'—as a kind of rote genuflection.

[2] The list of works arguing for this position is growing ever longer. It includes works written or edited by Kristana Arp, myself, Debra Bergoffen, Claudia Card, Elizabeth Fallaize, Sava Heinämaa, Sonia Kruks, Michèle Le Doeuff, Eva [Lundgren-]Gothlin, Toril Moi, Margaret Simons, Ursula Tidd, and Karen Vintges, listed in the Select Bibliography.

that feminist theory has relegated itself to the same no man's land, if you will, that contemporary philosophy occupies: a place so rarified and remote that it's very hard to see how it even could connect up with the world in which we actually live. The problem, in both cases, is that we have come to conceive of what we do along the lines of a science: the point of it, in both its feminist and non-feminist incarnations, has become the arm's-length discovery of objective truths. This is so, I think, even when the point of a theory is ostensibly to show that there are no objective truths: endorsements of relativism are themselves inevitably presented as a discovery of how things objectively are.

What is missing from our theories is a robust normativity, one that continues to infuse eastern philosophy and was a hallmark of its western incarnation for most of its history. Until recently no philosopher worth his salt would have dreamed of propounding a view of how things objectively are that was not bound up with a specific view of how things ought to be: how, most pertinently, human beings ought to live. Plato and Aristotle would not have been able to make sense of the idea that you could separate their ontologies or epistemologies from their ethics. You cannot fully understand what Kant thinks he is doing in the *Critique of Pure Reason* unless you grasp what he calls the practical side of his philosophy. Jeremy Bentham argued that human beings are intrinsically creatures who seek pleasure—the view of human nature that underlies his utilitarianism—not because he was in principle opposed to Kant's insistence on the idea that we are obliged to obey some purely rational moral law but because he was appalled at the arbitrariness of British common law and wanted to find a simple, fair way to make it consistent. It was not until the twentieth century, with the rise of the logic-driven 'analytic' tradition, that it became common for philosophers to conceptualize what they were doing as a search for truth that need not have any practical ramifications and ought not have any political motivations. In many cases this turn had honorable roots: the famous German logical positivist Rudolph Carnap, for example, embraced a kind of philosophical scientism in the wake of his horror of Naziism and his fear that philosophers had, in some cases inadvertently, provided the grist for Hitler's ideological mill.[3]

[3] For a brilliant discussion of Carnap's philosophy in relation to his progressive politics (and in comparison with Heidegger and his 'neo-conservatism') see Michael Friedman's important study of the origins of the analytic–Continental split in philosophy: *A Parting of the Ways: Carnap, Cassirer, and Heidegger* (Chicago, Ill.: Open Court, 2000), esp. 18–22, 156–7.

The idea that philosophy ought to respond to atrocities not by withdrawing from real life but rather by becoming 'committed' or 'engaged' tends to get associated with the so-called Continental or French/German tradition in philosophy. But at the end of the day, Continental philosophy leaves us with no more secure a mooring to our lives than does its analytic cousin. *Philosophie engagée* is often so theory-driven, not to mention jargon-laden, that it's difficult to know what to *do* with it. There is only so far you can go, practically speaking, with the idea that oppression has a fundamentally materialist component or that our motivations tend not to be fully transparent to us or that what counts as feminine is 'socially constructed'. Intellectual commitment to and fine-tuning of these ideas, however progressive, tends to float free of a *world*, of a full-blown vision of how things are and ought to be. Of course, the very idea of generating a grand vision of things is decidedly out of fashion: we tend to think of the aspiration to think big as in principle at odds with the hard work of acknowledging the plurality of experiences actual people have, especially people who have traditionally been rendered voiceless.[4] Philosophical work that aims to raise consciousness, to turn people around in their shoes, to change their gestalt of the world, tends to get branded these days as hopelessly apolitical, aestheticized, individualistic, and socially effete.[5] To retreat to one's study in an attempt to generate grand visions seems for many to entail leaving people to suffer on one's doorstep.

And yet, I submit, philosophy in the best sense of the term still has a role to play in getting individuals to take a serious interest in changing the world—that is to say, in making what needs changing visible. A truly engaging philosophical vision, one that you find haunting your everyday experience, can transform your life and, through you, the lives of others. This is true even if you find the philosophical vision that stops you in your shoes repellent—even if it strikes you as preposterous or immoral. Such a vision will draw its power from its author's ability to fuse the descriptive and the normative: to describe the world in a new way, one that makes the readers it attracts lead their lives in

---

[4] If we are analytic philosophers, we are likely to find all but the most exhaustively articulated and defended grand visions suspiciously coarse-grained, to boot.

[5] For a particularly strong attack on the idea that consciousness-raising ought to be a central feminist philosophical strategy see Kathy Miriam's 'Toward a Feminist Theory of "Action" and Re-theorizing the Political: A Comparison of Judith Butler and Hannah Arendt' (unpublished paper).

that world differently.[6] This, I am claiming, is the power of *The Second Sex*, at least when it is read carefully and well. To read the book carefully and well—even if you find yourself repulsed by it—is to be thunderstruck by the pervasiveness and intensity and mysteriousness of the history of women's oppression. It is to find your sense of what it is to be a woman in the world—and, therefore, your sense of yourself and your role in that world, whether you are a woman or a man—transformed.

But it is very hard for a feminist theorist today to read this book carefully and well. Part of the problem, as I've already suggested, is the English translation. It is the work of Howard Parshley, a retired professor of human biology at Smith College, who was commissioned by Alfred Knopf essentially to ratchet down the difficulty of *The Second Sex* for a mainstream American audience and to squeeze its two volumes into one book that, with luck, would become the next 'Studies in the Psychology of Sex', the scandalous series by Havelock Ellis.[7] Scholars disagree about how to apportion blame for the resulting travesty. My own inclination is to take the clearly well-intentioned Parshley off the hook: he should be credited with urging upon Knopf the philosophical seriousness of *The Second Sex* and then taking two years to try to educate himself in philosophy before attempting the translation. In any event, no one who works closely with the book is unaware of its woeful inadequacy. As is well documented in a landmark study by Margaret A. Simons, published a decade and a half ago, the English translation leaves out fully seventy-five pages of the original text.[8] None of the omissions is any way noted. Sometimes Parshley cuts out the end of one sentence and splices it on to the end

---

[6] Richard Rorty sometimes appears to share my understanding of how writing can effect change in the world. However, he does not construe the sort of writing he has in mind as philosophical: the grand visions he endorses are to abjure the (in his mind effete) project of limning the general features of the world or proposing what it means to be human. These visions are instead simply concerned with the practical question of how things could be better than they currently are (see Rorty's 'Feminism and Pragmatism', *Michigan Quarterly Review*, 30/2 (spring 1991), 231–58).

[7] The Havelock Ellis aspirations appear in a letter Knopf wrote to Parshley in November of 1951, from which Deirdre Bair quotes an excerpt on p. xv of her introduction to the 1989 Vintage edition of *The Second Sex*.

[8] Margaret A. Simons, 'The Silencing of Simone De Beauvoir: Guess What's Missing from *The Second Sex*?', *Women's Studies International Forum*, 6/5 (1983), repr. in Simons's *Beauvoir and* The Second Sex: *Feminism, Race, and the Origins of Existentialism* (Lanham, Md.: Rowman and Littlefield), 61–71. Despite Simons's work, Knopf refuses to relinquish

of another one, paragraphs away. He appears to get bored whenever Beauvoir starts documenting actual women's reports of their experience and so is especially prone to cut them.

This sort of butchery is bad enough. But if you are interested in what's going on philosophically in *The Second Sex* you will be even more disturbed to learn that Parshley often *adds* words to the book: he misrepresents or omits Beauvoir's philosophical terminology and substitutes his own understanding of what she means to say in formulations that are often greatly misleading or even philosophically incoherent. Take the passage in the introduction to the book in which Beauvoir is discussing a certain lack of solidarity among women and writes that 'elles ne se posent pas authentiquement comme Sujet' (*SS* 1989, p. xxv; *DS* 1986, i.19).[9] Parshley renders this as follows: 'They do not authentically assume a subjective attitude.' One needs only a passing familiarity with French to see that this translation is fast and loose; Beauvoir says, literally, that 'they do not pose themselves authentically as Subject'. Someone used to translating French philosophy books would have recognized, further, that the verb *se poser* is the French equivalent of the German *sich setzen*, ordinarily rendered in English as 'self-posit'—a centrally important philosophical technical term dating back at least to the late eighteenth century, when it was a centerpiece concept for, to name just the obvious instances, Fichte and Hegel. Were Parshley's translation better, readers trained in post-Kantian philosophy would understand that Beauvoir is here signaling her investment in analyzing women's lives in very specific philosophical terms. But even a reader with no philosophical background would be alerted that something philosophically serious is going on. Alas, there are literally hundreds of such examples in Parshley's translation. (I found this one by opening my heavily annotated English translation to a random page.) The upshot is that you really cannot read the English translation of *The Second Sex* and get a full or fully accurate understanding of what Beauvoir is doing philosophically.

---

its translation rights to the book. Toril Moi, in a splendid companion piece to the Simons classic, documents the story of a recent unsuccessful attempt on the part of Beauvoir scholars to persuade Knopf to change its mind (see 'While We Wait', reprinted in the present volume).

[9] Toril Moi discusses Parshley's shortcomings with respect to translating *se poser* in 'While We Wait'.

But the problematic English translation of *The Second Sex* is only part of the reason that it's hard to read the book well. An equally important factor is that, even in the original French, Beauvoir does not do very much philosophical hand-holding (hence, perhaps, Parshley's unfortunate attempt to do it for her). It's not quite that she assumes that her reader is conversant with Hegel, Marx, Freud, Husserl, and Heidegger and so will be able to discern the history and significance of her often unflagged appropriation of terms like 'self-posit'. Rather, it's as though she is so driven by what she's doing that she does not have time even to wonder who exactly might be in a position to appreciate the results. For *The Second Sex* is the product of an explosive alchemical reaction between Beauvoir's long-standing interest in various of her philosophical forebears and a brand-new investment in the question of what it means to be a woman. By the time she came to write the book Beauvoir had become a prominent woman in French intellectual circles. Her 1943 novel *L'Invitée*, translated into English as *She Came to Stay*, had been very well received, and she was well known, too, as a writer of philosophical essays. So, not surprisingly, she had been urged routinely by other women to put her gifts and reputation to work for women's rights.[10] But she did not find 'the woman question' interesting, she later noted, until in 1946 she began to reflect on her own life in preparation for writing a volume of memoirs: 'I became aware with a sort of surprise that the first thing I had to say was this: I am a woman.'[11] *The Second Sex* constitutes an epic meditation on this simple fact—not exactly that Beauvoir was a woman but that this fact was, she found to her surprise, the first thing she was inclined to adduce in a recounting of her life.

The reason, I think, that Beauvoir's digression from telling the story of her life ended up spanning a thousand pages rather than, say, ten is that her 'I am a woman' not only came as a moment of self-revelation but also served as a lens through which Beauvoir was finally able to get a clear view of her philosophical preoccupations. By 1946, when at

[10] In the 1940s French feminists were working particularly hard to gain the right for women to vote, which was finally granted in 1949, coincidentally the year *The Second Sex* was published.

[11] 'Une interview de Simone de Beauvoir par Madeleine Chapsal', in *Les Écrits de Simone de Beauvoir: la vie—l'écriture*, ed. Claude Francis and Fernande Gontier (Paris: Gallimard, 1979), 385 (my translation). In the third volume of her autobiography Beauvoir writes: 'Wanting to speak about myself, I realized that it was necessary for me to describe the feminine condition' (*La force des choses*, 1 (Paris: Gallimard, 1963), 257 (my translation)).

the age of thirty-eight she began writing *The Second Sex*, Beauvoir had been struggling for more than fifteen years to have her philosophical say. Her abiding interest at least from her graduate school days at the Sorbonne had been a set of quintessentially modern philosophical problems: how to come to grips, at the levels of metaphysics, epistemology, and ethics, with the fact of the self's profound metaphysical isolation. This isolation receives its epitomizing expression in the opening pages of Descartes's *Meditations*, which, as I have argued elsewhere, was a touchstone philosophical text for Beauvoir throughout her philosophical life.[12] The *Meditations* begins with Descartes working himself into what he identifies as a state of madness in response to the sense that nothing can guarantee the soundness of his sense of connectedness with the world. Descartes takes himself to bring this madness under control by the discovery, in the second meditation, that his very doubt is indubitably a proof of his own existence. In the third through sixth meditations Descartes attempts to establish, over and above this proof, that his sense of connectedness with the world is indubitably guaranteed by the existence of God. But, notoriously, readers in the 350 years since the *Meditations* was published for the most part have not found these further arguments anywhere near as vivid or convincing as the deep skepticism to which Descartes gives such poignant expression in meditations 1 and 2 and with which he at least symbolically ushers in the modern era in philosophy.

Cartesian skepticism in its purest form has expressed itself in two versions: the 'problem of the external world' and the 'problem of other minds' or, in the Continental philosophical tradition, the 'problem of the other'. The problem of the external world expresses the general worry that, given that all of our experience is mediated by our senses, we cannot know that our impressions of what actually exists are accurate. Perhaps we are hallucinating or dreaming or are disembodied spirits being tested in purgatory or brains being nourished in vats of organic chemicals and stimulated by the electrodes of evil scientists. The other-minds or 'problem-of-the-other' version of skepticism expresses the more specific worry that we cannot know that other people experience the world as we do. For analytic philosophers the problem of other minds is essentially epistemological: the concern is that we cannot know whether someone else is truly in pain, or sees

[12] See *Simone de Beauvoir, Philosophy, and Feminism*, ch. 2.

the color I call 'green' where I see the color red, or is genuinely adding numbers instead of fortuitously producing the right answers every time. For Continental philosophers the problem of the other is essentially metaphysical and ethical: you might say that the issue is how other people's essential separateness from me affects and ought to affect my own way of being in the world.

Given its prominence in the history of modern philosophy in Europe from Descartes onward, we should not be surprised that Beauvoir was interested in the problem of the other as a graduate student in philosophy in the late 1920s.[13] Some philosophers, most notably Margaret Simons, contend that the way Beauvoir thought about the problem essentially did not change from this early period right on through her writing of *The Second Sex*.[14] Simons makes this claim in the service of a project that has preoccupied all revisionist philosophical readers of Beauvoir over the last dozen years; namely, rescuing her from the long philosophical shadow cast by her life-long partner Jean-Paul Sartre. Beauvoir met Sartre during her final year of graduate school in 1929 when Sartre asked her on behalf of his study group— the members of which were all male, of course—to teach them what they needed to know about the early-modern rationalists for the *agrégation*, a critical comprehensive exam which, to everyone's shock, the hot-shot Sartre had failed the year before. Shortly thereafter Beauvoir and Sartre made their notorious temporary pact, which in effect became permanent, to be each other's 'essential' lovers but neither to marry nor to expect the other to remain sexually faithful. From this time onward, for the rest of her life, Beauvoir always appeared to insist that Sartre was the superior philosopher; and this claim of course has tended to get taken at face value.[15] (Hence, we have one more reason for the lack of serious philosophical interest in *The Second Sex* until very recently.)

---

[13] In 1929, at the age of 21, Beauvoir became one of the youngest *agregés* in the history of professional French philosophy. The best account of Beauvoir's intellectual and personal development as a young woman is in Toril Moi's *Simone de Beauvoir: The Making of an Intellectual Woman* (Cambridge, Mass.: Blackwell, 1994), esp. ch. 2.

[14] Simons draws this conclusion from her reading of Beauvoir's unpublished diaries of the period (see Simons, 'Beauvoir's Early Philosophy: The 1927 Diary', in her *Beauvoir and The Second Sex*, 185–243).

[15] I say 'appeared to insist' instead of 'insisted', since Beauvoir tended to hedge her apparent insistence in subtle ways. For example, during a series of interviews in the 1970s with a German feminist journalist named Alice Schwarzer, Beauvoir at one point says of

One way to establish that Beauvoir was not just slavishly following Sartre but had something important and novel to say philosophically is simply to take a fresh look at her writings and show that they have previously been poorly or under-read.[16] Another strategy, one inaugurated by the popular writings on Beauvoir by Kate Fullbrook, an English professor, and her husband Edward, a freelance writer, is to show that it was in fact Sartre who followed in the philosophical footsteps of Beauvoir. In 1994 the Fullbrooks published a widely publicized book on Beauvoir and Sartre subtitled *The Remaking of a Twentieth-Century Legend*, in which they claim, first, that we find all the important points Sartre makes in his existentialist tour de force *Being and Nothingness*, published in 1943, in the first sixteen pages of Beauvoir's novel *L'Invitée*, also published that year but written somewhat earlier than much of Sartre's book. In a tone of relentless outrage the Fullbrooks insinuate that Beauvoir allowed Sartre to pull the existentialist rug out from under her and then to take all the credit for 'inventing' French existentialism.[17] Let us put aside a priori doubt that the ins and outs of a densely argued, very long philosophical book could be epitomized in the first chapter of a novel. Let us also not bother here with the question of what we might expect when two writers who are passionately devoted not only to each other but also, and not coincidentally, to a certain way of conceptualizing things write books at roughly the same time. There is still the issue of whether philosophical originality is best conceptualized as a matter of who got there first: Sartre *or* Beauvoir. Even more worrisome, there is the question of whether we *want* Beauvoir to have invented Sartrean existentialism, which, as I and

Sartre that 'he is primarily a philosopher and I have adopted his philosophical ideas' (Alice Schwarzer, *After* The Second Sex: *Conversations with Simone de Beauvoir*, 1st American edn. (New York: Pantheon Books, 1984). She later says that with respect to philosophy 'he was creative and I am not'; 'I always recognised his superiority in that area'; and 'I took my cues from him'. But seconds later she notes that whereas in *Being and Nothingness* Sartre 'talked of freedom as though it were quasi-total for everybody', she 'insisted on the fact that there are situations where freedom cannot be exercised' (p. 109).

[16] This is the strategy I favor, and it is the strategy that is followed by a plurality of scholars interested in resuscitating interest in Beauvoir's philosophical merits, including Eva [Lundgren-]Gothlin, Karen Vintges, Michèle Le Doeuff, and Toril Moi, all cited in n. 2 above, as well as Hazel E. Barnes in her article, 'Response to Margaret Simons', *Philosophy Today*, 42 (suppl.) (1998).

[17] e.g. 'The major ideas behind *Being and Nothingness* were fully worked out by Beauvoir and adopted by Sartre before he even began his famous study' (*Simone de Beauvoir and Jean-Paul Sartre: The Remaking of a Twentieth-Century Legend* (New York: Basic Books, 1994), 3).

others have argued at length, is in crucial respects seriously at odds with the views that Beauvoir expresses in *The Second Sex* and that she is clearly at least groping toward in her earlier writings, including *L'Invitée*.

In claiming that we can draw a philosophical straight line from an unpublished diary Beauvoir kept in 1927, two years before she met Sartre, right through to *The Second Sex*, Margaret Simons unfortunately follows the Fullbrooks in construing philosophical originality in very narrow terms. I say that this move is unfortunate, not only because I think it entails an attenuated understanding of philosophical originality but also because of the great debt that every philosopher working on Beauvoir today owes Simons, not only for her revelation of the inadequacies of the English translation of *The Second Sex* but also for her pioneering conviction in the philosophical importance of Beauvoir's work.[18]

No one who admires Beauvoir as a philosopher would be uninterested in the fact, unearthed by Simons, that as a graduate student Beauvoir was clearly worried about the problem of the other and in particular about whether there is a hopeless tension between human self-interest and altruism—between self and other. The theme of a fundamental opposition between self and others is indeed prominent in *The Second Sex*, as Simons stresses. But Beauvoir specifically attributes her interest in this idea to Hegel's formulation of it in *The Phenomenology of Spirit*, and we see no striking precedent for this interest—other than perhaps a predilection for the problem of the other—in Beauvoir's juvenilia.[19] Simons asks us to believe that already, as a nineteen-year-old musing on self and other, Beauvoir was 'laying the foundations' of the 'phenomenology of interpersonal relationships' that Sartre details in *Being and Nothingness*.[20] But there is strong

---

[18] Much of the relevant work is collected in *Beauvoir and* The Second Sex: *Feminism, Race, and the Origins of Existentialism*. (Notice that the subtitle of this book hints at Simons's interest in the Fullbrookian claim that Beauvoir might have been instrumental in 'inventing' existentialism.)

[19] Read the introduction to *The Second Sex* for massive evidence of Beauvoir's intellectual indebtedness to Hegel in her conceptualization of self–other relations.

[20] 'Is *The Second Sex* Beauvoir's Application of Sartrean Existentialism?'—a paper delivered at the World Congress of Philosophy in August 1998. (A copy of the paper can be found at http://www.bu.edu/wcp.) By using the word 'phenomenology' Simons is alluding to Sartre's debt to Husserl, who in the early part of the twentieth century developed a way of thinking philosophically grounded in a careful study of the data of experience. Sartre spent a year in Germany in the early 1930s studying Husserl's work carefully, and his investment in the phenomenological method is everywhere in evidence in *Being and Nothingness*.

evidence even in Beauvoir's pre-*Second Sex* writings that she saw grave problems with this phenomenology and even stronger evidence that she was finally able to articulate her intuitions about self and other in their full glory only when she developed an interest in what it meant to say 'I am a woman'. While many serious philosophical readers of Beauvoir reject the strategy of Beauvoir resuscitation adopted by the Fullbrooks and Simons, I think I may be the only one who goes so far as to claim that until she began to think about her identity as a woman Beauvoir could not get clear on her own philosophical views.[21] My position is that it took a meditation on the question of what it meant to claim 'I am a woman' for Beauvoir to understand and articulate fully certain profound differences between her own and Sartre's ways of approaching the problem of the other.[22] Whether I am right about this or not, Beauvoir scholars are united in their conviction that at least by the time of *The Second Sex* we find a sharp difference between Beauvoir's articulation of and thoughts on the problem of the other and those of Sartre.

In *Being and Nothingness* Sartre had propounded the view that human beings are by nature split creatures: they are both subjects and objects.[23] This position of course was not new. But whereas most dualists since Descartes had been keen on showing that the split can somehow be overcome or, at least, domesticated, Sartre distinguished himself by denying that a human being can ever hope to synthesize the subject–object split. On Sartre's view the systematic study of human experience ('phenomenology') shows that a person never experiences himself at one and the same time as both an acting subject and a passive object. At times—paradigmatically when I am passing judgment on others—I experience myself as the center of the universe. Conversely, there are times—paradigmatically when someone else is

[21] Bergoffen (see n. 2) supports Simons's project, as does Eleanore Holveck, *Simone De Beauvoir's Philosophy of Lived Experience: Literature and Metaphysics* (Lanham, Md.: Rowman & Littlefield, 2002). Disagreement with Simons's project has shown up mostly in the form of silence on the part of other scholars of Beauvoir's philosophy, though see Barnes's 'Response to Margaret Simons' for an explicitly critical rejoinder.

[22] I do not mean to suggest here that before *The Second Sex* there are no signs of dissent. We certainly find glimmers of Beauvoir's reservations about Sartre's views not only in her novel *L'Invitée* but also in her earliest published philosophical writing, including *Pyrrhus et Cinéas* (1944) and *Pour une morale de l'ambiguité* (1947), as well as the essays collected in *L'Existentialisme et la sagesse des nations* (1948).

[23] I am working here with the 1966 Pocket Books version of Hazel Barnes's excellent translation of *L'Être et le néant* (New York: Washington Square Press).

explicitly or implicitly judging me—that I experience myself as one among many mere things in a universe organized around a consciousness that is completely alien to mine. For Sartre, these moments never coincide. In part III of *Being and Nothingness*, in which he spells out his view of self–other relations in great detail, Sartre considers apparent objections to this central claim. You might think that the phenomenon of love, to take only the most obvious instance, provides a counter example. But Sartre argues explicitly that it does not.[24] The basic argument here is that one cannot love someone else without reifying her in some way or another. What I want when I fall in love with someone else is for that person to acknowledge my subjectivity, which in principle cannot be done, Sartre claims, without my beloved's turning my subjectivity into a kind of object and my doing the same to him or her.

We cannot understand the nature of a claim like this unless we appreciate that Sartre thinks we find direct evidence for it in our everyday experience. He thinks that we will see, if we look carefully and without prejudice, that at every instant of our interaction with others we are either the object of the other's judgment or the judge ourselves but never both at the same time. The challenge is not to succumb to the temptation of imagining that the other's judgment of me, no matter how complimentary or otherwise welcome, can possibly be correct—can possibly, in other words, succeed in not reifying me. This dilemma of our lives with others is what Sartre notoriously calls 'the look': either I feel your eyes on me, metaphorically or otherwise, or you feel mine on you. And one lives a lie when one denies this condition—when one imagines that one has achieved reciprocity with someone else or has discovered oneself in any definitive way in the other's eyes or, on the other side of things, fails to acknowledge the power of another person's judgment.

Let us be a little more concrete here by turning to a famous example of Sartre's, one he uses in order to drive home the fact of our temptation to reify ourselves—to be, that is, in what he calls 'bad faith'.[25] He asks us to imagine that a man asks a woman on a date and

---

[24] See *Being and Nothingness*, pt. III, ch. 3, sect. I, 'First Attitude Toward Others: Love, Language, Masochism'.

[25] The example I'm about to discuss leads off the second section of the 'Bad Faith' chapter in *Being and Nothingness*. See also Toril Moi's illuminating discussion of this moment in chapter 5 of *Simone de Beauvoir: The Making of an Intellectual Woman* (see n. 13 above).

takes her at some point in the evening to a café. The woman is talking, and the man, anticipating what is to come later on, takes her hand in his. Here, the man expresses his subjectivity by implicitly announcing to the woman that she is an object of his sexual desire. But the woman continues to chat as though nothing has happened: she treats her hand as an inert thing over which she has no control and which is in no way connected with her own subjectivity. This woman, Sartre thinks it is obvious, is in bad faith in so far as she fails to acknowledge to herself, let alone to her date, that the man's action has marked her as a sexual object. In choosing to suppress this fact, the woman paradoxically fails to take responsibility for herself—treats herself, not just her hand, as a thing. On Sartre's view, what is required of the woman here is to 'look' back at the man by acknowledging and thereby transcending her own sexual desirability. In so doing, however, she is prevented by metaphysical necessity from acknowledging the man's own subjectivity, which will become known to her again only in so far as the man once again makes her an object in his own world.

Things are of course rather more complicated in Sartre's actual exposition of these matters in Being and Nothingness.[26] Still, my caricature perhaps suffices to point up at least two unattractive features of his view of subject–object relations. First, there is his conviction that we are fundamentally and hopelessly unable to achieve any sort of metaphysical—and, therefore, ethical or even epistemic—reciprocity with one another. (This predicament drives the play No Exit—the one in which a character notoriously exclaims 'Hell is other people!'— which Sartre wrote just after completing Being and Nothingness.) Second, on Sartre's view, any oppression a person might suffer can only be of her own making. I overcome the other when I 'look' at him; when I fail to do so I consign myself to the status of being an object in his universe. Another person cannot so consign me without my willing capitulation. As I have noted before,[27] Sartre was quite explicit about this position in Being and Nothingness. He wrote this book in the late 1930s and early 1940s, when Hitler's inhuman treatment of Jews was already well known to European intellectuals, and yet he was able to write: 'A Jew is not a Jew first in order to be subsequently ashamed or proud; it is his pride of being a Jew, his shame,

---

[26] I provide a chapter-long take on Sartre's views in Being and Nothingness on subjectivity and objectivity in chapter 4 of Simone de Beauvoir, Philosophy, and Feminism.

[27] Simone de Beauvoir, Philosophy, and Feminism, 116.

or his indifference which will reveal to him his being-a-Jew; and this being-a-Jew is nothing outside the free manner of adopting it' (p. 677).[28] A sympathetic reader might understand Sartre to be saying here that one's consciousness of 'being-a-Jew' is a function, rather than a cause, of the way one as it were bears one's Jewishness. But even this generous interpretation scarcely mitigates Sartre's failure, especially in the context of his times, even to consider 'being-a-Jew' as an identity *imposed* on individuals as part of an attempt to justify their systematic oppression.

I submit that no one who reads both *Being and Nothingness* and *The Second Sex*, even in English and without obsessive care, can fail to appreciate both Beauvoir's indebtedness to the terms in which Sartre thinks and, at least as importantly, the vast chasm between his thought and hers when it comes to the enormous issues I have just been discussing. On Beauvoir's view, the idea that we can strive to meet one another in genuine mutual respect—simultaneously regarding one another as both subjects and objects, as Beauvoir puts it[29]—is not only realistic but also constitutes a crucial part of living a fully human life. What gets in the way of our extending this respect to one another is not to be found at the level of metaphysics but at the level of human psychology and social reality: we are inclined to avoid the hard work of forging this respect because we find it too risky. Undertaking it requires that I abandon my fixed conception of myself—my various interests in self-objectification or perhaps even self-petrifaction—as well as bear up under another person's objectifying judgment of me. ('Bearing up' could of course take the form of thoughtfully rejecting such a judgment—and preparing myself for a potential redoubling of its force.) Where Beauvoir diverges most dramatically from Sartre on this front is her discovery that a crucial refuge in our flight from the project of mutual recognition is to be found in our investment in sex difference: men are socialized to conceive of themselves as subjects in some absolute, unassailable, objectified sense of the term, and women as objects of men's unidirectional judgment.

This brings me to the second major way in which Beauvoir's view is frankly at odds with Sartre's. Beauvoir argues forcefully that while

---

[28] I should note that according to Sartre human beings routinely react to the 'look' with either pride or shame (see pt. III of *Being and Nothingness*, especially the section on 'The Look').

[29] See e.g. *SS* 1989, 139–41; *DS* 1986, i. 237–9.

human reciprocity is possible in principle it is bound to misfire in the face of oppression, not least the systematic form imposed upon women since at least the invention of the tool in the Iron Age.[30] Following Hegel—whose model of thinking about human relationships, as should be obvious to anyone familiar with his 'master–slave dialectic', was enormously important to both Sartre and Beauvoir— Beauvoir thought that 'we discover in consciousness itself a fundamental hostility toward every other consciousness' (*SS* 1989, pp. xxii–xxiii; *DS* 1986, i. 16–17). By nature, she thought, we human beings yearn endlessly for confirmation of our importance and are inclined to resent other people both for their power to yield or withhold it and for their mirror claims on us. And yet experience endlessly brings us to relinquish our fundamental hostility toward at least certain others, as their own humanity is made manifest to us—often in the form of an expression of their own need for recognition. In so far as men and women are taught to constrain this acknowledgment with respect to one another, men play the social role of absolute 'Subjects' and women that of absolute 'Others', and their capacity for genuinely human being is therefore drastically attenuated.[31] This means, further, that the task of *The Second Sex* is not, as is ordinarily assumed, to achieve equality between men and women by raising women to the social level of men—although, of course, Beauvoir thought that overcoming women's oppression must entail a certain social and economic parity. Rather, Beauvoir's view is that nothing less than a revolution in our understanding of what it means to be human is required. The task of *The Second Sex* is to explore both men's and women's investment in the status quo and therefore to inspire us to resist it.

The best evidence I can muster for this reading of *The Second Sex* is the book itself—and in French, if you can manage it.[32] If you read the book carefully you will not be able to avoid a sense of Beauvoir's decidedly un-Sartrean commitments both to the possibility of genuinely reciprocal mutual recognition and to the rejection of any conception of freedom that can entirely escape the long arm of oppression.

---

[30] The relevant discussion is at *SS* 1989, 78; *DS* 1986, i. 131.

[31] The capitalization is Beauvoir's.

[32] Regardless of the state of your French, I urge you to demand of Knopf and of Gallimard (the French publisher) that they at bare minimum permit, if not actively support, a new, scholarly edition of what we all can at least agree is a centrally important book in the history of feminist thought.

You also will be unable to cling in good faith to the related dogma—invariably pressed upon me in one form or another when I speak to feminist audiences about Beauvoir—that her outlook is essentially 'masculinist', heartless, condescending, bourgeois, Eurocentric, racist, or otherwise morally or politically warped. Critics of the current revival of interest in Beauvoir in philosophical circles are fond of seizing upon various contradictions and tensions in *The Second Sex* and judging them to cripple the text.[33] These accusations of inconsistency are overblown. But I do not expect you to take my word for it. Read the book (again) for yourself and then judge.

The current outpouring of secondary literature on the philosophical bearings of *The Second Sex* and Beauvoir's other writings has barely begun to scratch the surface of the text. Most of the relevant authors, myself included, have been largely concerned to bring Beauvoir out from Sartre's philosophical shadow not only by providing evidence of her abjuring of this or that key Sartrean tenet but also by emphasizing the extent to which she was also heavily influenced—indeed, the claim often is that she was more influenced—by philosophers other than Sartre. Most often, comparisons are made with other writers in the phenomenological tradition—notably Husserl and Merleau-Ponty—and to Hegel, Marx, and Heidegger.[34] This is the same list of authors that one would adduce in tracing Sartre's own philosophical forebears. What those of us who are currently writing on Beauvoir are ordinarily

[33] See e.g. Céline T. Léon's vicious attack on Beauvoir in 'Beauvoir's Woman: Eunuch or Male?', in *Feminist Interpretations of Simone de Beauvoir*, ed. Margaret A. Simons (University Park, Pa.: Penn State University Press, 1995), 137–59. Léon: 'Beauvoir's contradictory statements... reproduce the power structure by which Western civilization has been shaped' (p. 155). Other critiques of Beauvoir's 'contradictions' include Penelope Deutscher, 'The Notorious Contradictions of Simone de Beauvoir', in *Yielding Gender* (New York: Routledge, 1997), 169–93; Tina Chanter, 'The Legacy of Simone de Beauvoir', in *Ethics of Eros: Irigaray's Rewriting of the Philosophers* (New York: Routledge, 1995), 46–79; and Moira Gatens, 'Woman as the Other', *Feminism and Philosophy: Perspectives on Difference and Equality* (Bloomington, Ind.: Indiana University Press, 1991), 48–59.

[34] See Arp, Vintges, Kruks, and Heinämaa (n. 2 above) for work that situates Beauvoir with reference to the phenomenological tradition. For work that draws connections with Hegel see Gothlin and Bauer (n. 2); Gothlin also analyzes Beauvoir's interest in Marx. Both Gothlin and I are also convinced that Heidegger is an important figure for Beauvoir (see the paper of mine cited in n. 35 below as well as Gothlin's 'Reading Simone de Beauvoir With Martin Heidegger', in Claudia Card (ed.), *The Cambridge Companion to Feminist Philosophy* (New York: Cambridge University Press, 2003), 45–65. To my knowledge, there is very little work on Beauvoir's indebtedness to Freud, Lacan, and Lévi-Strauss, even though their writings were clearly on her mind as she wrote *The Second Sex*.

at pains to show is how differently from Sartre she understands their philosophical pertinence.

Let me give you one example from my own recent work.[35] It concerns Sartre's and Beauvoir's differing interpretations of and investments in the Heideggerian notion of *Mitsein*, or 'being-with'. As with many of Heidegger's technical terms, the meaning of *Mitsein* is not obvious, and one will not understand it apart from careful exegesis of its role in Heidegger's *Being and Time*. What is clear enough is that *Mitsein* concerns the fact that we are fundamentally 'with' other people; what is disputed is the meaning of 'with'. On Sartre's understanding of Heidegger, *Mitsein* is a kind of 'solidarity', of the sort required for a set of rowers to do their job effectively: 'It is', Sartre writes in *Being and Nothingness*, 'the mute existence in common of one member of the crew with his fellows'.[36] Since Heidegger claims that *Mitsein* is a fundamental ontological state for human beings, it follows from Sartre's metaphor that, on Heidegger's view, we are all fundamentally in solidarity with one another. But Sartre flatly rejects this idea. If and when we find ourselves 'with' one another, it is at the level of what he and Heidegger both call the 'ontic', or the everyday, not at any ontologically deeper one. Indeed, Sartre says, the idea of some sort of fundamental human fellowship—some planet-wide boatload of scullers, as it were—is incoherent, since it leaves no room to explain why people are manifestly not in solidarity with one another much of the time. Since Sartre is deeply interested in the so-called problem of the other, the question of how self–other relationships are negotiated, he has no interest in the concept of *Mitsein*, which, at least on his construal of the term, doesn't even allow us to pose the problem. Sartre is absolutely clear on this point: 'The relation of the *mit-Sein* can be of absolutely no use to us in resolving the psychological, concrete problem of recognition of the Other' (p. 334).

Beauvoir's rejection of this dismissal is right on the surface of *The Second Sex*. In the last sentence of the famous introduction to the book, Beauvoir says, clearly in full voice, that her aim is to help women to 'participer au Mitsein humain'—that is, to 'participate in

---

[35] The relevant paper is 'Beauvoir's Heideggerian Ontology', in Margaret A. Simons (ed.), *The Philosophy of Simone de Beauvoir* (Indianapolis, Ind.: Indiana University Press, 2003).

[36] The idea of *Mitsein* as a kind of solidarity is on p. 333 of the 1966 version of *Being and Nothingness*. The longer quotation is from p. 322.

the human *Mitsein*' (*DS* 1986, i. 32; my translation).[37] But why does she accept what Sartre rejects? Both Sartre's interpretation of the concept of *Mitsein* and his flat-out disdain for it are driven by his general picture of human relations. Beauvoir's rejection of this picture stems from her radically different understanding of what Heidegger means by *Mitsein* and how we might go on with the concept. On Beauvoir's reading of Heidegger, *Mitsein* is not some sort of primordial human fellowship. Rather, it stands for the fact that human beings live in a world that is through and through marked by the existence of other people, so that we cannot understand the nature of even the simplest object (Heidegger's favorite example is a hammer) apart from a reference to what we, and not just I, do with it.[38] That we live in a 'with-world' (*Mitwelt*), as Heidegger sometimes puts it, does not imply that there is some grand human community.[39] To the contrary: the very publicity of the stuff of our lives puts us in danger of a kind of alienation, both from others and from ourselves. Far from finding others in the *Mitsein*, we can lose ourselves in it. We do this by failing to make the world our own—by succumbing to what Heidegger famously calls inauthenticity. And in losing ourselves we become incapable of authenticity with respect to our dealings with others.

I think that Beauvoir's appropriation of the concept of *Mitsein* reveals that her understanding of what's going on in *Being and Time* is considerably more accurate and nuanced than Sartre's is.[40] But more important than how close to or far from Heidegger's text her interpretation lies is the way that her project in *The Second Sex* positions her to extend the concept of *Mitsein* in directions that Heidegger clearly did not envision. Beauvoir's central concern in her book is to understand why the second-class status of women has been so long-standing and intractable and whether and how it might be overcome. Beauvoir takes

[37] Parshley has Beauvoir saying that she is going to help us see why women run into trouble when they 'aspire to full membership in the human race'. The four other instances of *Mitsein* that I address in 'Beauvoir's Heideggerian Ontology' are at: (1) *DS* 1986, i. 17 (compare *SS* 1989, xxiii, and note the fateful translation of *la réalité humaine*, the French term for Heidegger's *Dasein*, as 'human society' in Parshley's version); (2) *SS* 1989, p. xxv; *DS* 1986, i. 19; (3) *SS* 1989, 35; *DS* 1986, i. 75; and (4) *SS* 1989, 47; *DS* 1986, i. 89.

[38] A hammer happens to be a human artifact. But the point would be the same if we were to think about the nature of clouds or moral goodness or aesthetic judgment or the mind or a knowledge claim or the human being itself.

[39] Martin Heidegger, *Being and Time*, trans. John Macquarrie and Edward Robinson (New York: Harper & Row, 1962).

[40] My 'Beauvoir's Heideggerian Ontology' provides evidence for this claim.

from Heidegger a way of understanding human beings, in their inherent 'with'-ness, as endlessly tempted to fail to make their lives their own. The concept of the *Mitsein* serves as a resource for helping her articulate the problem of how a woman is to find the courage to be herself, to distinguish herself, to find her voice, in a world in which she is inevitably with—even smothered by—others, and particularly men. Beauvoir appropriates the concept of *Mitsein* in her quest to understand why men and women are inclined to exploit the fact of sex difference as a way of avoiding the hard task of finding themselves in the world.

This sketch of my work on Beauvoir and Heidegger is meant to help support the claim that the contemporary work on Beauvoir's philosophical influences, work that most philosophers interested in her are now undertaking, is important and needs to continue. However, to understand what's truly ground-breaking about *The Second Sex* we need to look carefully at what 'influence' comes to in this particular case. My *Mitsein* example suggests that what's of primary interest about Beauvoir's appropriations of other philosophers' writings is the way the lens of her inquiry into women's lives reveals entirely new dimensions of the fruitfulness of this work. The driving question of *The Second Sex*—'What is a woman?'—determines the form that Beauvoir's articulation of her philosophical investment in a Heidegger or Husserl or Merleau-Ponty will take.[41] And Beauvoir's provisional answer to this question—'*I* am a woman'—further constrains the extent to which this articulation will get mired in philosophical abstraction. Her concrete answer to an abstract question epitomizes what I believe is the greatest philosophical achievement of *The Second Sex*; namely, Beauvoir's holding her everyday experience as a woman, in all its concreteness, in the same space as her philosophical investigation into what it means to be a woman, in all its abstraction.

This is, not surprisingly, precisely the achievement of Beauvoir's that I think we philosophers—most importantly, we feminist philosophers, who by definition must be interested in the bearing of philosophy on our ordinary lives—continue to neglect almost entirely. Instead, we keep imagining that our theories will somehow magically transfigure themselves into political action against gender oppression, that we

[41] In *Simone de Beauvoir, Philosophy, and Feminism* I detail the way in which Beauvoir's inquiry in *The Second Sex* provides her with a way of articulating her investment in Hegel that had eluded her previously (see chs. 5–7).

needn't worry about whether or how we can *live* our theory. This sort of fantasy, I fear, drives the kind of high metaphysics that we find in the very influential work of Judith Butler, which, no matter how visionary or right-minded, at the end of the day has no obvious connections with the way we live our everyday lives. And our fantasies also drive an alternative understanding of philosophy as a kind of toolkit, one we can dig around in to construct buttressing argument for various feminist political positions.[42] But this strategy entails an abandonment of the age-old, not to say paradigmatic, philosophical task of posing big questions—about, for example, what it means to be a sexed human being. What contemporary feminist philosophy lacks is precisely what Beauvoir gives us: a way of doing philosophy that changes how people see the world. I do not exaggerate. Can we name a book that is recognizably philosophical that has done more to change actual women's lives? Can we name a book that has changed actual women's lives that is recognizably more philosophical? A way of doing philosophy that changes how people see the world: this is of course exactly what I've claimed non-feminist philosophy—the 'malestream' kind—has come sorely to lack. In undertaking the project of genuinely appropriating Simone de Beauvoir's achievements, difficult as that project will no doubt be, might we feminist philosophers position ourselves to become a philosophical vanguard? To answer this question, we must of course start by reading—really reading—*The Second Sex*.

ACKNOWLEDGEMENTS

I gave this paper as the keynote address at the annual meeting of the Eastern Division of the Society for Women in Philosophy at the University of Southern Florida in April 2003. I wish to thank Joanne Waugh and Christa Davis Acampora for inviting me to give this address and encouraging me to speak on Beauvoir, and I am indebted to the conference participants for valuable feedback. Special thanks to Toril Moi, Mark Richard, and Emily Grosholz for recommending important changes to the text.

---

[42] I have in mind work in various 'applied' forms of feminist ethics and social and political philosophy. See e.g. Rae Langton, 'Speech Acts and Unspeakable Acts', *Philosophy and Public Affairs*, 22/4 (1993). Here, Langton deploys what she takes to be arguments in J. L. Austin's classic *How to Do Things With Words* in order to defend the coherence of the idea that pornographic 'speech' should not be free. I discuss Langton's work at length in *How to Do Things With Pornography* (unpublished manuscript).

PART III

LITERARY CONTEXT

7

Meaning What We Say: The 'Politics of Theory' and the Responsibility of Intellectuals

Toril Moi

'The desire for a theory that guarantees political radicalism and, ideally, political effectiveness, has been strong in recent years', Jonathan Culler writes.[1] As a feminist literary critic and theorist I know what he means, for I belong precisely to the group of intellectuals for whom the question of the 'politics of theory' has been a cause of concern for a long time. Radical theorists often ask themselves whether the writing they do, which tends to be specialized and fairly abstract, really makes a political difference. Whenever I think about this I feel comforted by the thought that *some* intellectual works, at least, have had tremendous impact. *The Second Sex*, above all, is the very incarnation of committed writing. Here is a book of philosophy, a highly intellectual analysis of women's situation, that actually did change thousands of women's lives, and in so doing contributed to changing the values of whole societies.[2]

Yet the existence of incontrovertible examples (*Uncle Tom's Cabin* and *Das Kapital* are others) has hardly helped to settle discussions about the 'politics of theory'. In present-day debates it is as if Sartre and Beauvoir, once considered paradigmatic examples of committed intellectuals, have been entirely forgotten. In this essay I shall show that they still have thought-provoking contributions to make to our understanding of the relationship between politics and intellectual

---

[1] Jonathan Culler, 'Literary Theory', in *Introduction to Scholarship in Modern Languages and Literatures*, ed. Joseph Gibaldi, 2nd edn. (New York: MLA, 1992), 201–35, at 218.

[2] For some examples of lives changed by *The Second Sex* see Toril Moi, *Simone de Beauvoir: The Making of an Intellectual Woman* (Oxford: Blackwell, 1994), 179–81.

work. This essay, then, is not so much about *The Second Sex* as it is about some of the thoughts and attitudes that made Beauvoir want to write that book. In order to clear the way for a reconsideration of French existentialism, I shall start by taking a closer look at the phrase the 'politics of theory'.

DEMANDING THE ABSOLUTE

The perennial interest in the question of the 'politics of theory' among intellectuals on the left stems from anxiety about being intellectuals in the first place. Radicals wish to make the world better and more just. Yet we have chosen to work with words, ideas, and culture. For this we get paid so that we can lead comfortable middle-class lives. In a world full of suffering and injustice there is something unfair about this. The most attractive existential solution to the sense of guilt that this situation breeds is to find a way to justify intellectual work politically. No wonder that many succumb to the temptation and set out to prove either that theory in its broadest generality or that some particular theory is intrinsically political. If we can believe that theory (some theory) simply is political, then doing theory would carry its own political and existential justification at all times. What a relief for guilt-ridden theorists!

Unfortunately, this is not a very convincing strategy. We would be more politically effective, and happier too, if we could manage to wean ourselves from this fantasy. First of all, the question of the 'politics of theory' is far too general. There are all kinds of theories, used by all kinds of people in all kinds of contexts. A theory of truth and discourse does not have the same relationship to politics as a theory of capitalism or women's oppression. The question about the 'politics of theory' has in fact mostly been raised by post-structuralists, whose theories have to do with language, discourse, and subjectivity. (So the 'politics of theory' really means the 'politics of post-structuralism'?)

In the same way, the word politics means different things at different times, in different situations. In the 1930s a political play was likely to be about class, or fascism. Now a political play may be about AIDS or race or gender or sexuality. To the question 'Is theory political?' all one can reply is 'It depends'.[3]

---

[3] Cora Diamond puts the phrase 'it depends' to good philosophical use in 'Knowing Tornadoes and Other Things', *New Literary History*, 22 (1991), 156–60.

In short, to ask about the 'politics of theory' is to impose a demand for absoluteness on a human activity that will yield no such thing. To such a question, any answer we could give would either be metaphysical or meaningless, or both. Stanley Cavell writes:

We impose a demand for absoluteness... upon a concept, and then, finding that our ordinary use of this concept does not meet our demand, we accommodate this discrepancy as nearly as possible. Take these familiar patterns: we do not really see material objects, but only see them indirectly; we cannot be certain of any empirical proposition, but only practically certain; we cannot really know what another person is feeling, but only infer it.[4]

Cavell's examples are all taken from classical cases of philosophical skepticism, but the symptom he alerts us to (the demand for absoluteness) is rife in contemporary literary theory too: Whenever something turns out not to be absolute, in our disappointment we turn around and declare that it is nothing at all. So if we can't have absolute, ultimate truth, for example, then we declare that 'truth' (or 'certainty') does not exist at all.

As we have seen, Jonathan Culler's diagnosis is that contemporary theorists are looking for a 'theory that guarantees political radicalism'. The very idea of a 'guarantee' requires further investigation, alongside the notions of 'theory' and 'politics'. What picture of the relationship between politics and theory must one have to make it look as if a 'guarantee' of radical effects (or should this be radical intentions?) can be had? Is this not another version of Cavell's 'demand for absoluteness'?

To ask about the 'politics of theory' is not the only way to think about the political value of intellectual work. Nor is the demand for absoluteness confined to contemporary literary theorists. To show what I mean, I shall now turn to two statements by Sartre and Beauvoir.

SARTRE'S MELODRAMA

'Faced with a dying child, *Nausea* does not tip the scales', Sartre said in 1964, the year in which he published *The Words*.[5] At roughly the same

---

[4] Stanley Cavell, 'Aesthetic Problems of Modern Philosophy', in *Must We Mean What We Say?* (Cambridge: Cambridge University Press, 1969), 73–96, at 77.

[5] 'En face d'un enfant qui meurt, *La Nausée* ne fait pas le poids.' Sartre made this statement in an interview with Jacqueline Piatier entitled 'Jean-Paul Sartre s'explique sur *Les Mots*', published in *Le Monde* 18 April 1964. My quotation comes from the reprint in Michel Contat and Michel Rybalka, *Les Écrits de Sartre* (Paris: Gallimard, 1970), 398.

time, in 1963, Simone de Beauvoir wrote: 'I am an intellectual, I take words and the truth to be of value.'[6] There are two different attitudes towards politics and words at work in these statements. I now want to show why I think of Sartre's image as *metaphysical* and *melodramatic*, in contrast to what I shall call Beauvoir's *ordinary* view of intellectual commitment. (My choice of words is meant to indicate my debt to Stanley Cavell, and through him, to Wittgenstein.)

At the time, many took Sartre's statement to mean that he thought there was no justification for literature in a starving world. It is unclear whether Sartre himself thought this, or whether he just meant to raise the question of the political effects of writing by saying something provocative. I shall ascribe the common, extreme interpretation to 'Sartre', but it may well be that what I am describing is not Sartre, but those who take his statement in this way, then and now.

In 1964 Sartre was 59, he was slowly going blind, and he suffered from alarming levels of hypertension. He was also a world-famous intellectual, tirelessly campaigning for radical causes. Given his specific circumstances, the most politically effective thing he could do was to continue to write, which is exactly what he did. Yet the image of the dying child is immensely more powerful than any pragmatic consider-ations. However justified he may have been in his choices, that image makes Sartre's intellectual life appear insufficient, even callous. The image tells us that regardless of what he does as an intellectual Sartre is painfully aware that it is not always enough.

The phrase 'not always enough' reveals what the problem is. *Of course* writing is not always enough. How could it be? What human activity is 'always enough'? Enough for what? In the vague, unspecific, and generalized turn of phrase 'not always enough', metaphysics—Cavell's 'demand for absoluteness'—rears its head. For if we are faced with a dying child, we tend to her. We feed her, care for her, hold her, provide as much medicine and comfort as we possibly can. In such a case tending to the child is simply what we do. Only a cold-blooded murderer would turn her back and return to her desk.

But if this is right then Sartre's image tells us nothing about the political and ethical value of intellectual work. We all know that novels and theory don't feed the hungry or heal the sick. To whom was he

---

[6] Simone de Beauvoir, *Force of Circumstance*, trans. Richard Howard (Harmondsworth: Penguin, 1987), 378. 'Je suis une intellectuelle, j'accorde du prix aux mots et à la vérité', Simone de Beauvoir, *La Force des choses* (Paris: Gallimard (Coll. Folio), 1963), ii. 120.

speaking? Who would feel illuminated by the thought that *Nausea* will not save a dying child? The answer is clear: only someone who once fervently hoped that it would. Sartre's youthful faith in salvation through literature, which happens to be a major preoccupation of *The Words*, instantly comes to mind. But the same attitude can be found in those present-day intellectuals who have excessive faith in the power of theory to put everything politically right, as if every kind of oppression would vanish if only we could elaborate the right theory of subjectivity, or discourse, or truth.

In Sartre's example of the dying child there is an immensely seductive fantasy of being able to produce writing powerful enough to save a dying child. There is no middle ground here: either writing does it all, or it does nothing. I don't mean to overlook the fact that Sartre's statement has the form of a negation, that his claim is that *Nausea can't* do anything for a dying child. In my view, the very form of the statement carries out psychic work; its task is to *negate* the fantasy of the omnipotence of writing, a fantasy Sartre himself so masterfully explored in *The Words*. 'Negation is a way of taking cognizance of what is repressed . . . A negative judgment is the intellectual substitute for repression', Freud writes.[7] By saying that his writing is *not* justified, Sartre keeps the dream of justification by literature alive, but the affect has shifted, from exuberant jubilation at the omnipotence of writing to abject disappointment and guilt at the failure of writing.

The very intensity of the image reinforces and expresses the contrasting affects contained in the negated fantasy. Juxtaposing a dying child and an ageing male intellectual, Sartre pits wronged innocence against guilt and decay. Pressing the question of intellectual responsibility to the extreme, he trades in the stark absolutes, the all-or-nothing logic, of melodrama.[8] In this way he invites us to believe that politics is the only possible *raison d'être* of writing, and that if writing doesn't save a dying child it is of no use at all.

---

[7] Sigmund Freud, 'Negation' (1923), in *The Standard Edition of the Complete Psychological Works*, trans. and ed. James Strachey, xix (London: The Hogarth Press, 1953–74), 233–9 at 235–6.

[8] In his influential study *The Melodramatic Imagination* Peter Brooks writes: 'The connotations of the word [melodrama] include: the indulgence of strong emotionalism; moral polarization and schematization; extreme states of being, situations, actions; overt villainy, persecution of the good' (Brooks, *The Melodramatic Imagination: Balzac, Henry James, Melodrama, and the Mode of Excess* (New York: Columbia University Press, 1985), 11).

Among intellectuals today the tell-tale symptoms of Sartre's anxiety-inducing fantasy are excessive feelings of anguish and guilt about the political failure or impotence of intellectuals. The inevitable flip side of this is excessive optimism about the power of theory. Once we lose faith in that, we are ripe for Sartre's melodrama. Unless we can find an alternative to see-sawing between these equally intense and affect-laden positions, we will become embittered and lose all faith in the value of intellectual work. The irony is that the more intensity we invest in our quest for political justification, the more we court ultimate political disaffection.

BEAUVOIR AND THE ORDINARY

How do we get off the see-saw? Beauvoir's 'I take words and the truth to be of value' rings truer to me than Sartre's melodrama of the intellectual and the dying child. It is significant, for example, that she simply says 'of value', and not 'of absolute value', or 'always of *political* value'. To my ears, Beauvoir invites us to consider what value words and the truth have in a given situation, no more, but also no less. Beauvoir's approach enables us to discuss the relationship between theory and politics in ordinary, everyday terms, and not in the empty terms of metaphysics.

For her, then, the question of where, when, and how the intellectual should commit herself becomes a concrete, individual, and practical (as opposed to an abstract, general, and metaphysical) one: Can I justify doing what I do? How good am I at it? Do I have the talents and skill required to do something else? Could I acquire them? Is the cause I believe in better served by a mediocre guerrilla fighter or a first-rate writer? Let us say that I really want to know what intellectuals can do to save dying children. I read in the paper that: 'The United Nations calculates that the world population's basic needs for food, drinking water, education and medical care could be covered by a levy of less than 4% on the accumulated wealth of the 225 largest fortunes [in the world].'[9] It would seem that the people who can do the most to help dying children are not intellectuals, but the owners of those 225 fortunes.

[9] Ignacio Ramonet, 'Politics of Hunger', trans. Barry Smerin, Le Monde diplomatique, November 1998, 1 (supplement to Manchester Guardian Weekly, week ending 22 November 1998).

As intellectuals we can spread this knowledge. But we also need to acknowledge that unless we are a certain kind of economist or doctor our daily work is not going to be concretely concerned with the prevention of famine and death. Intellectuals working in the humanities shouldn't simply ask what intellectuals in general can do, but what we can do that people from other disciplines can't do better.

The advantage of Beauvoir's approach is that it enables us to acknowledge the distress that fuels Sartre's stark image, without having to give up the thought that words and writing have political significance. The only alternative to political guilt and anguish is not complaisant acquiescence in the death of children. It is part of intellectual life constantly to ask what the political, ethical, and existential value of one's work is. My point is that there doesn't have to be one answer to that, let alone one answer to be given once and for all. Moreover, there is no need to raise those questions in melodramatic terms.

The question of justification nevertheless remains. Are we justified in speaking about theory? Or about anything at all? (Can we defend writing novels, essays, travel books, poetry?) Even if we don't think that children are dying because we are writing, we may feel vaguely guilty about giving ourselves the right to speak and write when so many millions cannot. Isn't there an unbearable arrogance here? Since we are no better and no worse than anyone else, what justifies our 'arrogation of voice' (as Stanley Cavell calls it)?[10]

I'll be blunt: the answer is *nothing*. Our speaking—even the most passionate political call to arms—is never justified by anything but our own wish to speak: 'Who beside myself could give me the authority to speak for us?', Cavell writes.[11] To ask for *general* justification is to ask for a metaphysical ground beneath our feet. There *is* something arrogant and something unjust about writing anything at all. How can I write when millions of others cannot? How can I justify my arrogation of voice? How can anyone? If we do decide to write, it is pointless to consume ourselves in guilt about the 'exclusionary' effects of writing per se. The question, therefore, is not how to justify writing anything

---

[10] The term 'arrogation of voice' stresses the unfounded moment of arrogation contained in any theoretical or philosophical speech act, as well as the arrogance of the act of claiming for oneself the right to appeal to the judgment of others (see Stanley Cavell, *A Pitch of Philosophy: Autobiographical Exercises* (Cambridge, Mass.: Harvard University Press, 1994), 1–51; see also Toril Moi, *What Is a Woman? And Other Essays* (Oxford: Oxford University Press, 1999), 233–5, 249–50).

[11] Cavell, *Pitch*, 9.

at all, but rather what one aims to do with one's writing. (I shall return to this.)

I can spend my life feeling guilty about having more opportunities to express myself than millions of other women, or I can try to write in ways that embody my own commitments. Beauvoir says that to write is to appeal to the freedom of the other.[12] If we follow the implications of that, we will realize that ultimately we can't control the political effects of our own writing. Of course, we will try to be as persuasive as possible, to make our case as well as we can, but readers are still free to meet our appeals with anything from enthusiasm to indifference, contempt, and silence. To appeal to the freedom of others is to risk their rebuff. If we want to be politically committed, all we can do is to say what we have to say, and take responsibility for our words. In short, we have to mean what we say.

MEANING WHAT WE SAY: INTENTIONS AND RESPONSIBILITY

So, readers might object, the answer to the question of the 'politics of theory' is that we have to mean what we say? What's so political about that? Does what we aim to do with our writing really matter? Is this not just a return to the dreaded 'intentional fallacy', the belief that the author's intentions are the key to the meaning of the text. And is there not here a belief that 'meaning' is something else than the words that express it?

In *What Is Literature?* Sartre[13] asks the committed writer two crucial questions: 'What aspect of the world do you want to disclose? What

---

[12] 'Language is an appeal to the freedom of the other, because the sign only becomes sign when it is grasped by a consciousness', Beauvoir writes in *Pyrrhus et Cinéas*. 'I can only appeal to the other's freedom, not constrain it', she also writes (Beauvoir, *Pyrrhus et Cinéas* (Paris: Gallimard, 1944), 104, 112, my translations). For further discussion of the idea of the appeal to the other see Moi, *What Is a Woman?* 226–37. These pages also contain some discussion of the idea of arrogation of voice.

[13] Although I shall speak of Sartre's *What Is Literature?*, because the book has his name on the cover, it is probably more accurate to say that the concept of committed literature was jointly developed by Beauvoir and Sartre in the 1940s. At the time, they appeared to share what I have called the 'ordinary' view of commitment, a view to which Beauvoir (probably unlike Sartre) remained faithful for the rest of her life. The roots of the concept go back to Beauvoir's understanding of writing and speech as generous *appeals* to the other's freedom, which she first developed in *Pyrrhus et Cinéas* in 1944. (For a pioneering investigation of the concept of the 'appeal' in Sartre and Beauvoir see Eva Gothlin, 'Simone

change do you want to bring into the world by this disclosure?' (p. 37).[14]
Clearly Sartre takes the writer's intentions to be relevant to the question
of her political commitment. The very mention of the word intentions,
however, makes literary critics recoil. They take the word to commit the
speaker to the belief that intentions are, as it were, spiritual entities, and
as such the thin edge of the wedge of two commonly despised literary
theories, namely the expressivist theory of meaning and the traditional
communication model.[15] The disreputable picture of meaning and
writing that contemporary critics want to avoid is this: The writer's
intentions correspond to a vision, or 'message', in her head, which she
then proceeds to clothe in the appropriate words. The reader faithfully
decodes the writer's message, so as to reproduce in her own head the
writer's original vision. Bad writing interferes with the decoding, good
writing ensures a seamless process of communication.

Sartre may or may not have shared this view. (His understanding of
the relationship between intentions and words is opaque to me, and I
won't even try to discuss it here.[16]) But Sartre does not raise the

de Beauvoir's Notions of Appeal, Desire, and Ambiguity and their Relationship to Jean-Paul
Sartre's Notions of Appeal and Desire', *Hypatia*, 14/4 (1999), 83–95.) In October 1945 both
Beauvoir and Sartre signed the editorial manifesto of *Les Temps modernes*, which contains
the first published reference to 'committed literature'. (The manifesto has been translated
as Jean-Paul Sartre, 'Introducing *Les Temps modernes*', in *'What Is Literature?' and Other
Essays*, ed. Steven Ungar, trans. Jeffrey Mehlman (Cambridge, Mass.: Harvard University
Press, 1988), 249–67.) In the spring of 1947 Beauvoir gave a number of lectures in the
United States in which she spoke of the commitment and responsibility of writers in ways
that appear to have been very similar to those put forward in Sartre's texts on the subject
(see Claude Francis and Fernande Gontier, *Les Écrits de Simone de Beauvoir* (Paris: Gallimard,
1979), 143–50). Finally, the concept of committed writing was further developed by Sartre
in *What Is Literature?*, written in 1947 and published in 1948. His text actually incorporates
most of the *Temps modernes* manifesto. If we want to know what committed literature looks
like, *The Second Sex*, written in the period between 1946 and 1949, is the fullest and best
example of the kind, unless one believes that 'committed literature' has to mean fiction or
drama. Sartre's examples are mostly novels, but the questions he asks of the writer seem
perfectly suited to writers of essays as well. I can't see why commitment should be limited
to specific genres.

[14] All references to Sartre, *'What Is Literature?' and Other Essays*, ed. Ungar will be given
in the text, preceded by the abbreviation *WIL*.

[15] Adorno too implies this when he writes: 'For Sartre, the atheist...the conceptual
meaning of the literary work remains the precondition for commitment' (Theodor W.
Adorno, 'Commitment', in *Notes to Literature*, ed. Rolf Tiedemann, trans. Shierry Weber
Nicholsen, ii. (New York: Columbia University Press, 1992), 76–93, at 78).

[16] In *What Is Literature?* Sartre sometimes sounds as if he is committed to the idea that
we think without words: '[I]t is a matter of knowing whether [words] correctly indicate a

question of intentions simply because he has outmoded or mistaken ideas about meaning and words. Even if he does have such ideas, and even if we strongly disagree with him on those issues, it should be possible to see that the question of intentions remains crucially important to a theory of intellectual commitment, simply because it is impossible to assess *responsibility* without referring to intentions. There is a difference between invoking the author's intentions as the only true *meaning* of the work, and invoking them as a source of her *responsibility* for the work.

This resonates with Stanley Cavell's Wittgenstein-inspired understanding of meaning. For him—and these brief remarks do no justice to the rich, concrete detail of his argument—our meanings are always there, in the words we speak. If we want to find out what a sentence means, we need to ask 'what we should say when', not postulate the existence of accompanying mental acts. Moreover, because speech and writing are *acts*, we are as responsible for our meanings as we are for anything else we do:

> [T]he 'pragmatic implications' of our utterances are (or if we are feeling perverse, or tempted to speak carelessly, or chafing under an effort of honesty, let us say *must be*) *meant* . . . they are an essential part of what we mean when we say something, of what it is to mean something. And what we mean (intend) to say, like what we mean (intend) to do, is something we are responsible for.[17]

Of course, we may not always realize what we are saying (this sort of thing keeps psychoanalysts, philosophers, and literary critics in work), but this is another matter entirely. If or when it dawns on us that we have said something we don't want to mean, we usually *do* something (we apologize, admit our mistake, do what it takes to change the situation). This is precisely what Cavell means when he speaks of 'owning our words', or 'taking responsibility for what we say'. If we fail to do this, words such as irresponsibility, evasion, avoidance, shiftiness, inauthenticity, and bad faith will usually not be absent from the conversation.

---

certain thing or a certain notion. Thus, it often happens that we find ourselves possessing a certain idea that someone has taught us by means of words without being able to recall a single one of the words which have transmitted it to us' (*WIL* 35). But on the same page he also writes: 'We are within language as within our body', which conjures up far more interesting perspectives. To unravel Sartre's theory of language would be an arduous task.

[17] Stanley Cavell, 'Must We Mean What We Say?', in *Must We Mean What We Say?* (Cambridge: Cambridge University Press, 1969), 32.

At this point, Anne Stevenson's fine response (see Ch. 8 below) made me realize that I need to explain more carefully what I mean by saying that we are responsible for our words. I agree with her that it is difficult to say what one means. Everyone who writes knows how many drafts and how much sweat it takes to convey just the right things in just the right way. Of course Beauvoir chose her subject, her style, her readers, her words, and of course she labored intensely over her drafts. Everyone who writes has intentions and aims, and they matter deeply. My point, however, is that we need to distinguish between intentions as the source of *responsibility* and intentions as the source of *meaning*.

Intentions matter for the question of responsibility. The author's intentions, however, are not the source of the meaning of her words. To deny this is simply to deny that there can be a private language. The language we all speak gives meaning to our words. Every speaker of the language participates in the production of meaning. As long as it has speakers, a language will continue to evolve and change. No speaker invents her own meanings: if she did, we would not understand her. This is precisely *why* it takes so much hard work to get to the point where we actually can say what we mean.

But once we have said something we must mean it, that is to say take responsibility for it, 'own our words'. Thus we are responsible for unintended as well as intended meanings. In everyday life we often show that we know this. Say some ambiguous sentence about the dress, hairstyle or sex life of one of my friends escapes me. My friend blushes furiously, starts to cry, and I feel acutely embarrassed. I suddenly realize that I didn't mean to say *that*, that it came out all wrong, that of course it would be misunderstood.

Freud would surely tell me that my slip of the tongue reveals some truth about my relationship to my friend, or to hair, dress, or sex. I don't disagree with that. But what I'm interested in here is what I *do* once the unfortunate comment has escaped. Usually I apologize, make excuses, or perhaps try to explain that I didn't mean it, or at least not in *that* way. These reactions all acknowledge that the words mean what they meant, that they gave rise to my friend's tears, and that I am responsible for this. (Paradoxically, then, to say 'I didn't mean it', is precisely to acknowledge that my words mean exactly what I say I didn't mean to say.)

To make excuses, to explain, to apologize are ways of taking responsibility for our words. It is also a way of honoring Freud's insight that ambiguous utterances are ours, that, however difficult it may be, we need to own them, not simply disavow them. (In Freud's case this means 'working them through', analyzing them until we realize that we really are capable of saying, thinking, meaning what we said.) What we usually don't do in such situations is to say: 'Since I really didn't *intend* to say anything bad about you, my words just can't mean what you take them to mean. So I have done nothing wrong. I am not responsible. You have no reason to cry.' I realize that I have said something I don't mean when I realize that I don't want to own *those* words. And to acknowledge this (to apologize, regret, etc.) *is* to own those words. We are responsible for the situation that arises from our words, whether we like it or not. We must mean what we say.

Sartre and Beauvoir's theory of committed literature (*littérature engagée*) makes some very similar connections between speaking, meaning, and responsibility, no doubt because the French existentialists too start from the idea that to speak is to act. 'The committed writer knows that words are action', Sartre writes in *What Is Literature?* (p. 36). It is striking to see just how close Sartre comes to formulating a speech-act theory of language in this much maligned book:

Prose in essence is utilitarian. I would readily define the prose-writer as a man who *makes use* of words. M. Jourdan made prose so that he could ask for his slippers, and Hitler, so that he could declare war on Poland. The writer is a *speaker*; he designates, demonstrates, orders, refuses, interpolates, begs, insults, persuades, insinuates. (*WIL* 34)

Here Sartre sounds almost like J. L. Austin; the idea of the 'performative' or 'illocutionary' aspects of speech acts appears to be just around the corner. But Sartre never turned his theory of prose into a theory of language, surely because of his unfortunate decision to start his essay by drawing a fundamental distinction between poetry and prose, in which prose becomes action and poetry a kind of iconic object-language.

Sartre's principal aim in *What Is Literature?* is to draw attention to the writer's social and political responsibility. Given his own historical situation this is not surprising. The essay was published less than three years after the 1945 execution of Robert Brasillach, the writer and editor of the fascist newspaper *Je suis partout*. In her compelling essay on the trial, entitled 'Eye for Eye', Simone de Beauvoir reveals that although she detested Brasillach and everything he represented, she too was fascinated by the spectacle of a writer whose life was at stake because of his writings.[18]

As we have seen, intentions are crucial for a discussion of responsibility, if not meaning. Drawing on Cavell, we can say that although the author's intentions may be largely irrelevant when it comes to deciding what a text means (the meaning of our words is not a private matter), they do not remain irrelevant when it comes to the question of the author's responsibility for her text. In a court of law the difference between murder and manslaughter is a matter of intentions. If I can convince the judge that I did not intend to steal the stopwatch, but simply forgot to pay for it because my head was full of thoughts about writing and commitment, she may let me off the charge of shoplifting.

The difference between a crime and liability in tort also turns on intentions. If I intended to burn your house down, I am a criminal. But if I burnt your house down because my own kitchen caught fire when I was trying to make potato chips in my uniquely inept way, I have certainly been negligent, but I have probably committed no crime. The result of my act is not here in dispute: whatever I intended, the fact is that your house is now a smouldering heap of embers. When it comes to deciding what *degree of responsibility* I bear for this state of affairs, however, my intentions have to be taken into account.

To ask what you intend to do with your book, then, is to ask about the degree of responsibility that you are prepared to take for it. This responsibility is always personal; it is a matter of *your* words. Moreover, as Sartre points out, *silence* is also an act for which you are responsible:

Silence itself is defined in relationship to words, as the pause in music receives its meaning from the group of notes round it. This silence is a moment of language; being silent is not being dumb; it is to refuse to speak, and therefore to keep on speaking. Thus, if a writer has chosen to remain silent on any aspect whatever of the world, or, according to an expression which says just what it means, to *pass over* it in silence, one has the right to ask him ... 'Why have you spoken of this rather than that, and—since you speak in order to bring about change—why do you want to change this rather than that?' (*WIL* 38–9)

---

[18] See Mary McCarthy's translation of Simone de Beauvoir's 'Oeil pour œil' (*Les Temps modernes*, 1 (1946), 813–30) as 'Eye for Eye', in *Politics*, 4/4 (1947), 134–40. My understanding of the Brasillach trial has been greatly enhanced by my colleague Alice Kaplan's outstanding study *The Collaborator: The Trial and Execution of Robert Brasillach* (Chicago, Ill.: University of Chicago Press, 2000).

PERSONAL RESPONSIBILITY

For Sartre and Beauvoir, then, political commitment is a matter of personal and individual engagement. (In this context there can be no question of declaring the death of the author.) To say that political commitment and political responsibility are personal, however, is not to postulate the existence of some radically unfettered inner self. Rather it means that our political choices are not separable from the kind of persons we are. What makes us the persons we are is a vast complex of influences. To put it in existentialist terms: the social and historical situation I am in, as well as my personal situation in all its complexity—in short, my lived experience—determines the kind of commitments I will be able to make. But this is no full-blown determinism, for lived experience arises from what we continually make of what the world makes of us. It is the full range of situated experiences of a given person, her subjectivity.[19] The personal, then, is not just those experiences conventionally labelled private or sexual, or those that can be related to a social 'identity'.

Attention to the personal does not entail denial of the historical or the social. We do not have to picture the individual as an isolated monad in order to speak of personal commitment and responsibility. I do not need to deny, for example, that what I find intellectually interesting to the point of wanting to write about it is to a large extent determined by the values and protocols of the intellectual field of which I am both a product and an agent. Nor do I have to deny that in the big scheme of things my own subjectivity may be but a moment in the working of some larger dialectics. But the fact that I am a product of my social and historical position does not absolve me from having to make up my own mind about political and existential questions. My position in history deeply affects the question of my personal responsibility, but it does not abolish it.

How responsible am I for my sexism if I live in a place and a time where everyone assumes that women are less valuable, have a lesser share in humanity, than men? Aristotle might be a good example. He thought women were naturally inferior to men and often categorized them with slaves. In the introduction to *The Second Sex* Beauvoir quotes Aristotle's claim that women are inherently defective (see *SS*

---

[19] See the title essay of Moi, *What Is a Woman?*, for further discussion of these terms ('lived experience', 'subjectivity', 'making something of what the world makes of us', etc.).

1989, xxii; *DS* 1986, i. 15).[20] It seems wrong to say he is not at all responsible for his ideas about women, yet it also seems wrong to say that egalitarian ways of thinking were readily available to him. The question here is not the meaning of Aristotle's words, but the degree of responsibility he bears for them. If some famous philosopher in 2003 spoke of women (and ignored women) in the way Aristotle did, he would surely provoke an outrage. Today there could be no mitigating circumstances for a philosopher who chose to speak in this way.

The question of responsibility, in other words, takes us straight to the question of *situation*. (Tort lawyers have always known this.) We aren't responsible to eternity, or to some abstract entity, we are responsible to those human beings with whom we share a world: 'Whether he wants to or not, and even if he has his eyes on eternal laurels, the writer is speaking to his contemporaries and brothers of his class and race', Sartre writes (*WIL* 70). (Speaking of responsibility, I note the 'he' and the 'brothers' in this sentence, but this was France in the 1940s. Even Beauvoir did it: the last word of *The Second Sex* is 'brotherhood'.) The question for the committed writer, then, cannot just be: 'What do you want to change?' It also has to be: 'Who are you writing for?'

WHO ARE YOU WRITING FOR?

When it comes to judging what kind of (political) act our writing constitutes, then, the question of whom we imagine that we are writing *for* becomes as important as the question of what we are writing *about*. For Sartre these two questions are in fact inextricably linked.[21] '[A]ll works of the mind contain within themselves the image of the reader for whom they are intended', Sartre writes (*WIL* 73). To choose a subject is to choose one's readers; and to choose one's readers is to choose one's subject.

The writer is responsible for her writing, yet her text is nothing without a reader. The writer can only appeal to the reader's freedom,

[20] For the classical feminist treatment of Aristotle see Susan Moller Okin, *Women in Western Political Thought* (Princeton, NJ: Princeton University Press, 1992), 73–98.

[21] Some writers carefully work to eradicate the image of the reader in their texts (Nathalie Sarraute comes to mind). This says as much about the world the writer takes herself to be addressing as any other form of writing. Ann Jefferson's marvellous book on Sarraute truly sheds new light on her relationship to identity (see Ann Jefferson, *Nathalie Sarraute, Fiction and Theory: Questions of Difference* (Cambridge: Cambridge University Press, 2000)).

to her decision to read or not to read the text. The reader is necessary to the writer; the writer cannot write without explicitly or implicitly imagining a reader with whom she shares a world (I shall return to the idea of 'sharing a world'.) This world, Sartre writes, is the concrete terrain where commitment plays itself out:

[E]ach book proposes a concrete liberation on the basis of a particular alienation. Hence, in each one there is an implicit recourse to institutions, customs, certain forms of oppression and conflict...to hopes, to fears, to habits of sensibility, imagination, and even perception, and, finally, to customs and values which have been handed down, to a whole world which the author and the reader have in common. It is this familiar world which the writer animates and penetrates with his freedom. It is on the basis of this world that the reader must bring about his concrete liberation; it is alienation, situation, and history. It is this world which I must change or preserve for myself and others. (WIL 72)

Sartre is here placing a very existentialist emphasis on the everyday world that readers and writers have in common, just as Beauvoir in *The Second Sex* pays close and concrete attention to women's common and ordinary experiences.

I shall go on to show that it is easy to see for whom Beauvoir wrote *The Second Sex*. But why am I not using myself as an example here? For I claim that responsibility is always personal, and several readers of drafts of this essay have therefore asked me about myself. They have also asked me to be more specific. Why can't I say clearly what kind of responsibility I take for my own writing? In what way are my own texts committed? I agreed. The problem was that however much I tried to develop these questions, I failed. All I came up with was vague and nebulous prose. Now I think I finally know why. First of all, my fundamental claim is that the author's *text* is the key to the author's intentions. (To find out for whom Beauvoir wrote *The Second Sex* I read *The Second Sex* and not her memoirs.) I have no special access to the meaning of my own words that other people don't have. (This explains why authors are rarely the best critics of their own writing.)

But what about responsibility? In my drafts I was trying to say something about my own responsibility in the general and the abstract, just because I felt it ought to be said. The result was dismal. The reason why turns out to be theoretically significant, for it points to a limitation in Sartre's theory. For the question of the degree of responsibility one bears for one's texts is not, in fact, a general and abstract question. Sartre is right to say that an author must always and at all times be ready to explain himself. But he forgets that the question of political responsibility is just as situated, just as specific, as the question of who one is writing for. One is not always responsible to all for everything, regardless of what Sartre and Beauvoir say.[22] Or, in other words: One doesn't demand an explanation unless a problem has arisen. It is therefore not a coincidence that all my examples have to do with shoplifting, arson, and murder.

On this point Cavell and Wittgenstein think very differently from Sartre. For them, the question of meaning—the need to ask questions about the meaning of our words—only arises when something has gone wrong. 'The sign-post is in order—if, under normal circumstances, it fulfils its purpose', Wittgenstein writes in *Philosophical Investigations*.[23] To demand a general explanation for how meaning can be possible at all is to reintroduce the demand for the absolute. But the same is true for the question of responsibility. If nobody has asked me 'How could you write *this*?' I can't tell what it is I am supposed to be responsible for. If I then try to say something about my own responsibility, the result will inevitably be vague and general. It is like trying to defend oneself without knowing what the accusations are.

When it comes to *The Second Sex*, however, there is one accusation I would like to address. Many feminists have accused Beauvoir of being ethnocentric, of only being interested in white Europeans. I want to go further and say that she is only interested in a certain group of French men and women. But this, in my view, is precisely the reason why *The Second Sex* has had so much to say to women and men all over the world.

---

[22] The epigraph to Beauvoir's second novel, *Le Sang des autres* (*The Blood of Others*) is 'Everyone is responsible for everything to everyone' (Simone de Beauvoir, *Le Sang des autres* (Paris: Gallimard (Coll. Folio), 1945); Simone de Beauvoir, *The Blood of Others*, trans. Yvonne Moyse and Roger Senhouse (Harmondsworth: Penguin, 1964/86)). The novel is about the occupation of France, and deals, among other things, with the fate of the French Jews. In this horrendous situation the epigraph must have felt right. But as a general maxim it is metaphysical and absolutist.

[23] Ludwig Wittgenstein, *Philosophische Untersuchungen/Philosophical Investigations*, 2nd bilingual edn. (New York: Macmillan, 1958), §87. This is the point where Wittgenstein and Cavell differ most profoundly from post-structuralist thinkers such as Jacques Derrida. For Derrida the letter may always not arrive. His theory of language is geared to emergencies and failures, whether or not they have actually arisen. Wittgenstein on the other hand starts from a sense of wonder at the fact that we so frequently do understand each other. For a subtle and thorough investigation of the relationship between Derrida and Wittgenstein see Martin Stone, 'Wittgenstein on Deconstruction', in Alice Crary and Rupert Read (eds.), *The New Wittgenstein* (London and New York: Routledge, 2000), 83–117.

In *The Second Sex* Beauvoir takes no pains to reach readers outside France. Her text is peppered with sardonic references to local luminaries such as Claude Mauriac and allusions to contemporary newspaper and magazine stories. In the introduction she refers, for instance, to a defunct and ephemeral magazine called *Franchise*, a September 1948 issue of *Le Figaro Littéraire*, and the most recent issue of *Hebdo-Latin* (a local student rag). Beauvoir's creativity was nourished by and directed towards a community of readers with whom she had just shared the gruelling experience of the German occupation.

At the time, however, the French were deeply divided by the occupation and the post-war purges, and *The Second Sex* makes it abundantly clear that the readers Beauvoir imagines to be sharing her everyday experiences are not all of the French, just the ones more or less on the left, the people often referred to at the time as 'men and women of goodwill'. Thus *The Second Sex* is explicitly not addressed to members of the 'conservative bourgeoisie', since they 'still see in the emancipation of women a menace to their morality and their interests' (*SS* 1984, p. xxx; *DS* 1986, i. 25). Beauvoir's explicit criticism of Julien Benda, Claude Mauriac, and Henri de Montherlant, for example, demonstrates that she is not writing for people who rate these writers highly; that is to say, people the existentialists would qualify as the 'reactionary forces' of the bourgeoisie.[24]

Although the example of *The Second Sex* shows that in order to write well we need to be able to imagine readers who share a situation with us, it also demonstrates that this is no guarantee of a friendly reception. In France *The Second Sex* was savaged by the critics. Beauvoir's sexuality and morals were publicly denounced. The book was placed on the Index by the Vatican. The French reception contrasted sharply with the far more balanced and positive American reception of the book in 1953.[25] Yet *The Second Sex* is explicitly not addressing American women. Beauvoir's frequent references to the habits and opinions of American women are directed to the French, for whom a trip to the United States was still a rare adventure in 1949. American readers of the French text would have discovered that Dorothy Parker is made out to exemplify their own misguided nominalism:

[24] For references to these writers in the introduction see *SS* 1989, xxii, xxx, xxx–xxxi, xxviii; *DS* 1986, i. 15; i. 23; i. 26.

[25] For the French reception see chapters 3 and 7 of Moi, *Simone de Beauvoir*; for the American reception see Jo-Ann Pilardi, 'The Changing Critical Fortunes of *The Second Sex*', *History and Theory*, 32/1 (1993), 51–73.

American women, in particular, are prepared to think that there is no longer any place for woman as such; if a backward individual still takes herself for a woman, her friends advise her to be psychoanalyzed and thus get rid of this obsession. In regard to a work, *Modern Woman: The Lost Sex*, which, incidentally, is highly irritating, Dorothy Parker has written: 'I cannot be just to books which treat of woman as woman...My idea is that all of us, men as well as women, should be regarded as human beings.' (SS 1989, xx; DS 1986, i. 12, translation amended)[26]

Moreover, Beauvoir continues, American women aren't even properly philosophical in their nominalism; it is no more than an expression of their own discomfort with the fact of being women: 'The clenched attitude of defiance of American women proves that they are haunted by a sense of their femininity' (SS 1989, xx; DS 1986, i. 13, translation amended).[27] None of this prevented *The Second Sex* from becoming far more politically influential in the United States than in France. Beauvoir, it would seem, reached women in other countries *through* her French readers, not in spite of them.[28] Precisely because she managed to make her French readers' way of being in the world, their specific situation, unusually evident, her French readers can recognize themselves in her words. At the same time, however, the clarity and force with which she describes the French situation (which is also her own) allows other people to *respond to* her text, to examine their own situation in the light of hers. The gesture of *The Second Sex* is: 'This is what I see. Can you see it too?'.[29] The better the description of what Beauvoir sees, the easier it is for readers to agree or disagree with her.

The Second Sex, then, is intensely French in its address and frame of reference. The enormous international influence of Beauvoir's essay demonstrates that what makes a text important to readers of different nationalities, races, and classes cannot be reduced to the question of

---

[26] Beauvoir writes 'Les Américaines en particulier', but the published American translation has 'Many American women'. Elsewhere I have shown that it is by no means certain that Dorothy Parker said anything at all about *Modern Woman* (see Moi, *What Is a Woman?* 181–4).

[27] 'L'attitude de défi dans laquelle se crispent les Américaines'. The published American translation tones down Beauvoir's text: 'The attitude of defiance of many American women', Parshley translates.

[28] Sartre writes about Richard Wright that he never explicitly intended to reach European readers: 'He is addressing himself to the cultivated negroes of the North and the white Americans of goodwill (intellectuals, democrats of the left, radicals, C.I.O. workers). It is not that he is not aiming through them at all men but it is *through them* that he is thus aiming' (WIL 79).

[29] This is a version of Stanley Cavell's compelling account of the attitude of the ordinary-language philosopher: 'The philosopher appealing to everyday language turns to the reader

whether their own race or nationality is represented in it. What matters is whether the text shows the reader some aspect of the world that he or she can *respond to*. To respond to a text the reader does not have to identify with it or recognize herself in it, or feel represented by it; she needs to feel stirred, moved, challenged by its appeal. In *The Second Sex* Beauvoir shows us what the world looks like to her: as a place in which women are oppressed in particular ways, by particular methods. Women and men all over the world have responded to that vision.

In short, *The Second Sex* teaches us that political effects are not necessarily a matter of representation. Sartre's point is that we never write for *everyone*; rather, we write for (or against) readers we can concretely imagine. Through them—but only through them—we reach others. Toni Morrison has often said that she writes with black American readers in mind. Through them, however, she reaches her other readers, including the white men and women of the Swedish Academy.

THE RISK OF WRITING

Simone de Beauvoir did not set out to write an important feminist book. On the contrary, she had never thought much about feminism, or about being a woman, until one day in June 1946 when she decided to write her memoirs. At this point, for the first time in her life, the question of what it had meant to her to be a woman occurred to her:

I realized that the first question to come up was: What has it meant to me to be a woman? At first I thought I could dispose of that pretty quickly. I had never had any feeling of inferiority, no one had ever said to me: 'You think that way because you are a woman;' my femaleness had never been irksome to me in any way. 'For me,' I said to Sartre, 'you might almost say it just hasn't counted.' 'All the same, you weren't brought up in the same way as a boy would have been; you should look into it further.' I looked, and it was a revelation: this world was a masculine world, my childhood had been nourished by myths forged by men, and I hadn't reacted to them in at all the same way I should have done if I had been a boy. I was so interested in this discovery that I abandoned my project for a personal confession in order to give all my attention to finding out about the condition of woman in its broadest

not to convince him without proof but to get him to prove something, test something, against himself. He is saying: Look and find out whether you can see what I see, wish to say what I wish to say' (Cavell, 'Aesthetic Problems', 95–6).

terms. I went to the Bibliothèque Nationale to do some reading, and what I studied were the myths of femininity.[30]

The Second Sex was written at a time when there was no women's movement in France.[31] When Simone de Beauvoir took the risk of writing about women from the point of view of her own experience as a woman in a patriarchal society she could not possibly have known what the outcome of her act would be. In particular, she could not have known how political, and how historically significant, *The Second Sex* was to become for readers in the 1960s and 1970s.

Change is produced, Sartre says, when the writer's reflections on her experience inspire others to think about their own situation in new ways: to write is to appeal to the other's freedom. But to be a politically committed writer is not necessarily to be a politically significant writer. Only writers who occupy a situation of some historical significance can hope to be able to make an important difference in the world. This happened to be the case of Simone de Beauvoir. Her own situation as an independent intellectual woman was paradigmatic of changes already under way in women's situation all over the western world. Although it may not have been apparent in the late 1940s, the generation of women born in the 1940s and 1950s would leave home, seek an education, set out to claim independence, sexual freedom, and serious careers. 'The free woman is only just being born', Beauvoir wrote in 1949 (*SS* 1989, 715; *DS* 1986, ii. 641). Whether she knew it or not, her reflections on her situation as a woman captured the spirit of a century.

The same is unlikely to be true for most of us. However committed we are, we can't be sure that we will have anything of historical significance to say. There is nothing much we can do about this. We shall have to accept that we cannot predict the political effects of our writing. On this point we must simply use our best judgment, take our chances, and write about what really matters to us. That is to say, we need to take our writing seriously, to stake ourselves in it. The difficulty of doing this is the difficulty of meaning what we say.

So where does this leave us, you ask? Can I still write theory with a clear political conscience? Well, I just said that that's for you to figure out. I

---

[30] Beauvoir, *Force of Circumstance*, 103, translation amended. For the French text see Beauvoir, *La Force des choses*, i. 136.

[31] In *Women's Rights and Women's Lives in France 1944–1968* (London: Routledge, 1994) Claire Duchen gives a thorough overview of women's situation and women's organizations in France in this period.

could not advise you any further without knowing who you are and what your situation is. What I do know is that any attempt to lay down theoretical requirements for what politically correct writing *must* look like is bound to be hopelessly dogmatic. Ask yourself instead what you want to change and who you are writing for. Then ask yourself whether what you have to say is worth saying. If you think it is, write about it as well as you can. This will not protect you against criticism, nor will it guarantee the importance of your intervention. On the other hand, it does maximize your freedom. Even so, you may never say anything of world-shattering importance. That is the risk you take when you choose to write. But when others violently disagree, when they accuse you of any number of political and personal sins, you will know how to own your words.

This theory of committed writing starts with Beauvoir's idea that writing is an appeal to the other's freedom. Thus writing becomes an invitation to dialogue. The committed writer's gesture is: 'This is what I see. Can you see it too?'[32] If the reader can't see it she may, if you are lucky, take the time to explain what *she* sees. Then your appeal is answered. Of course we want everyone to see what we see. But when they can't the disagreements and conflicts that arise can be deeply enlightening in their own right. To adapt a phrase of J. L. Austin's: 'A disagreement . . . is not to be shied off, but to be pounced upon: for the explanation of it can hardly fail to be illuminating.'[33]

ACKNOWLEDGEMENTS

This essay started life as a draft towards a projected third chapter in my book *What Is A Woman?*, but I decided against using it. Then it became a brief paper on 'The Politics of Theory', presented at a panel called 'Cynical Theory Revisited' at the MLA conference in Chicago, December 1999. An excerpt from the beginning appeared as part of the 'Afterword' in Toril Moi, *Sexual/Textual Politics: Feminist Literary Theory*, 2nd edn. (London and New York: Routledge, 2002), 180–5. The whole essay was published in Norwegian as 'Å mene det vi sier: Om de intellektuelles ansvar', *Samtiden*, 1 (2003), 60–75. I have made some further, slight revisions to the English text published here. I want to thank Anne Garréta, Emily Grosholz, Anne Stevenson, Live Cathrine Slang and Knut Olav Åmås for inspiring comments on various drafts.

[32] This particular gesture was first analyzed by Stanley Cavell in 'Aesthetic Problems'. See also my discussion of Beauvoir's view of writing as dialogue and appeal in Moi, *What Is a Woman?*, 226–50.

[33] J. L. Austin, 'A Plea for Excuses', in *Philosophical Papers*, 3rd edn. (Oxford: Oxford University Press, 1979), 175–204, at 184.

8

Saying What We Mean

Anne Stevenson

Disciples of J. L. Austin may well be disappointed by this response to
Toril Moi's 'Meaning What We Say: The "Politics of Theory" and the
Responsibility of Intellectuals', for there is no way in which I can
'pounce upon' an illuminating disagreement with its salient points. I
agree with Moi that intellectuals would do well to abandon their search
for a general theory of literature that guarantees political radicalism (or
even specific political results). Her arguments against demanding an
absolute 'politics of theory' (whatever that may mean) and for sup-
planting such an intangible generality with a willingness to engage with
particular, down-to-earth situations seem to me irrefutable and wonder-
ful. I applaud Moi's emphasis on what, after Stanley Cavell, she identifies as Beauvoir's commitment to 'ordinary' language in her pursuit of
'truth and value'. All I can do is approach the question of 'Meaning
What We Say' at a tangent, as it were. At one point in her essay, Moi
refers to Sartre's 'unfortunate decision' to draw a distinction between
poetry and prose by excluding from poetry the 'performative' or active
elements of language (see p. 150 above). Like Moi, I take issue with this
view, but I would also suggest that the question of how language relates
to conscience and political commitment is part of a larger issue having
to do with how words equip us both to express and to disguise (from
ourselves and others) the ways in which we think.

   Toril Moi opens her argument by citing Beauvoir's 'I take words and
the truth to be of value', as a useful starting point if we want to justify
literature's age-old link with non-utilitarian purposes. Comparing
Beauvoir's modest, *'ordinary'* view of intellectual commitment with
Sartre's *'metaphysical* and *melodramatic'* remark, 'Faced with a dying
child, *Nausea* does not tip the scales', Moi dismisses Sartre's all-or-
nothing view as a seductive fantasy. *'Of course'*, she writes, 'writing is
not always enough. How could it be? What human activity is "always

enough?" ' (p. 142 above). And though she concedes that the philosopher's implied condemnation of all non-utilitarian and therefore
'worthless' political writing may not express a considered opinion on
Sartre's part (the remark may only have reflected a moment of self-
disgust), Moi is right to insist that intellectual breast-beating leads
nowhere. So, with Moi, let's discard that piece of acting, and turn
instead to the more rewarding question of how politically committed
writers—or, more challenging from my point of view—how *morally
concerned* writers should approach their craft.

Literature that sets out to 'do people good' has always had a reputation for being suspect as entertainment. In the nineteenth century
serious writers—writers with a message—were expected to slip hom-
ilies into their poems and novels (think of Browning, Wordsworth,
George Eliot, Dickens). Today's up-front authors give their readers
more freedom of interpretation. It's not only that outright moralizing
strikes them and their publishers as banal or condescending; it's more
that the right to preach has passed under their noses into the hands of
critics and journalists. Radical political opinion is certainly something
contemporary criticism is looking for, but writers themselves—poets,
novelists, playwrights—tend to be politically concerned without
wanting to commit themselves to specific ideologies. Perhaps this is
because Sartre's clique of French intellectuals, together with the
communist-inspired program they set up for creating a *littérature engagée*, has fallen out of fashion; or perhaps, with the advent of television,
it's because most radical ideologies have changed their tune of late,
and the language of public politics (as distinct from the discourses of
political theory) is more than ever suspect—certainly not to be trusted
as a vehicle of serious commitment to anything.

The state of affairs described above, however, could hardly have
been imagined when Simone de Beauvoir's *The Second Sex* was first
published, scandalizing French conservative society in 1949. Here, Moi
suggests, was a radical, theoretical book that, in the middle years of
the century, actually changed thousands of women's lives. Why, we
might wonder, do so few feminist texts today have a like effect? One
answer, surely, is that Beauvoir hardly thought of herself as a feminist
until she began to write her book. Like no woman theorist today, she
more or less stumbled into feminism. Margaret Crosland, in her introduction to the Everyman's Library edition (1993), tells us that Beauvoir
only began to think about problems of femininity during the war,

when she found herself in a baffling situation arising from complex relationships with both men and women. When she told Sartre that she had never thought of herself as female, only as a philosopher, he told her to look again: 'she had been brought up as a girl, not as a boy; should she not examine precisely how this had influenced her life and work so far?' (*SS* 1993, p. xiii).

So *The Second Sex* was an adventure, a personal exploration that needed documentation at every step, and it was written, as Moi points out, not as a generalized feminist text for thinking women of the future—however much it has (or has not) become that today—but specifically for French women of Beauvoir's own generation and class. Writing of Beauvoir when she almost by accident began to write *The Second Sex*, Moi importantly points out the difference between 'invoking the author's intentions as the only true *meaning* of the work, and invoking them as a source of her *responsibility* for the work' (p. 148 above). In 1949 Beauvoir could not have foreseen that her richly researched, radical book written mainly for French Catholic women readers who, surviving the Nazi occupation, had emerged into a changed world, would find its most appreciative audience first in America, and ultimately in the world of the future. Nevertheless, by 'meaning' to write such a book and taking responsibility for her intentions Beauvoir became, like Virginia Woolf, a 'politically significant' author to whom generations of women (and men) are still indebted.

That distinction between an author's intended *meaning* (which may or may not be the reader's) and the *responsibility* a writer assumes for what she actually says is the keynote of Moi's essay. Praising Beauvoir for using plain, jargonless language and a mode of discourse appropriate to political writing that aims to challenge or change the social status quo, Moi advises modern feminists to follow Beauvoir's example and say what they mean while taking responsibility for their intentions. Such advice, however, implies that we believe we know what we mean. Either we work it out as we go along, weighing the documentary evidence and testing our deductions against it (as Beauvoir did), or we assume we know in advance the gist of what we are going to say. Too often in the second or third stage of an ideological revolution (as I take the twentieth-century feminist movement to have been) the heavy intellectual spadework done at its outset gets taken for granted. After thirty, forty, fifty years the foundational thinking has been done, once radical propositions have been set in stone, as it were; and as more and

more proselytes flock to the fold fewer and fewer original contributions to the cause seem possible. It is at this point that theory moves
in, discarding plain language that will now seem repetitive or outdated
and substituting for it a novel, seemingly sophisticated system of tag-
words that tend to bury any changes in social attitude or improve-
ments that may occur beneath the discourse of an exclusively
intellectual in-group. Toril Moi's paper 'Saying What We Mean' suggests—at least to me—that radical political theory may have reached
this point. Many of its core assumptions may have to be reassessed,
thrown out, or redefined; and where better to begin than with a return
to Beauvoir's practical example and to her clear 'appeal to the freedom
of the other' to accept or reject some of our seemingly most sacred
doctrines.

One way in which we can open ourselves to fresh ideas is to look
again at how we came to accept the old ones. At one point in her
paper Toril Moi admits that even when we intend to mean what we
say and take pains to be responsible for our words 'it is difficult to say
what one means' (p. 149 above). Moi seems here to be stepping into an
area that neuroscientists, cognitive psychologists, and linguists have
opened up in the last decade or two. Steven Pinker, for example, in a
breakthrough book called *The Language Instinct: The New Science of
Language and Mind*, devotes an entire chapter to refuting the popular
misconception that we always think in words, that consciousness is
impossible without language, and that therefore 'the foundational categories of reality are not "in" the world but are imposed by one's
culture'. Such a belief, writes Pinker, when you come to test it through
experience, 'is an absurdity. Don't we all share the frequent experience
of writing a sentence, then stopping and realising that it wasn't exactly
what we meant to say? To have that feeling, there has to be a "what
we meant to say" that is different from what we say.'[1]

For someone like myself, for whom writing *anything* is a painful
struggle to find words and word patterns that will give at least *some*
meaning to my mostly inarticulate feelings, Pinker's common-sense
belief that we do not fill our consciousness with words and sentences
but with a sort of proto-verbal sense language or 'mentalese' comes as
a relief. It gives fresh authenticity to the 'stream of consciousness'

---

[1] Steven Pinker, *The Language Instinct: The New Science of Language and Mind* (London: Penguin Books, 1994), 57.

theory that inspired Proust and Joyce, among others, over a century ago. But many writers have realized that language does not invent or determine or contain the world 'out there', it names it. Or, rather, language makes possible certain parameters of nature and reality that human minds need understandingly to share if human beings are to communicate and thrive as a species. Of course, as Virginia Woolf knew, there is always more going on, both 'out there' and in our heads, than she or Proust or Joyce could put into words.[2] Nor is the world that we know through our senses, or that we believe in in terms of our ideas, fixed and objective. The state of relatedness between 'us' and 'things', as between 'us' and 'us', is in constant flux. No matter how many definitions and identifications we make, no language can absolutely keep pace with the shiftings of reality—for which it essentially finds metaphors. With good reason, Shelley wrote (in *A Defence of Poetry*) of 'metaphorical language that marks the before unapprehended relations of things'. In a modernist critic's words, 'metaphor attempts to arouse cognition of the unknown by suggestion of the known'.[3] Eliot said much the same thing when he identified the 'objective correlative', and Shakespeare put it best of all in *A Midsummer's Night's Dream*: 'And as imagination bodies forth | the forms of things unknown, the poet's pen | Turns them to shapes, and gives to airy nothing | A local habitation and a name' (v. i. 14–17). Which is not to deny that the poet's (and critic's) pen is capable of describing as many distortions and lies as it is of creating imaginary felicities and marvels.

Such considerations suggest that teachers of literature will have to think again about the so-called iniquities of some standard literary devices. Consider, for instance, 'the intentional fallacy'.[4] When we

---

[2] Woolf's ideas cannot really be equated with a contemporary linguist's notion of 'mentalese', though a famous passage from her essay 'Modern Fiction' is worth quoting here as an example of how conscious the modernists were of their need to break with theoretical rules for writing fiction in order to satisfy the requirements of reality. Here is the passage: 'Life is not a series of gig-lamps symmetrically arranged; life is a luminous halo, a semi-transparent envelope surrounding us from the beginning of consciousness to the end. Is it not the task of the novelist to convey this varying, this unknown and circumscribed spirit, whatever aberration or complexity it may display, with as little mixture of the alien and external as possible?' (Virginia Woolf, *Collected Essays*, ii (London: Hogarth Press, 1966), 106).

[3] Owen Barfield, *Poetic Diction: A Study in Meaning* (London: Faber & Faber, 1928), 110.

[4] From the Greater Oxford English Dictionary: 'Intentional fallacy: in literary criticism, the fallacy that the meaning or value of a work may be judged or defined in terms of the writer's intention. 1946, Wimsatt & Beardsley in *Sewanee Review*, LIV, 482.'

consider the success or value of a piece of writing, is it really such a bad idea to take seriously its author's intentions? Surely what Pinker sees as preverbal mentalese has to include some form of intention. True, there may be no such thing as a pure mental 'message' that, clothed by a writer in appropriate words, gets passed from writers to readers like a baton in a relay race. But that's a terribly simplistic view of intention. Once we acknowledge that we human beings are born with a need (or an instinct) to name things and to communicate among ourselves, then intention can hardly be separated from our conscious, conscientious search for words that will say what we mean. For the purposes of everyday exchange, languages spare their speakers a good deal of interpretive trouble. Sharers of a common tongue understand each other most of the time automatically, without thinking about their indebtedness to a surrounding culture. But when words or phrases are not 'there' in the language, ready-made, when we have thoughts for which we rack our brains but can find no appropriate words, then we are thrown into that frustrating but creative state of imagination that (often subconsciously) attaches 'airy nothings' to 'a local habitation and a name'.

When the word 'intention' is used in this psychological sense and means intending to find words for thoughts that otherwise would remain impotent in the realm of 'mentalese', it refers to a relationship between meaning and language that is the matrix of all theory. Toril Moi believes that to write as committed women we must 'use our best judgment, take our chances, and write about what really matters to us... The difficulty of doing this is the difficulty of meaning what we say' (p. 159 above). This must mean, too, that when an author takes responsibility for her intentions those intentions must have at least something to do with the meaning of what she writes. Intentional fallacy? A fallacy, perhaps, only when it denies freedom to the reader. Beauvoir paid it no more heed than Sartre did, when in *What is Literature?* he confronted the engaged political writers of his time with two 'crucial questions': (1) 'What aspect of the world do you want to disclose?' and (2) 'What change do you want to bring into the world by this disclosure?'[5] When Beauvoir set about writing *The Second Sex* these were questions she addressed, and they are reflected in the kind of book she wrote. And, though it may seem unusual to associate

[5] See Moi's Ch. 7 nn. 13 and 14 above on Sartre's *What is Literature?*

Sartre's ideas with pragmatic ends, from a practical point of view they served her well. It is not hard to argue that *if* an individual is free to act as she intends, and *if*, as a politically committed writer, she intends to act (write) in order to revolutionize women's lot in the world, then she is a 'good writer' when she puts her intentions into words as directly and responsibly as she can. I believe Toril Moi is right to insist on 'speech acts' that say plainly what they mean. Whether she is right to question the intentionality of such acts and yet require their writers to take responsibility for them is another matter, and I shall come to it later.

Now, I want to switch course and turn the direction of this discussion away from political writing and its commitments back to my earlier observations concerning the relationship of ideas and language in a creative context. Texts such as *The Second Sex* are like most forms of heuristic exposition; they ask to be read at the level of their intentions. To complicate their effectiveness by asking whether an author's intentions matter is perhaps to muddy the water. Political *poetry*, however, like poetry of any kind, seems to ask for a different approach. I want to suggest that to write 'good' poetry (and by poetry I mean any form of imaginative writing that draws, for its meaning, on the ambiguities latent in experience and behaviour) does call for the kind of needling anxiety that seems so superfluous when we read Beauvoir's prose. I hope to show by example that it may be the vagueness, the flexibility, the very wordlessness of an author's state of mind at the inception of a poem—and not a set program of articulated intentions—that determines its success.

I am going to use a poem of my own to demonstrate how 'airy' unexpressed thoughts can solidify into words, but this is not because I think my poem is necessarily successful (though I wouldn't cite it if I didn't), but because only by showing how difficult it is for me to 'mean what I say' can I begin to 'say what I mean' about the creative process. Though I don't often write poetry with a political subject, I do, like most thinking people who watch television and read newspapers, respond with more or less unceasing despair to a lot of what I see happening in the world. I can't remember if the following poem was written after watching a programme on floods in Mozambique or after finishing J. M. Coetzee's 1999 Booker Prize-winning *Disgrace*. In any case, I was unhappy with the easy piety of an American politician interviewed on television (I can't even remember who it was) and upset in general by the way the First World preaches to the Third World without being willing to sacrifice any of its comforts. When Sartre observed that his novels couldn't prevent children from dying, he wasn't speaking only for himself.

Anyway, I know that before 'Report from the Border' became a poem it lay in my mind, a cluster of uncomfortable feelings. At the time I had been asked to contribute a poem to a yearly publication called *New Writing*, and without that motivation I might not have tried to put these inchoate feelings into words. After an hour or two of sitting at my desk—and this after lying on my bed letting ideas 'jiggle around' in my mind for a day or so—I came up with four stanzas that stand today more or less as they did then. I couldn't really tell you how they got themselves on paper, except to say that they came rhythmically; the sound came first.

A Report from the Border

Wars in peacetime don't behave like wars.
So loving they are.
Kissed on both cheeks, silk-lined ambassadors
Pose and confer.

Unbuckle your envy, drop it there by the door.
We will settle,
We will settle without blows or bullets
The unequal score.

In nature, havenots have to be many
And havelots few.
Making money out of making money
Helps us help you.

This from the party of good intent. From the other
Hunger's stare,
Drowned crops, charred hopes, fear, stupor, prayer
And literature.[6]

---

[6] 'A Report from the Border' is the title poem of my latest collection (Newcastle upon Tyne: Bloodaxe Books, 2003), 33. The printed version differs slightly from that given in this paper, but for the sake of my argument I have not changed the wording here.

Rather than go into the details of small changes I made after writing the first draft of 'Report from the Border', let's look at the way in which intentions steered me in directions I hadn't anticipated. The poem doesn't *only* accuse the wealthy nations of doing down the poor ones, though its ironic tone can hardly be missed. Cliché pop words like 'loving' and 'kissed' are undermined by the contempt suggested by 'silk-lined' and 'pose'. The stanzas in italics do not represent direct speech; they invite censure by callously stating the terms of an economic policy that soothes the conscience of the rich while seeming to explain a sensible economic policy to the poor. The irony is further emphasized by the sounds and meanings of those invented words, 'havenots' and 'havelots'.

But in the last stanza the poem changes course. To call representatives of the First World 'the party of good intent' sounds ironic—and it may be. Still, to my ear, the phrase isn't altogether condemnatory; capitalism, after all, is not fascism. America, for all its faults, does in fact help undeveloped countries, sending aid in the form of loans, teachers, doctors, economic advisers, and so forth. Such policies rarely make headlines, but, since members of my family have devoted their lives to working as Third World advisers for the American government, I couldn't in conscience allow my poem absolutely to condemn American policies. Had I been writing a story I might have chosen to show how an American peace worker of very good intent is frustrated into adopting harsh colonialist policies when caught between sides in a Third World civil war. As it is, all I could do—unless I were to loosen the tension set up by the form and spoil the poem as a poem—was to let the last line, the last two words, suggest my story for me. 'From the other [party] | Hunger's stare, | Drowned crops, charred hopes, fear, stupor, prayer | *And literature.*'

So what of my intention? Certainly I had no idea when I began writing that I would let this poem turn around and bite me at the end. And yet, there was no other way to acknowledge the complexities of the situation as I knew it to exist. A conscientious reporter—say, for *The Economist*—would have covered both the good and bad aspects of the American aid programme. Some contemporary Graham Green might have enlisted the reader's sympathy with, or fury against, individual characters by imagining how they would respond to a virtually lived-through Third World crisis, not just to a text book case. But as a poet I was stuck with a tight form that put *every single word* under the truth spotlight, and I had to be responsible for all of them.

Saying what we mean, then, seems to be the way we tell ourselves truths that can be contradictory. And this implies that the hinterland of our impressions and emotions is latticed with paths that lead in all sorts of unknown, unexplored directions. Pinker's 'mentalese' turns out to be a jungle full of half-thoughts and unnamed feelings, an uncultivated country through which our minds jog daily, but which can also be the feeding ground of superstition, prejudice, fear, and misconception. Matching thoughts and words is like transforming a patch of this wilderness into a garden, casting out unwanted thought-weeds and singling out for growth the word-plants we live on.

Even so, once we have a garden going according to our taste we can't be sure that everyone else is going to like it. Let's say, for instance, that I really do believe I said what I meant in 'Report from the Border'. I even wrote it down for you in prose, in case you should mistake my full meaning. But you're the left-wing editor of a socialist poetry magazine, and you think everything America does is evil. There's no way in which you're going to accept my poem's equivocation at the end. You're going to echo Sartre, perhaps, and tell me that if literature is the result of innocent suffering caused by capitalist exploitation then literature is not worth having. Or perhaps that 'literature' suggests demagoguery, propaganda, or advertising. So there we are, you and I, confronting each other with opposing beliefs, each of us meaning what we say but neither of us able to say what we mean without infuriating the other. And lo, the intentional fallacy looms once more, for it may be that you read the entire poem as a piece of cynical irony, including the last line. In which case you happily accept the poem for your magazine, not realizing that the poem I intended you to read in one way you have interpreted in another. Whose interpretation is right? Well, we have all been thoroughly indoctrinated: once the poem leaves the author's mind and exists on the page it is up for grabs—though that doesn't, of course, entail that it can mean *anything*. What I understand the intentional fallacy to mean, really, is that *the* right interpretation of a text can never be certain. And surely that's true, although some readings must be 'righter' than others if the text is to be generally understood. Sometimes two or three interpretations seem valid, and that's fine with me, too. Yet somehow the intentional fallacy has come to be one of the bugaboos of literary theory, and no one has quite got up courage enough to strip it of its pretensions.

So what, finally, do I want to conclude in this paper that has carried me such a long way away from Beauvoir and *The Second Sex* into the jungles of 'the meaning of meaning'? What, to ask a loaded question, is my *intention*? In part, perhaps, to look again at the theory of responsibility that Toril Moi found in Stanley Cavell: 'We can say that although the author's intentions may be largely irrelevant when it comes to deciding what a text means (the meaning of our words is not a private matter) they do not remain irrelevant when it comes to the question of the author's responsibility for her text' (p. 151 above). This is to argue that writers should take responsibility not only for saying what they mean but for saying things they may not have meant. And, although Moi makes a good (Freudian) case for taking responsibility for saying things we don't mean, this doesn't seem fair. I am not sure I can subscribe to a theory that gives an author responsibility for ideas she may not know she has expressed and for which other people, in her own time or in the future, may blame her. If the intentional fallacy strips me of control over my meaning, I cannot, logically, be held responsible for unintended meanings others read into my work. Yet, rather than reject Moi's healthy respect for responsibility, let's try instead to get rid of the idea that an author's intentions don't matter. Let's grant every author at least as much autonomy as her critics. Let's admit that without intentions, without a fierce struggle to make words say what she meant, including the ambiguity she intended, the author of my poem 'Report from the Border' wouldn't have written a thing, and the text wouldn't exist.

No. Rather than batter our heads against the ramparts of the intentional fallacy, I suggest we broaden the meaning of intention to give political theorists as well as imaginative writers credit for *intending to say what they mean*, for intending to connect words with what they have experienced as reality, for intending to name, however symbolically or metaphorically, as much as possible of what they think or experience. If we could manage to define intention in terms of the writer's instinct to find shareable words to convey meaning, then we could applaud every creative urge to seek, among other revelations, Shelley's 'metaphorical language that marks the before unapprehended relation of things'. Such a policy would take literature out of the hands of theorists and put it back into the hands of scholars and artists where it belongs. Nobody who writes with imagination and insight needs to justify their theories, whether to the left, right, or center of the spectrum, so long as what he or she writes bears some relevance to an actual human situation in all its humanness, and not to an idealized prescribed programme. All we authors can do to persuade our readers to trust us is to say what we mean and mean what we say—in so far as that is possible within the limits of our language and culture.

Toril Moi ends her paper with the question with which she began it: 'Can I still write theory with a clear political conscience?' (p. 159 above). The argument of her paper has by this time cleared it of dogma by refusing to lay down theoretical requirements for what politically correct writing *must* look like. Before answering yes or no to any such question, she says, every writer must determine the serious-ness of the particular situation that compels her (him) to write. This descent from the universals of theory on the part of a very well-known feminist theorist is welcome and should set an example for generations of critics to come. And if critics can learn to appeal to the freedom of the other, to be less doctrinaire and less ready to fall back on instant political correctness, then poets and writers of fiction will feel free to admit to themselves the full complexity of their imaginative undertak-ings. No art can thrive when artists persuade themselves that theory comes first. If the example of *The Second Sex* can at least partly per-suade radical artists of all kinds to *look* at actual human situations without prejudice and to open themselves to particular experiences before they even begin to theorize at large—I'm particularly thinking of the way some avant-garde visual artists have, in the last decade or two, become self-promoting slaves of social disillusion in Britain—its revival as an essential text is all the more to be celebrated.

9

The House We Never Leave: Childhood, Shelter, and Freedom in the Writings of Beauvoir and Colette

Emily R. Grosholz

In the second volume of *The Second Sex*, chapter II of the first part is entitled 'The Young Girl', following 'Childhood' and preceding 'Sexual Initiation'. There, Simone de Beauvoir writes about a precious moment of freedom in a young girl's life. Just at the onset of adolescence she is old enough to exercise some autonomy and to range beyond the confines of the family house, but she has not yet fallen into the adult constraints of married life. She is still well protected, but she is at liberty: optimal circumstances for cultivating imagination. However, this moment may not last; she is well aware of its transience, and so are those around her, the adults who hope she will soon give up her unladylike exuberance and settle down into a marriageable young woman. So she is a figure, for Beauvoir, full of hope and yet somehow tragic. 'With puberty', Beauvoir writes of the young girl,

the future not only draws near: it takes residence in her body; it becomes the most concrete reality. It retains the fatal quality it has always had...The present seems only a transition to her, already detached from the past of childhood; for she can find no valid aims in it, only occupations. In a more or less disguised fashion, her youth is used up in waiting. She is awaiting Man. (*DS* 1986, ii. 89)[1]

This chapter is, remarkably, one of the most vivid and poetic chapters in *The Second Sex*, whose prose is otherwise often weighed down

---

[1] All translations from texts by Beauvoir and Colette are mine.

by Beauvoir's understandable sadness about the status of women, and her own erudition, her determination to so thoroughly document the plight of women that it cannot be ignored. The young girl is not just a tragic figure; she is a poet, reflective, critical, and creative. She also becomes a figure of the modern age, who resembles at once both Hamlet and Ophelia, and the former more than the latter. Indeed, the situation of the young girl forces her into the attitude of the poet, of the poetically introverted Hamlet, precisely because it is paradoxical and intractable. Refusal, Beauvoir observes,

is the trait which defines the young girl, and which gives us the key to most of her actions; she doesn't accept the destiny that nature and society assign to her; and nonetheless she doesn't positively reject it: she is internally too much at odds to do battle with the world. She limits herself to fleeing the world, or to contesting it symbolically. Each of her desires is coupled with an anxiety: she is intensely eager to possess her future, but she dreads breaking completely with her past. (DS 1986, ii. 122)

In the ordinary life of every woman, Beauvoir seems to imply, there is a moment that demonstrates her imaginative, intellectual, spiritual, and erotic potential, and she has only to remember that moment in order to revive it. The conflict between the vitality and ambition of the young girl and the absence of obvious social forms for her energy leads not just to frustration but also to insight, for she learns about irony and pretence earlier than her brothers:

The young girl is secretive, turbulent, prey to difficult conflicts. This complexity enriches her; her interior life is more profoundly developed than that of her brothers. She is more attentive to the movements of the heart, which therefore become more nuanced, more diverse; she has more psychological sense than the boys who are directed towards external goals... She can give meaning to those revolts which oppose her to the world, and avoid the traps of the 'serious' and of conformity. The combined falsehoods of those around her encounter her irony and clairvoyance. (DS 1986, ii. 133)

To illustrate her point, Beauvoir discusses *inter alia* George Eliot's Maggie Tulliver in *The Mill on the Floss*, Colette's heroine Vinca in *Wheat in the Blade (Le Blé en herbe)* and, most significant, the invocations of her own younger self in *My Mother's House (La Maison de Claudine)* and *Sido*, those beautiful memoirs in which memory is revised by art.

As Beauvoir announces, when the young girl does not find or refuses love she may find poetry: 'Quand elle ne rencontre pas l'amour, il lui arrive de rencontrer la poésie' (*DS* 1986, ii. 135). The figure of the modern man (Marlowe's Dr Faustus, Shakespeare's Hamlet, Rousseau's Emile, Goethe's Werner) and of the poet in modernity displays two ironic involutions. On the one hand, he is plunged in self-consciousness and subjectivity; yet in a certain sense this leads him to become more objective: Descartes's *cogito* becomes Kant's transcendental ego that reflects upon what it has itself contributed to the object of knowledge. On the other hand, he is plunged in the passivity of reflection, which, however, often transforms itself into symbolic action that then comes to claim its place as the most important—or at least the most characteristic—kind of human action: Kant's erotic reason, striving for the impossible, manages after all to generate an ethics and an aesthetics in the second and third *Critiques*. And this is just what Beauvoir says of the young woman as poet:

Because she doesn't act, she looks, she feels, she takes in; a color, a smile evoke deep echoes in her, because her destiny is already dispersed far away from her, in cities already built, in men already shaped by life . . . Being poorly integrated into the human universe, adapting to it only with difficulty, she is, like an infant, capable of *seeing* it; instead of being concerned solely with her mastery of things, she fastens on their meaning, discovering thereby unusual cross-sections, unexpected metamorphoses. (Ibid.)

Viewed this way, Beauvoir's young woman arrogates modernity to herself, along with its task of remaking the world in words.

For Beauvoir, this all entails that the young girl stands in a special relation to nature, a relation at once grandiose, empty, and regulative, as indeed erotic reason does in the first *Critique*, the *Critique of Pure Reason*. My invocation of Kant here is just to show how fully Beauvoir's young girl takes on the traits of modernity; the reference is inexplicit, but Beauvoir uses Kant's vocabulary, taken over by Hegel, when she writes:

she projects herself towards things with fervor, because she hasn't yet been shorn of her transcendence; and the fact that she doesn't accomplish anything, that she is nothing, only makes her enthusiasm more passionate: empty and infinitary, that which she tries to attain from the seat of her nothingness is Everything. This is why she feels a special love for Nature: even more than the adolescent boy, she worships it. Unsubdued, inhuman, Nature sums up most clearly the totality of what is. Since she hasn't yet acquired title to any part of the universe, it is her kingdom in its entirety, thanks to this very dispossession; when she lays claim to it, she lays claim just as proudly to herself. (*DS* 1986, ii. 135–6)

A page later she invokes Emily Brontë's Catherine, and might just as well have invoked Charlotte Brontë's Jane Eyre, each of whom sought to attain everything 'from the seat of her nothingness' by wandering out on the Yorkshire moors, that terrestrial ocean.

Immediately afterward, Beauvoir invokes Colette, and quotes a long passage from *Sido*:

For I already loved daybreak so much that my mother would give it to me as a reward. I got her to wake me up at three-thirty in the morning, and I set out with an empty basket on each arm towards the little market gardens hidden in the narrow loop of the river, towards the strawberries, the currants, and the bearded gooseberries. At three-thirty, everything lay asleep in the blue of genesis, humid and vague, and as I walked down the sandy path, the mist—landlocked by its own weight—bathed first my legs, then my sturdy little torso, finally rising to my lips, my ears, and my nostrils, all of them more sensitive than the rest of my body... It was on this path and at this hour that I became aware of my own worth, of an ineffable state of grace and of my own complicity with the first breeze that stirred, the first bird, the sun once again oval, distorted by its blossoming on the horizon... I returned when the church bells announced the first mass. But not before having eaten my fill, not before having described a great circuit in the woods like a dog out hunting by himself, not before having drunk at two hidden springs which I worshipped...[2]

Beauvoir makes two observations about this passage and another, similar in tone and theme, from a novel by Mary Webb. First, she sharply distinguishes nature from the house of childhood:

The texts that I have cited clearly show what a refuge the adolescent girl finds in the fields and the woods. In the paternal house, mother, laws, custom, routine, together rule; she wishes to tear herself away from this past, to become in turn a sovereign subject. But in a social milieu she can accede to adult life only by making herself into a woman, by paying for her liberation with an abdication; whereas in the milieu of plants and animals she is a human being, freed at once from her family and from men, a subject, a free being. (*DS* 1986, ii. 341)

This polarity, so strong in Beauvoir, is lacking in Colette, where the natal house opens up into the garden, which in turn gives on the surrounding countryside, where the house itself is full of animals and plants, and where the figure of Sido blesses the freedom of her

[2] *Oeuvres de Colette*, iii (Paris: Flammarion, 1960), 259–60 (hereafter *OC*). The works I refer to in volume iii are *La Maison de Claudine* (whose more accurate title in English is *My Mother's House*) and *Sido*.

children, even as she waits anxiously for them to return. I will discuss the meaning of this contrast between the two writers in the following sections.

Second, Beauvoir gives this phase in the life of a woman special prominence. Invoking Emily Brontë, Anna de Noailles, Catherine of Siena, Theresa of Avila, and Joan of Arc, as well as Mme Roland and Rosa Luxembourg, Beauvoir writes that a youthful desire for the absolute was

the flame that fed their lives. In her servitude, in her destitution, from the depths of her refusal, the young girl can draw up the greatest daring. She encounters poetry; she also encounters heroism. One way to take up the fact that she is badly integrated into society is to surpass her limited horizons. The richness and the force of their nature, and fortunate circumstances, have permitted certain women to pursue the passionate projects of adolescence into their adult life. But they are exceptions . . . (*DS* 1986, ii. 139)

Thus early adolescence is an occasion for real creativity (and of the kind typical of modern man, subjectively objective and symbolically active); it has inspired works of genius from nineteenth- and twentieth-century women writers and political figures; and it can serve as a topic in the reflections of every woman to help her locate the sources of her own power: What was I doing when I entered adolescence? What did I have then that I have lost? How might I regain that vibrant potential? So it is not surprising to notice that both Beauvoir and Colette wrote memoirs about that crucial period in their childhood—*Memoirs of a Dutiful Daughter* (1958, when Beauvoir turned 50) and *My Mother's House (La Maison de Claudine)* (1922, when Colette turned 49) and *Sido* (1930)—just at the point in their adult lives when they were reassessing their own sense of themselves, after great achievements combined with great conflict and loss.

In the next section I will examine the sense of the 'jeune désir d'absolu' in the *Memoirs of a Dutiful Daughter*, and the way in which it is worked out in terms of a polarized city house and provincial countryside in Beauvoir's writings, as well as the construction of her mother as enforcer of patriarchal law. This contrasts with the integration of house and countryside in *My Mother's House* and *Sido*, where Colette's mother emerges as a figure at once warm, critical, and autonomous, in whose eyes a daughter has as much right to bloom as the geraniums, foxgloves, begonias, and roses in her garden and window boxes. To this I will turn in the subsequent section. In the very last section I will try to elicit from the two memoirs a revision of the existentialist approach, along lines both suggested by and departing from some remarks by Gaston Bachelard, where the truth of mortality is balanced against the truth of natality, and the courage of launching oneself over nothingness—of living with no ground under one's feet—is balanced against the courage of building a house and sheltering one's children there.

BEAUVOIR'S *MEMOIRS OF A DUTIFUL DAUGHTER*, PARTS I AND II

Simone de Beauvoir was raised in Paris, living first in an apartment on the boulevard Raspail and then on the rue de Rennes. The churches, parks, bookstores, and theaters of Paris were well known to her from childhood, and her devotion to the city never changed throughout her life. And yet she claims in part I of *Memoirs* that the happiest times of her earliest years were the two and a half months she spent every summer in the country, where she was left alone and at liberty to explore the 'immensity of the horizons' which surrounded the manor house of her grandfather, called La Grillère, in Meyrignac. She seems to have encountered her parents there only at meals; the rest of the time she devoted to reading and exploring.

Early on in her description of life at La Grillère Beauvoir echoes the passage from Colette cited above.

First of all my joys was to watch the meadows wake up, very early in the morning; book in hand, I left the sleeping house and pushed the gate open. I couldn't sit on the grass, misted over with white frost, but walked down the avenue, along the meadow planted with select trees which grandfather called 'the landscaped garden'. I read a little, taking small steps, and felt against my skin the coolness of the air begin to soften; the delicate glaze that covered the earth gently began to melt; the purple beech, the blue cedars, the silvery poplars, shone with a radiance as fresh as the first morning in paradise: and I, I alone was the bearer of the world's beauty and the glory of God—though all the while hungrily dreaming of hot chocolate and toast. When the bees began to buzz, and the green shutters opened out onto the scent of wysteria warmed by the sun, I had already shared a long, secret past with this new day which for the others had barely begun.[3]

[3] *Mémoires d'une jeune fille rangée* (Paris: Gallimard, 1958), 110–11 (hereafter *MJFR*).

Beauvoir does not typically evoke subtleties of color, touch or scent in her prose: the writing here is modelled on Colette's.

So too is the passage which follows a page later, where Beauvoir describes afternoon rambles with her sister.

Scratching our legs on gorse and our arms on brambles, we explored for miles round about the chestnut orchards, the fields, the moors. We made great discoveries: pools, a waterfall, and, in the middle of a heath, blocks of gray granite which we scaled in order to discern far away the blue line of the Monédières. En route we tasted the hazelnuts and blackberries in the hedges, arbutus berries, cornel berries, and the acidic berries of the berberis; we sampled the fruit of all the apple trees; but we were careful not to suck milky sap from the euphorbia, or to touch the beautiful red spikes which haughtily bear the name 'Solomon's Seal'. Dazed by the smell of freshly mown hay, of honeysuckle, of buckwheat in flower, we lay down on moss or grass, and read. (*MJFR* 111–12)

Beauvoir remarks: 'Although the presence of my sister usually didn't bother me, solitude I found thrilling' (*MJFR* 113). Her communion with nature was hers in solitude and freedom.

Beauvoir's musings on life at La Grillère are followed immediately by an account of her initiation into the mysteries of puberty and sex, gleaned from friends, from the perusal of Colette's *Claudine at School*, and from her cousin at La Grillère. The confused pronouncements of her cousin, she records, led her and her sister into 'wild verbal debaucheries', which included carolling, much to the distress of the grown-ups, 'Your white breasts are lovelier by far to my greedy mouth—than the wild strawberries of the woods—whose milk I sip there'. This popular song, left lying on the piano by her Aunt Helen, sounds like a sexualized version, with the same vocabulary, of Beauvoir's explorations in the forest. In the next few pages she describes her intense identification with Jo March in Louisa May Alcott's *Little Women* ('I became in my own eyes a character out of a novel' (*MJFR* 125–6)), and then with the little girl Zaza, her first passionate attachment, whose death at the very end of *Memoirs* will mark the end of childhood. The recognition that she loves Zaza, both selflessly and irrevocably, ends part I.

All of these themes, summers at La Grillère, the complex intersection of life in books and life on earth, the advent of puberty in Beauvoir's flesh and in her soul, are revisited in part II, and their interrelations more profoundly explored. Just as her adolescence began,

Beauvoir's family moved from the boulevard Raspail to the rue de Rennes, a step down on the social and economic ladder caused by her father's inability to succeed in his professional life. This change made Beauvoir realize that one day she would also lose her country house, since her grandfather had bequeathed it to her uncle; the association of change with loss invested the metamorphosis of her body (from girl to woman) and of her relation to her parents (from trust to suspicion) with great anxiety.

I had lost the security of childhood, but had gained nothing in return. The authority of my parents remained inflexible and, as my own critical spirit was now awakened, I endured it with increasing impatience. I no longer saw the usefulness of formal visits, family meals, all the chores and duties that my parents regarded as obligatory. The responses: 'This is required', 'This just isn't done', no longer satisfied me at all. My mother's solicitude began to weigh on me. (*MJFR* 146)

Her mother, unable to offer reasons for the principles and rules she imposed, began to seem to Beauvoir like a petty tyrant, as well as a rival for her father's attention.

Trying to determine her own fate in her own way, unconstrained and unregulated by her mother, Beauvoir turned to characters in books: Alcott's Jo in *Little Women* and its sequel, Colette's Claudine, George Eliot's Maggie in *The Mill on the Floss*. Reflections on these beloved books and their heroines led Beauvoir to the question of why and how she decided to become a writer. Even early in part I she had addressed the question: 'I had a spontaneous urge to turn everything that happened to me into a story. I talked a great deal, and wrote willingly. If I recounted an episode from my life in an essay it escaped from oblivion, became interesting to others, was once and for all redeemed' (*MJFR* 197). To write and to represent her own life in writing were for Beauvoir coeval impulses. Thus here she says that she (and her father) had always admired writers; that she loved to communicate; that she loved to teach; but the real motivation for writing was a desire to invent, legitimate, and immortalize her own life. 'By writing a work based on my own history, I would create myself anew and justify my own existence . . . This project reconciled everything' (*MJFR* 199).

In *Simone de Beauvoir: The Making of an Intellectual Woman* Toril Moi observes that Beauvoir moved from 'union' with her parents to an engulfing relationship with Zaza, and thence to another, even more engulfing, relationship with Sartre, in part because she vacillated between a fantasy of unity or oneness and devastating feelings of abandonment—absolute happiness or absolute despair. 'The intensity of her happiness', writes Moi, 'is clearly caused by the experience of an overwhelming unity with a dominant other... But if her bliss rests on a fantasy of merger with a dominant other, the slightest threat to that profoundly satisfying and exhilarating sense of unity might produce an equally violent experience of desolation and abandonment.'[4] Thus as Beauvoir's trust in her parents is eroded, entering adolescence, she seeks solace in the immortality of books and writing, and more than ever before in the countryside at Meyrignac. Recall that Beauvoir claims in *The Second Sex* that the young girl 'feels a special love for Nature: even more than the adolescent boy, she worships it. Unsubdued, inhuman, Nature sums up most clearly the totality of what is' (*DS* 1986, ii. 136).

The peculiar cast of Beauvoir's personality thus structures in part her account of the 'universal' experience of the young girl. In any case, it is manifest in the description of her own experience at Meyrignac.

My love for the countryside took on mystical colors. As soon as I arrived at Meyrignac the walls crumbled, the horizon receded. I was lost in the infinite while always remaining myself. I felt on my eyelids the warmth of the sun which shines on everything and yet which, here and now, caressed only me. The wind whirled around the poplars: it came from elsewhere, from everywhere, it jostled space and I turned in my own vortex, immobile, out to the edges of the earth. When the moon rose in the sky I communed with distant cities, deserts, seas, villages which all at the same moment were bathed in its light. I was no longer an empty consciousness, an abstract perspective, but rather the rough smell of buckwheat, the intimate odor of the heath, the thick heat of midday or the chill of evening; I weighed heavily on the earth, and yet I rose into the blue sky like vapor, without boundaries. (*MJFR* 174)

This is precisely the structure of Beauvoir's 'melancholia', her oscillation beween radical absorption and absolute emptiness. It also includes a Cartesian moment where, using the vocabulary of the first and second *Meditation* and even perhaps of the *Principles*, the isolated *cogito* finds itself to be a kind of vortex.

---

[4] Moi, *Simone de Beauvoir: The Making of an Intellectual Woman* (Oxford: Blackwell, 1994), 224.

Moi points out that Beauvoir's melancholia affected her view of her mother, and of mothers in general. Her oscillation—that of a girl on the threshold of adulthood—is also an oscillation between someone who wishes to become independent and at the same time succumbs to the seductions of dependence. It turns the figure of mother into a death-dealing Medusa, internalized in the daughter: it kills Zaza, and threatens to do the same to Simone.

It is not Simone's triumph at the *agrégation* or her meeting with Sartre that ends the book [*Memoirs*], but her account of the death of Zaza, who dies for love at the hands of a selfish and petty-minded mother. In Beauvoir's version of the story, Zaza becomes the ultimate little mermaid; her mother the Medusa incarnate. Simone's independence is paid for by Zaza's dependence and ultimate death.[5]

Thus the young girl can find refuge in nature only by setting out alone, indifferent to or against the wishes of the mother. As Beauvoir insists in *The Second Sex*: 'The texts that I have cited clearly show what a refuge the adolescent girl finds in the fields and the woods. In the paternal house, mother, laws, customs, routine, together rule; she wishes to tear herself away from this past, to become in turn a sovereign subject' (*DS* 1986, ii. 341). One night at La Grillère Beauvoir stayed out late in the countryside, reading and watching the moon rise, so late in fact that she missed the evening meal: 'By way of punishment, my mother ordered the next day that I not be allowed outside the boundaries of the estate. Frankly, I did not dare disobey. I spent the day sitting on the lawn or pacing up and down the avenues with a book in my hand and fury in my heart' (*MJFR* 176).

It was also at Meyrignac that Beauvoir discovered that she no longer believed in God. The argument recalls not so much Descartes's *Meditations* as the *Thoughts* of Pascal, for Beauvoir recasts his wager. Pondering the asceticism of Christianity, Beauvoir realized that if she must choose between earthly joys and God she would choose forbidden apples, the warm fragrance of the stables, the sexy novels of Balzac (and by implication Colette, in whose style she is writing). 'I had always thought that in comparison with eternity this world counted for nothing; but it did count, because I loved it, and suddenly it was God who no longer weighed in the balance' (*MJFR* 192). But the liberation of this insight also entailed a certain terror: 'Suddenly, every-

5 Moi, *Simone de Beauvoir*, 218.

thing fell silent. What a silence! The earth rolled through a space that no look could penetrate, and, lost on its immense surface in the midst of a blind ether, I was all alone. Alone: for the first time I understood the terrible meaning of this word. Alone: without witness, without interlocutor, without recourse' (*MJFR* 193).

This revelation, moreover, she could not reveal to her pious mother, her father (atheist, but deeply concerned with respectability), or even Zaza. The dark side of oneness with erotic nature is isolation. She wonders whether the emptiness can ever be filled when the moment recurs again later in Paris. The end of part II suggests that the answer to the question lies in books, in the vocation of writing and the rejection of the role of dutiful daughter to her mother—in particular, the pursuit of philosophy and indeed of a philosopher, 'someone who would guarantee my existence without taking away my powers of self-determination' (*MJFR* 205). 'My life', she writes as the last line of part II, 'would be a beautiful story come true, a story I would make up as I went along' (*MJFR* 237). Yet the image of her mother as destructive and intrusive would continue to haunt the story for many years to come.

COLETTE'S *SIDO*

The world of houses for the adolescent Beauvoir is a constrained, constraining world, where daughters are forced into domestic service and blind devotion. The worst thing about her own mother was that all these duties, to husband, God, and family, didn't seem to bother her, so that she passed them along to her daughters with no ambivalence, no perspective. At La Grillère the house is the setting for 'passionate discussion of the quality of the cantaloups', and boredom brought on by lack of competences; in Paris, the house becomes a prison:

I would go out on the balcony: there would be nothing but roofs. The heavens would be reduced to a geometrical locus, the air was no longer perfume or caress, but merged with naked space. The noises of the street did not speak to me. I would stand there with an empty heart and my eyes full of tears . . . Back in Paris, I was again under the thumb of adults. (*MJFR* 177–8)

And it is defined by its opposition to the world of nature, the way in which it closes its doors and shutters: Beauvoir's moments of spiritual rebellion often take place by an open window or on a balcony.

By contrast, the house of Colette's childhood, the house on the rue de l'Hospice in a small village in Burgundy, is quite porous: there are no firm boundaries where nature and domestic culture exclude each other. At the back of the house the sitting room opened on to a flagged terrace whose roof was 'a mantle of wisteria and begonia too heavy for the trellis of worn iron-work, which sagged in the middle like a hammock'; the terrace opened on to the upper garden, the upper garden to the lower. And the lower garden was supposed to be demarcated from the rue des Vignes by 'a strong iron railing', but, Colette writes, 'I never knew that railing except twisted and torn from the cement of its wall, carried off and brandished in the air by the unconquerable arms of a hundred year old wysteria vine' (OC iii. 147). Much of the life of the house spilled out into the garden: 'Those rear gardens gave the village its character. We lived there in the summer, we did our laundry; we chopped wood in winter, we did chores there in every season, and the children, playing in the sheds, perched on the side rails of the unhitched hay wagons' (OC iii. 258). Down the road lay the fields, beyond the fields the meadows and the woods. The garden served as the middle term that brought them into relation with the house.

And the house itself was full of flora and fauna. Returning home after a week in Paris, the sixteen-year-old Colette professed her aversion to 'houses without animals', and sought the familiars of her home: the dog with a new puppy, the new litter of kittens, the pet swallows, the spider who descended at three in the morning to drink the dregs in her mother's cup of cocoa, the carefully tended, extravagently fed caterpillar who one day would become an emperor moth; and the pots of delicate geraniums, dwarf rose bushes, spiraea, succulents and cacti, or lupin, narcissus, hibiscus, winter-cherry, sweet pea, and crocus getting started ahead of time for spring (OC iii. 175–8; 255–65). The presiding spirit over all these creatures, the one who brought them all inside for shelter, was of course Colette's mother, Sidonie, whose presence these books so vividly evokes:

Everything is there before my eyes, the garden with its sun-warmed walls, the last sombre cherries hanging from the tree, the sky barred with long rosy clouds, it is all there under my fingers: the vigorous revolt of the caterpillar, the thick, moist, leathery leaves of the hydrangea, the small, calloused hand of my mother. The wind, if I wish, creases the stiff paper of the false bamboo and sings, in the thousand rivulets of the air combed through the yew tree, a fitting accompaniment for the voice that spoke that day—and all other days up to its silence at the very end—words like these: 'Someone must take care of that child . . . Can't we save that woman? Do those people have enough to eat? But of course I can't stop feeding the creature . . .' (*OC* iii. 178)

Beauvoir sees in her mother only a dutiful wife and parent, a devout Catholic who never questions the priest, and a devout wife who echoes her husband's opinions and values Simone only as long as she plays the role of dutiful daughter. There is little evidence in her mother of a critical or creative spirit, or even of curiosity and generosity: to enter a realm where she, Simone, can flourish she must leave her mother behind. By contrast, what Colette admires most in her mother Sido is precisely the independence of her opinions, the depth of her know- ledge of nature and society, her ability to create and sustain the earthly paradise of her home garden, and her discriminating generosity. A whole chapter of *My Mother's House*, 'My Mother and the Curé', chron- icles the very funny, subversive relation Sido carried on with the local priest, who always succumbed to her gentle tyranny in the end.

She was never afraid to scandalize the neighbors, if it meant shelter- ing a pregnant, unmarried servant girl, or refusing her most beautiful flowers for the adornment of altar or tomb.

But she willingly sacrificed an especially lovely flower for an especially small child, a child not old enough to talk, like the little boy of a neighbor who lived in the house just east of us and brought him over to our garden one day to show him off. My mother criticized his baby outfit as too tight, undid his tripartite bonnet, the useless woollen scarf, and contemplated at her leisure his bronze curls, fat cheeks, the black, severe, and fathomless eyes of a ten-month-old infant, truly more beautiful than every other ten-month-old infant. She gave him a rose called 'thigh of excited nymph' which he accepted with delight, carried to his mouth and sucked on, then kneaded the flower in his strong little hands, pulled off the petals, curved and red, the image of his own lips . . . (*OC* iii. 264)

Beauvoir's mother is described mostly in relation to Beauvoir her- self, and increasingly throughout *Memoirs* as a person uncomprehend- ing of and opposed to her daughter. Indeed, throughout she is referred to as 'Mama'; it is only in passing that we learn that her name is Françoise, in the half-page description of her life before the advent of her children. Neglected by her parents and sent off young to a convent school, she learned early, Beauvoir explains, to be resentful and docile, timid and dictatorial.

My mother never dreamed of protesting—in any way—against the illogic of social conventions. She acquiesced in many other compromises: they never undermined her principles; perhaps it was to make up for these concessions that she inwardly held to her strict intransigence . . . Since social customs forced her to excuse the indiscretions of certain men, she concentrated her severity on women. (*MJFR* 52)

What was her mother's life like when Beauvoir was not around? There is no suggestion of this in *Memoirs*, which is mostly concerned with the day-to-day life of Beauvoir, as she struggles to untangle herself from the bad faith of middle-class Parisian existence.

Colette's Sido on the other hand is often objectively depicted and indeed celebrated, independent of the needs and desires of Colette herself: in relation to her uncles, a first husband, Colette's father, the other siblings, and, finally, as a solitary being. One day her mother installed a scarecrow in their cherry tree to frighten the blackbirds; the next day Colette discovered her admiring a blackbird, green and violet glinting in his wings, as he gorged himself on cherries oblivious to the new scarecrow, just as Sido stood there oblivious to the protests of her child:

'The cherries? Oh yes, the cherries . . .' A kind of laughing wildness crossed her face, a universal scorn, a dancing disdain that ran roughshod over me along with all the rest of us, lightly . . . It was only for a moment, though it happened more than once. Now that I understand her better, I can explain those flashes in her eyes. It seems to me that a need to escape from everybody and everything lit them up, a leap towards the heights, towards an order written for herself alone. If I am wrong, let me err. Under the cherry tree, she came back down to earth one more time amongst us, ballasted by worries, by love, by the children and husband who clung to her; she became once again good, plump, and humble in the face of ordinary life: 'It's true, the cherries . . . You must have your cherries too, little girl . . .' (*OC* iii. 265)

The very first thing that we learn about Sido in *My Mother's House* is that she lets her children be: they may lie for hours hidden in shed or tree, reading, or range over the countryside, far out of earshot. She has raised them as free creatures, though their freedom costs her many hours of uncertainty and even sometimes of grief. Thus the home she has organized for them lies open to elsewhere, to the countryside she permits them to explore and to Paris, which she sometimes visits and does not despise: she has always provided them with a passport to travel beyond the porous boundaries of home. She herself has sent them out in the world, with her blessing. This relation of mother and daughter is what Beauvoir excises from the passage of Colette's she quotes in *The Second Sex*.

Here is the passage again, with the parts Beauvoir left out in italics:

For I already loved daybreak so much that my mother would give it to me as a reward. I got her to wake me up at three-thirty in the morning, and I set out with an empty basket on each arm towards the little market gardens hidden in the narrow loop of the river, towards the strawberries, the currants, and the bearded gooseberries. At three-thirty, everything lay asleep in the blue of genesis, humid and vague, and as I walked down the sandy path, the mist— landlocked by its own weight—bathed first my legs, then my sturdy little torso, finally rising to my lips, my ears, and my nostrils, all of them more sensitive than the rest of my body... *I went alone, this free-thinking countryside held no dangers.* It was on this path and at this hour that I became aware of my own worth, of an ineffable state of grace and of my own complicity with the first breeze that stirred, the first bird, the sun once again oval, distorted by its blossoming on the horizon... *My mother let me go, after having called me 'Beauty, Jewel-all-of-gold'; she watched her 'chef-d'oeuvre,' as she called me, run off and disappear down the slope of the garden. I was perhaps pretty; my mother and pictures of me at that time do not always yield the same judgment... But I was pretty at that moment, because of my age and because day was dawning, because of my blue eyes made sombre by the shadows of foliage, and my blond hair that would not be smoothed down until my return, and my childish sense of superiority, to be awake before all those other sleeping children.* I returned when the church bells announced the first mass. But not before having eaten my fill, not before having described a great circuit in the woods like a dog out hunting by himself, not before having drunk at two hidden springs which I worshipped... (*OC* iii. 259–60)

'My mother let me go.' Notice how just at this point the narrative point of view shifts to Sido, who watches her child vanish at the end of the garden. 'The countryside was safe.' Yes, but what countryside is ever completely safe for a ten-year-old girl? It was hard every time for Sido to see her masterwork, her beautiful and vulnerable child, go off alone, but every time she let her go. And that was the gift, just as much as the vision of daybreak.

Colette, like Beauvoir, saw her parents forced from the beloved house of childhood through reduced circumstances; and, like Beauvoir, but a generation earlier, she left her mother's house forever, to go to Paris to become a writer, hemmed in and encouraged by a powerful, overweening man. But whereas Beauvoir stands on the balcony of her house—degraded into a kind of prison—to look down on Paris through rebellious tears, Colette revisits her provincial house from the garden, entering always through the terrace, remembering its lighted windows as a refuge and her mother as a lighthouse, one of the *phares* that Colette in her old age invoked as a series of beacons that led her through the storms of life.

The little girl, tired out, mechanically repeats, 'When I shall travel around the world...' as if she were saying, 'When I shall go shake chestnuts from the trees...' A spot of red lights up inside the house, behind the windows of the sitting room, and the little girl starts. Everything that was green an instant before has become blue, around that red, immobile flame. The child's hand, trailing in the grass, senses the dew of evening. It is the hour of lamps. The lapping sound of running water rises in the leaves; as if by a wintry gust, the door of the hayloft begins to bang against the wall. The garden, all at once hostile around the sobered little girl, brushes back the cold leaves of the laurel, flourishes the sabres of the yucca and the barbed caterpillars of the araucaria. A great oceanic voice groans from the direction of the Moutiers where the wind, unobstructed, runs in gusts over the swell of the woods. The little girl in the grass fixes her eyes on the lamp, which a brief eclipse has just veiled: a hand has passed in front of the flame, a hand that wears a shining thimble. (*OC* iii. 159)

Throughout these books Colette often describes her mother's hand: strong, work-worn, elegant, and capable: 'Why did no one ever model, paint, sculpt, that hand of Sido's, tanned, wrinkled early by household work, gardening, cold water and sunlight, the long, tapered fingers, with their beautiful nails, curved and perfectly oval' (*OC* iii. 263). By synecdoche, the hand sums up the mother as the lighted lamp seen through a window sums up and organizes the world.

THE HOUSE WE NEVER LEAVE

Beauvoir revisits the house of childhood in her *Memoirs of a Dutiful Daughter*, in order to unmask and analyze its illusions, and to recount the long journey out of it, away from it. Her perspective is by and large first person, and she contrasts her own life with that of Zaza, who succumbed to, instead of escaping from, the natal house presided over by threatening mothers who must always demand repetition. Imagination takes flight when the young girl roams off into the countryside unaccompanied, unprotected, on her own initiative; it recoils from houses where mothers bring their children into the world. Colette by contrast finds the house of childhood in *My Mother's House* and *Sido* a refuge for imagination, and the mother who inhabits it a model of creativity. Colette's house opens up on to the countryside, and her mother is the one who sends her off on adventures in the morning, an empty basket on each arm to be filled with whatever she finds, and beckons her home at evening with a lighted lamp. The perspective in these books flits about from person to person like a blackbird from tree to tree, each angle giving depth and shadow to the life of garden, terrace, sitting room. A judgment is hard to draw here, and must in any case be nuanced by Beauvoir's later, more sympathetic view of her mother in *Une Morte très douce* (*A Very Easy Death*), but it seems that Colette was luckier in her family circumstances than Beauvoir.

In his book *The Poetics of Space* Gaston Bachelard observes that all of us carry with us, in the memory of both body and spirit, the house of our childhood. The protection afforded by our childhood home and the adults who watched over us, Bachelard argues, is vitally important in infancy—the cultural extension of the natural protection of the womb—and continues to be so throughout life, for the dream house provides a kind of psychic refuge where imagination is fostered: 'The house shelters day-dreaming, the house protects the dreamer, the house allows one to dream in peace. Thought and experience are not the only things that sanction human values. The values that belong to day-dreaming mark humanity in its depths.'[6] Memory and imagination are here allied in the organization of experience. We do not simply progress towards the future, but also constantly circle around and reinhabit our past; our being is not uniformly oriented towards death, but also towards birth. Moreover, just because human shelter isn't eternal doesn't mean it isn't real; we are, most of us, really protected in infancy and this 'being housed' is essential to our lived reality, just as essential as our later voyages outward, away from home. Why should we value voyage and war—Achilles' and Odysseus' Trojan war, for example—over home and hearth?

Bachelard challenges the presuppositions of his peers (perhaps Heidegger and Sartre) when he writes:

From my viewpoint, from the phenomenologist's viewpoint, the conscious metaphysics that starts from the moment when the being is 'cast into the world' is a secondary metaphysics. It passes over the preliminaries, when being is being-well, in the well-being originally associated with being. To illustrate

---

[6] Gaston Bachelard, *The Poetics of Space*, trans. Maria Jolas (Boston, Mass.: Beacon Press, 1994), 6 (hereafter *PS*).

the metaphysics of consciousness we should have to wait for the experiences during which being is cast out, that is to say, thrown out, outside the being of the house, a circumstance in which the hostility of men and of the universe accumulates. But a complete metaphysics, englobing both the conscious and the unconscious, would leave the privilege of its values within. Within the being, in the being of within, an enveloping warmth welcomes being. Being reigns in a sort of earthly paradise of matter, dissolved in the comforts of an adequate matter.[7]

The problem with Bachelard's formulation is that he assents too quickly to the master polarity, or ratio, of home and world, and then to its way of governing other ratios in a series of related proportions. Thus home is to world as unconscious is to conscious, matter to spirit, female to male, undifferentiated unity (reverie) to distinctions (science). These proportions subtly undermine the value and importance of home by aligning it, and women, with the indistinct and inarticulate.

What is most attractive about Colette's revisiting of the house of childhood is how deftly she throws these proportions into question, along with their reigning polarity or ratio, while still asserting the importance of natality vis-à-vis mortality, and of being housed vis-à-vis being cast out into the world. For Sido is at once scientific and passionate, critical and generous: 'her critical sense was sturdy, changeable, warm and gay as a young lizard'. And Colette in her reverie writes a prose as highly constructed, self-conscious, and rigorous as that of Proust, where the material world of her childhood is magically conjured up by the richest vocabulary and subtlest turns of phrase, to become the most precise expression of spirit:

Those massive lilacs whose compact flowers, blue in the shade and purple in sunlight, faded early, smothered by their own exuberance, those lilacs, long since dead: I can't make them rise up again towards the light, or revive the terrifying moonbeams—silver, lead-gray, mercury, facets of sharp amethyst, cutting sapphire that wounds—refracted by a certain pane of blue glass in the little pavilion at the end of the garden. (OC iii. 147–8)

Indeed, it is the house that makes exploration of the world possible, both because of its protective walls and evening lamps, and because of its windows and garden, as does Sido herself, sending her children out and then anxiously watching for their return. Beauvoir, it seems, neglected two important resources in her courageous attempt to reclaim

[7] Bachelard, The Poetics of Space, 7.

reason, freedom, and autonomy for women: her own mother Françoise, and her literary mother Colette who—though stemming from a different class, educated in an informal way, and committed to a different genre—had many profound and original insights to offer on the problematic life of women.

ACKNOWLEDGEMENTS

This essay is dedicated with affection to Seyla Benhabib, Eleni Fourtouni, and Catherine Iino, who helped me thread my way through the labyrinth of the 1970s; and with love to my daughter Mary-Frances.

Select Bibliography

Primary Works by Simone de Beauvoir, with
English Translations

Le Deuxième Sexe, 2 vols. (Paris: Gallimard, 1949).
Le Deuxième Sexe, 2 vols. (Paris: Gallimard (*Coll. Folio*), 1986).
The Second Sex, trans. H. M. Parshley (New York: Alfred A. Knopf, 1952; repr. New York: Bantam Books, 1961; New York: Vintage Books, 1974; Harmondsworth: Penguin, 1984; with introd. by Deidre Bair, New York: Vintage Books, 1989; with introd. by Margaret Crosland, New York and London: Alfred A. Knopf (Everyman's Library), 1993).

In chronological order:

L'Invitée (Paris: Gallimard, 1943).
She Came to Stay, trans. Yvonne Moyse and Roger Senhouse (New York: World, 1954; repr. Harmondsworth: Penguin, 1986; New York: Norton, 1999).
Pyrrhus et Cinéas (Paris: Gallimard, 1944).
Le Sang des autres (Paris: Gallimard (*Coll. Folio*), 1945).
The Blood of Others, trans. Yvonne Moyse and Roger Senhouse (Harmondsworth: Penguin, 1964/86).
Les Bouches inutiles (Paris: Gallimard (*Coll. Le Manteau d'Arlequin*), 1945).
Who Shall Die?, trans. Claude Francis and Fernande Gonthier (Florissant, Mo.: River Press, 1983).
Tous les hommes sont mortels (Paris: Gallimard (*Coll. Folio*), 1946).
All Men are Mortal, trans. Leonard M. Friedman (Cleveland, Ohio: World, 1955), rev. trans. Euan Cameron and Leonard M. Friedman (London: Virago Press, 1995).
Pour une morale de l'ambiguité (Paris: Gallimard, 1947).
The Ethics of Ambiguity, trans. Bernard Frechtman (New York: Citadel Press, 1948/1970/2000).
L'Existentialisme et la sagesse des nations (Paris: Les Editions Nagel, 1948).
L'Amerique au jour le jour (Paris: Morihien, 1948).

America Day by Day, trans. Carol Cosman (Berkeley, Calif.: University of California Press, 1999).

Les Mandarins (Paris: Gallimard (*Coll. Folio*), 1954).

The Mandarins, trans. Leonard M. Friedman (Cleveland, Ohio: World, 1956; repr. London: Fontana 1986; New York: Norton, 1991).

Privilèges (Paris: Gallimard, 1955). (Also published in the *Coll. Idées* under the title *Faut-il brûler Sade?*)

La Longue Marche (Paris: Gallimard, 1957).

The Long March, trans. Austryn Wainhouse (Cleveland, Ohio: World, 1958).

Mémoires d'une jeune fille rangée (Paris: Gallimard, 1958).

Memoirs of a Dutiful Daughter, trans. James Kirkup (Cleveland, Ohio: World, 1959; repr. Harmondsworth and New York: Penguin, 1963; New York: Harper and Row, 1959/74).

La Force de l'age (Paris: Gallimard, 1960).

The Prime of Life, trans. Peter Green (Cleveland, Ohio: World, 1962; repr. New York and Harmondsworth: Penguin, 1965/88; with introd. by Toril Moi, New York: Paragon House, 1992).

La Force des choses (Paris: Gallimard (*Coll. Folio*), 1963).

The Force of Circumstance, trans. Richard Howard (New York: Putnam, 1965; repr. with introd. by Toril Moi, New York: Paragon House, 1992).

Une Mort très douce (Paris: Gallimard (*Coll. Folio*), 1964).

A Very Easy Death, trans. Patrick O'Brian (New York: Warner Books, 1964/73; repr. Harmondsworth: Penguin, 1983; New York: Pantheon Books, 1985).

Les Belles images (Paris: Gallimard (*Coll. Folio*), 1966).

Les Belles Images, trans. Patrick O'Brian (New York: Putnam, 1968; repr. New York: HarperCollins and London: Fontana, 1985).

La Femme rompue (Paris: Gallimard (*Coll. Folio*), 1968).

The Woman Destroyed, trans. Patrick O'Brian (New York: Putnam, 1969; repr. London: Fontana, 1987).

La Vieillesse (Paris: Gallimard (*Coll. Folio*), 1970).

The Coming of Age, trans. Patrick O'Brian (New York: Putnam, 1972; repr. Harmondsworth: Penguin, 1986; New York: Norton, 1996).

Tout compte fait (Paris: Gallimard (*Coll. Folio*), 1972).

All Said and Done, trans. Patrick O'Brian (New York: Putnam, 1974; repr. Harmondsworth: Penguin, 1987 and Marlowe, 1994).

Quand prime le spiritual (Paris: Gallimard, 1979).

When Things of the Spirit Come First, trans. Patrick O'Brian (New York: Random House, 1984; London: Fontana, 1986).

La Cérémonie des adieux (Paris: Gallimard (*Coll. Folio*), 1981).

Adieux: Farewell to Sartre, trans. Patrick O'Brian (New York: Pantheon Books, 1984; repr. New York: Knopf, 1985; Harmondsworth: Penguin, 1986).

Lettres à Sartre, 2 vols. (Paris: Gallimard, 1990).

Journal de Guerre (Paris: Gallimard, 1990)

Letters to Sartre, trans. Quintin Hoare, Pref. Sylvie Le Bon de Beauvoir (New York: Arcade, 1991).

Lettres à Nelson Algren (Paris: Gallimard (*Coll. Folio*), 1999).

A Transatlantic Love Affair: Letters to Nelson Algren, trans. Kate Leblanc (New York: New Press, 1998).

Books in English on Simone de Beauvoir

ARP, KRISTANA, *The Bonds of Freedom: Simone de Beauvoir's Existentialist Ethics* (Chicago, Ill: Open Court, 2001).

BAIR, DEIRDRE, *Simone de Beauvoir: A Biography* (New York: Simon and Schuster, 1990).

BAUER, NANCY, *Simone de Beauvoir, Philosophy, and Feminism* (New York: Columbia University Press, 2001).

BERGOFFEN, DEBRA B, *The Philosophy of Simone de Beauvoir: Gendered Phenomenologies, Erotic Generosities* (Albany, NY: State University of New York Press, 1997).

CARD, CLAUDIA, (ed.), *The Cambridge Companion to the Philosophy of Simone de Beauvoir* (Cambridge: Cambridge University Press, 2003).

CROSLAND, MARGARET, *Simone de Beauvoir: The Woman and her Work* (London: William Heinemann, 1993).

EVANS, MARY, *Simone de Beauvoir: A Feminist Mandarin* (New York: Tavistock, 1985).

EVANS, RUTH, (ed.), *Simone de Beauvoir's The Second Sex: New Interdisciplinary Essays* (Manchester: Manchester University Press, 1998).

FALLAIZE, ELIZABETH, *The Novels of Simone de Beauvoir* (London and New York: Routledge, 1988).

FULBROOK, KATE, and FULBROOK, EDWARD, *Simone de Beauvoir and Jean-Paul Sartre: The Remaking of a Twentieth-Century Legend* (New York: Basic Books, 1994).

HOLVECK, ELEANORE, *Simone de Beauvoir's Philosophy of Lived Experience: Literature and Metaphysics* (Lanham, Md.: Rowman & Littlefield, 2002).

KRUKS, SONIA, *Situation and Human Existence: Freedom, Subjectivity, and Society* (London: Unwin Hyman, 1990).

LE DOEUFF, MICHÈLE, *Hipparchia's Choice: An Essay Concerning Women, Philosophy, etc.* trans. Trista Selous (Oxford: Blackwell, 1991).

LEIGHTON, JEAN, *Simone de Beauvoir on Woman* (Rutherford, NJ: Fairleigh Dickinson University Press, 1975).

LUNDGREN-GOTHLIN, EVA, *Sex and Existence; Simone de Beauvoir's Second Sex*, trans. Linda Schenck (Hanover, NH: Wesleyan, 1996).

MOI, TORIL, *Feminist Theory and Simone de Beauvoir* (Oxford: Blackwell, 1990).

—— *Simone de Beauvoir: The Making of an Intellectual Woman* (Oxford: Blackwell, 1994).

—— *What is a Woman? And Other Essays* (Oxford: Oxford University Press, 1999).

O'BRIEN, WENDY, and EMBREE, LESTER (eds.), *The Existentialist Phenomenology of Simone de Beauvoir* (Dordrecht: Kluwer Academic Publishers (Contributions to Phenomenology, 43), 2001).

OKELY, JUDITH, *Simone de Beauvoir* (New York: Pantheon, 1986).

PILARDI, JO-ANN, *Simone de Beauvoir Writing the Self: Philosophy Becomes Autobiography* (Westport, Conn.: Praeger Publishers, 1999).

SCHWARZER, ALICE, *After The Second Sex: Conversations with Simone de Beauvoir* (New York: Pantheon Books, 1984).

SIMONS, MARGARET A. (ed.), *Feminist Interpretations of Simone de Beauvoir* (University Park, Pa.: Pennsylvania State University Press, 1995).

—— *Beauvoir and The Second Sex: Feminism, Race, and the Origins of Existentialism* (Lanham, Md.: Rowman & Littlefield, 1999).

—— (ed.), *The Philosophy of Simone de Beauvoir* (Indianapolis, Ind.: Indiana University Press, 2003).

SULLIVAN, SHANNON (ed.), *The Work of Simone de Beauvoir*, special issue of *The Journal of Speculative Philosophy*, 13/1. (1999).

TIDD, URSULA, *Simone de Beauvoir, Gender, and Testimony* (Cambridge: Cambridge University Press, 1999).

—— *Simone de Beauvoir* (New York: Routledge, 2004).

VINTGES, KAREN, *Philosophy as Passion: The Thinking of Simone de Beauvoir*, trans. Anne Lavelle (Bloomington, Ind.: Indiana University Press, 1996).

Name Index

Cottingham, John G., 77 n.
Coudenhove-Kalergi, Richard de, 27, 27 n.
Courtivron, Isabelle de, 38 n.
Crary, Alice, 155 n.
Crosland, Margaret, 162
Culler, Jonathan, xxv, 139, 139 n., 141

Darrow, Clarence, 63
Dasgupta, Partha, 93, 93 n.
Davis, David Brion, 109 n.
De Gaulle, Charles, xiii, 26, 28
Deitz, Paula, v
Delphy, Christine, 38 n., 39 n.
Derrida, Jacques, 155 n.
Descartes, René, vii, ix, xi, xv, xvii, xviii, xxii, xxiv, 6, 56, 77 n., 122-123, 126, 175, 182
Destler, Louise, xxvii
Deuber-Mankowsky, Astrid, 46 n.
Deutscher, Penelope, 56, 56 n., 131 n.
Devaney, M. J., 66 n.
Diamond, Cora, 140 n.
Dickens, Charles, 162
Diderot, Denis, 34
Du Bois, W. E. B., vii, viii, xxi, xxiv
Duchen, Claire, 60 n., 159 n.

Edwards, Mary-Frances Grosholz, 191
Edwards, Robert R., viii
Einstein, Albert, 19
Eliot, George, 162, 165, 174, 180
Ellington, J. W., 95 n.
Ellis, Havelock, 119, 119 n.
Ellmann, Mary, 65, 65 n.
Engels, Friedrich, 105
Englund, Sheryl A., 39 n.
Evans, Ruth, 38 n., 74 n.

Fallaize, Elizabeth, xiv, 38, 38 n., 40, 40 n., 41 n., 42, 42 n., 43, 43 n., 61-62, 68, 116 n.
Fanon, Frantz, xxiv
Farnham, Marynia L. Foot, 67 n.
Fawcett, Dame M. Garrett, 25
Ferry, Jules, 4, 4 n.
Fichte, Johann Gottlieb, 120
Flaubert, Gustave, x, 14
Fourtouni, Eleni, 191
Francis, Claude, 34 n., 121 n., 147 n.
Frege, Gottlob, ix
Freud, Sigmund, 9, 54 n., 121, 131 n., 143, 143 n., 149-150, 171
Friedan, Betty, xxix, 40 n., 115
Friedman, Michael, 117 n.
Fullbrook, Edward, 38 n., 39 n.
Fullbrook, Kate, 38 n., 39 n., 124

Gage, Matilda Joslyn, 35 n.
Gallie, W. B., xxix
Galster, Ingrid, 36
Garapon, R., 85 n.
Garréta, Anne, 160
Gatens, Moira, 103 n., 131 n.
Gauss, Johann Carl Friedrich, ix
Gibaldi, Joseph, 139 n.
Gillman, Richard, 39 n., 40, 41 n., 61 n., 63, 63 n., 64, 64 n., 65 n.
Goethe, Johann Wolfgang von, xxx, 175
Gontier, Fernande, 34 n., 121 n., 147 n.
Gothlin, Eva, xvi, xvii, 49, 49 n., 66, 68, 74, 75, 116 n., 124 n., 125 n., 131 n., 146 n.; see also Lundgren-Gothlin, Eva
Gracia, Jorge, xvii
Green, Ashbel, 61
Green, Graham, 169
Greer, Germaine, xxix
Grosholz, Emily, 61, 68, 135, 160

Habermas, Jurgen, xxiv
Harvey, J., 99 n., 100 n.
Hatcher, Donald L., 109 n.
Hegel, Georg Wilhelm Friedrich, x, xii, xv, xvii, xviii, xxii, xxiv, 9-11, 16, 18, 20, 29, 33, 43, 43 n., 44, 45 n., 47-48, 51-53, 71-73, 73 n., 74-76, 78-79, 88-89, 120-121, 125, 125 n., 130-131, 131 n., 134 n., 175
Heidegger, Martin, xiv, xv, xxiii, xxiv, xxix, 17, 49, 49 n., 55-56, 117 n., 121, 131, 131 n., 132, 132 n., 133, 133 n., 134, 189
Heinämaa, Sava, 116 n, 131 n.
Hill, Thomas E., 98, 98 n., 99, 99 n.
Hitler, Adolf, 19, 117, 128, 150
Hobbes, Thomas, xvii
Holveck, Eleanore, 126 n.
Houlding, Elizabeth A., 20 n.
Howard, Richard, 142 n.
Hsieh, Li Li, 68
Huppert, Isabelle, 60 n.
Husserl, Edmund, xv, 121, 125 n., 131, 134

Iino, Catherine, 191
Imbert, Claude, vii, ix, x, xi, xii, xv, xxiv, xxx
Irigaray, Luce, 30, 37, 45 n.

Jacobus, Mary, xxvi
James, Henry, 143 n.
James, Susan, vii, ix, xv, xvii, xviii, xix, xxii, xxiv, 77 n.
Jaurès, Jean Léon, 6
Jefferson, Ann, 153 n.